Persephone's Girdle

Gian Lorenzo Bernini, *Rape of Persephone,* 1622. Courtesy of the
Galleria Borghese, Rome

PERSEPHONE'S GIRDLE

Narratives of Rape in

Seventeenth-Century

Spanish Literature

MARCIA L. WELLES

Vanderbilt University Press
Nashville

04 03 02 01 00   5 4 3 2 1

A grant from Barnard College helped meet production costs.

Publication of this book was supported by generous grants from the Del Amo Foundation and from the Program for Cultural Cooperation between Spain's Ministry of Culture and Education and United States' Universities.

Library of Congress Cataloging-in-Publication Data

Welles, Marcia L.
    Persephone's girdle : narratives of rape in seventeenth-century Spanish literature / Marcia L. Welles. — 1st ed.
    p. cm.
    Includes bibliographical references (p.) and index.

    ISBN 0-8265-1335-2 (alk. paper)
    ISBN 0-8265-1351-4 (pbk. : alk. paper)
    1. Spanish literature—Classical period, 1500–1700—History and criticism. 2. Spanish drama—Classical period, 1500–1700—History and criticism. 3. Rape in literature. I. Title.
    PQ6066 .W45 2000
    860.9'355—dc21   99-6745
Published by Vanderbilt University Press
Printed in the United States of America

To my family

My husband, David, our daughter Dede and our son-in-law, Mark Gimbel,
our son, Michael, our daughter Margaret. And Aki.

To my mother
Louise Stevenson Andersen

and

To my father
Henry Testman Andersen

in memoriam

Contents

ILLUSTRATIONS

Frontispiece Gian Lorenzo Bernini, *Rape of Persephone* (1622)

Acknowledgments

I thank my professional friends and colleagues Mary S. Gossy, Yvonne Jehenson, Helen B. Levine, and Gridley McKim-Smith for their generous willingness to listen and advise. I thank Frances Kazan for her unfailing support. Wendy Gimbel's steadfastness and humor have helped me along the way. Portions of this study were written in Toronto. This would not have been possible without the friendship of Lynn and Skippy Sigel, Deena and Michael Sigel.

The Spanish Department of Barnard College has played a crucial role in my life. Margarita Ucelay, my teacher, inspired me to continue my studies; Mirella Servodidio, my colleague, has consistently encouraged me. To them I give thanks, and to my students.

Gonzalo Sobejano continues to set an example for me of personal integrity, intellectual rigor, and professional responsibility. As a mentor, colleague, and friend, I thank him.

Translations

The editorial decision to include only the English in cited materials made it especially important to provide accurate renditions of the Spanish, as well as of several French and Italian quotations. I owe an enormous debt of gratitude to my friend and colleague Helene F. Aguilar of Columbia University, for her translations of materials not published in English. Every effort has been made to approximate the original as faithfully as possible. For any errors I alone am responsible.

Permissions

I have previously published versions of materials here included as articles in the following journals or collections of essays. I gratefully acknowledge the editors' permission to reprint them:

"The Anxiety of Gender: The Transformation of Tamar in Tirso's *La venganza de Tamar* and Calderón's *Los cabellos de Absalón.*" *Bulletin of the Comediantes* 47, no. 2 (1995): 341–72.

"The Rape of Deianeira in Calderón's *El pintor de su deshonra.*" In *The Perception of Women in Spanish Theater of the Golden Age,* edited by Anita K. Stoll and Dawn L. Smith, 184–201. Lewisburg, Pa.: Bucknell University Press, 1991.

"Rojas Zorrilla's *Lucrecia y Tarquino:* 'The Taming of Lucretia' or 'The Staging of Perverse Desire.'" *Romance Languages Annual* 3 (1991): 622–29.

"Violence Disguised: Representation of Rape in Cervantes's *La fuerza de la sangre.*" *Journal of Hispanic Philology* (special issue) 13, no. 3 (1989): 240–52.

To the Reader

Persephone's Girdle refers to a detail in Ovid's version of the rape of Persephone (*Metamorphoses* 5.425ff.). After Persephone was kidnapped by Pluto and taken to be his queen of the world of darkness, her mother, Demeter, searched for her in vain. A Sicilian nymph, Cyane, who tried to stop the maiden's abduction, came to the aid of the grieving mother. Having neither lips nor tongue, she could not speak. Nevertheless, she provided Demeter with evidence of the crime. There, on the surface of the sacred waters of the nymph's pool, lay Persephone's girdle.

Violence always, and forever, leaves a trace, whatever effort may have been made to erase it. The calmness of the water's surface, the smoothness of a seamless text respond to a strategy of interference and allow their secrets to be recovered.

Persephone's Girdle

Introduction

A friend recently asked me how I developed an interest in the subject of rape in literature. When I responded that it was due to a rereading of Ovid's *Metamorphoses,* he was startled. He knew the tales well, but *rape?* Rape is brutal, dark, tragic; Ovid is sweet, witty, light. This is true, but there are, in fact, some fifty rapes or "sexual extortions" in Ovid, which prompted the classicist Charles P. Segal to suggest that the poem might be more properly considered an epic of rape than one of love (93). The poet's landscapes of sylvan beauty provide the setting for terrifying pursuit—both venatic and erotic—and death, either literal or by metamorphosis into a nonhuman form. Places of refuge become sites of violence. This is not as paradoxical as it at first may seem: "Rape is violence of an elemental kind, and defloration in this context is an elemental act with potentially violent repercussions, a mystery akin to the ferocity of nature herself" (Parry 277–78).

As readers of the *Metamorphoses,* we may be forgiven for our failure to recognize immediately the tragic side. After all, we are heirs to the literary and artistic tradition of ancient Greece, which had consecrated long ago the concept of the "heroic" rape (Brownmiller 313–42), perpetrated most notably by the great Jupiter himself (on males and females—Europa, Leda, Danaë, Ganymede, to cite but a few of the better-known examples), or by mortal heroes (such as Peleus's seizure of the sea nymph Thetis). From its emergence in the fifth century B.C. as a popular subject for Greek vase painting, heroic rape has been characterized by a lack of explicit violence or blatant sexuality, an elegance of posture and feature.[1] Titian's *Danaë with Cupid* (1545–1546) and *Danaë* (with Nursemaid; 1553–1554; fig. 1)[2] and Correggio's Jupiter series are later, increasingly eroticized versions of

I

the tradition: Norman Bryson describes Corregio's *Io* (between 1530 and 1534)[3] as "ravishment by a divine cloud which caresses every single pore of skin, and thus surpasses the limitations of a natural lover" (164). The offspring can be exceptional: the beautiful Helen is born to Leda, whom Jupiter possessed in the form of a swan; and Danaë gives birth to the mighty Perseus, forcibly conceived by Jupiter in the form of a golden cloud. A counterpoint to this tradition of the heroic rape in ancient Greece is that of the scenes of amorous pursuits of the maenads by satyrs, or the various pursuits by the centaurs, or scenes between men and prostitutes, which in their explicit eroticism are quite removed from the lofty Olympian realm (Wolfthal, "The 'Heroic' Rape"). In its iconography, Greek pictorial tradition does not ignore the difference between consensual sexual relations and seizure by force (Cohen), and, though rare, literary tradition is not insensitive to the traumatic impact of rape, even though the rapist be a god. In Euripides' *Ion,* Kreousa's confession of her violation by Apollo that led to the birth of Ion is marked by shame and fear of disgrace. Only at a moment of profound despair does she break her silence and speak of her sorrowful past (Scafuro).

In his important study of Calderón's richly elaborated myth plays, Thomas A. O'Conner, noting the playwright's foregrounding of female resistance in scenes of sexual violence and the negative impact on the victim, concludes: "Rape represents such basic evil in the theater of Calderón that the notion of a 'heroic' rape finds no place therein" (*Myth and Mythology* 90). Although the subtleties he perceives in Calderón's dramatic elaborations of these received legends certainly belie a unidimensional allegorical reading,[4] the heroic impulse remains: it is the status of the rapist that determines such a characterization, not the reaction of the victim (resistance, flight, fear, and sorrow by the pursued females are depicted in the Attic ceramics as well as in Ovid's poem).[5] And in Calderón's plays the children born of such unions, however unlawfully achieved, remain extraordinary or semidivine, as the case may be: Narcissus, offspring of the nymph Liriope's rape by the wind-god Zephyr in Calderón's

Figure 1. Titian, *Danaë,* 1553–1554. Courtesy of the Museo del Prado, Madrid

Eco y Narciso (Echo and Narcissus) or by the river-god Cephisus in Ovid, is uncommonly beautiful; in *El monstruo de los jardines* (The Monster in the Gardens), defying the efforts of his mother, the sea-nymph Thetis, to avoid his foreseen destiny in the Trojan War, Achilles, begotten by force, is animated by the call to war and duty to the country bequeathed to him by his father, the hero Peleus (himself a grandson of Jupiter), whose achievements the son will surpass.[6] In *Las fortunas de Andrómeda y Perseo* (The Fortunes of Andromeda and Perseus), Perseus, though seemingly an ordinary villager, has intimations of greatness, of the royal blood that runs through his veins ("such lofty blood" [2.642a]). His intuitions are verified. Bequeathed special gifts by Mercury and Pallas Athene, he routs the power of the allegorized *Discordia* and achieves peace by beheading Medusa and saving Andromeda, heroic feats beyond the powers of mere mortals for which he is acclaimed at the end: "Long live, long live, the glory of great Perseus / The son of Jupiter, worthy to be so!" (3.653c). This is court drama, and the use of coercive force by the father/king figure represented by the god Jupiter has complicated political implications in an absolutist state such as that of Habsburg Spain.[7] Decorum demands that emphasis fall not on the sexual violence of the father but on the spiritual and physical greatness of the divine heir.[8] Within the specific political context of the first performance of *Fortunas,* Margaret Greer (98) suggests that the heir represented by Perseus is the distinguished illegitimate son of Philip IV, don Juan José of Austria, who had secured peace for Spain by achieving a successful end to the twelve-year-long Catalan separatist rebellion in the fall of 1652.

Although the use of myths of rape in Calderón may not be celebratory, it nevertheless retains an aura of distinction, appropriate to this special realm where the divine and human meet: the musical setting of *Fortunas,* a semiopera (Stein), employs recitative exclusively for the deities, which functions to accentuate their divine difference from humans (Greer 69–71; Stein 144–67). In the world of mere mortals playing out their lives in history (as in *El alcalde de Zalamea [The Mayor of Zalamea],* for example), Calderonian drama unambiguously exposes the female's abduction and rape as a manifestation of unfettered animal sexuality.[9]

A variant of the aestheticization that characterizes the heroic rape is found in the romantic rape of the courtly love tradition, according to Kathryn Gravdal's definition of "romantic" as "that which blurs the distinction between seduction and aggression" (14). An illustration of this strategic elision of violence is found in the *Penitencia de amor* (Penitence of Love) by Pedro Manuel Jiménez de Urrea, a sentimental romance of frustrated love (Grieve xviii) that ends in the lovers' castigation by imprisonment.[10] Initial (futile) protests against intercourse by the maiden Finoya ("Alas, I am killed! Alas, you murder me! Alack, alack, regard my honor, Darino! Alack, alack, you murder me! Oh wretched that I am! Would I had arms to stay you or slay myself! [53]) are followed by her assenting to a subsequent meeting with Darino—"At this same time that you came. O misery, how can I say it?" (56). The protests seem perfunctory, meant rather to assuage a guilty conscience ("for I have done no wrong, I have been forced" [67]) than repulse a bodily attack. The substratum of misogyny underlying the tragic tale, liberally sprinkled with denigrating opinions about women by such classical authors as Aristotle, Juvenal, Seneca, and Terence, reinterprets the defloration scene. The blurring between forced and voluntary sex colludes with an ideology that, while idealizing, simultaneously represents woman as weak, vain, and hypocritical: "she has cause to repent" (18) contests the lover's servant, cynically countering arguments pertaining to a young woman's appearance of virtuous modesty. This effects a semantic reversal, whereby "no" becomes "yes" and sexual violence is eroticized.

If we turn from myth to ancient history—book 1 of Herodotus (fifth century B.C.)—to be exact, we learn that the origin of the struggle between Greeks and barbarians is none other than rape: first the Phoenicians seized Io, daughter of the king of Argos, and bundled her off to Egypt; then, and I quote, "giving them like for like" (1.2.4), some Greeks carried off Princess Europa from Tyre. Not satisfied, the Greeks then abducted Medea, daughter of the king of Colchis. Some forty or fifty years later Priam's son Paris, "having heard of these occurrences, determined to procure himself, by force, a wife out of Hellas; being fully convinced that he should not be compelled to make any reparation, inasmuch as the Hellenes themselves had not done so" (I.3.4.). The rest of the story we know. Citing Persian opinion, Herodotus adds that the Trojans considered the Greeks to be the aggressors, for the following reason: "now they hold it to be the crime of a wicked man, to ravish women; but that of a simpleton, to trouble one's self about revenge; for prudent men ought to take no account of such females; since it is evident, that, without their own consent, they could not be forced: the Persians consequently declare, that they of Asia never troubled themselves about women that are stolen away" (1.4.5). Peter Walcot wryly notes in his article on this topic that "[t]owards the end of his story of mutual rape Herodotus, respectable historian that he is, mentions what he calls a Phoenician alternative of the Io tradition: according to this version the Phoenicians did not rape the princess, but she went to Egypt with them willingly enough; being pregnant by the captain of the Phoenician vessel she joined their company in order to escape detection and in shame of her parents (1.5.2.)" (140). Walcot shows that this prejudice that victimizes the victim, craftily ascribed to other cultures, is also both Herodotean and, in general, Greek (141).

Rape also has a place in the science, or art, of politics. In *The Discourses,* Machiavelli includes a chapter (3.26) entitled "How Women Have Brought about the Downfall of States," in which he writes: "First, we see how women have been the cause of many troubles, have done great harm to those who govern cities, and have caused in them many divisions" (477). He cites the example of the rape of Lucretia as the precipitating factor in the downfall of the Tarquins and warns princes and rulers of republics concerning "the disorders that such events may occasion and look to the matter in good time, so that the remedy applied may not be accompanied by damage done to, or revolts against, their state or their republic" (478).

Early Spanish history could have provided Machiavelli with another stunning example of the political troubles women cause. The Muslim invasion of 711 and the eight centuries of reconquest that follow mark the definitive moment of difference for the peninsula: neither its politics nor its art and architecture, literature, or religiosity replicate the patterns of the rest of western Europe. In their explanation of the event, historical sources point to yet another chapter in the bloody annals of the elective Visigothic monarchy: the followers of Witiza, wishing to wrest the throne from King Rodrigo, facilitate the invasion from North Africa. But legend would have it otherwise, and presents another, more colorful and memorable version: King Rodrigo rapes the maiden Florinda la Cava, and her father, Count Julian, the governor of Ceuta, wreaks his revenge by calling in the enemy troops and allowing them passage across the Strait of Gibraltar. Spain is lost to the infidels. The *romancero* tradition records multiple versions of the affront. The differences in the assignment of blame are captured with fine irony in the final stanza of the "Romance nuevamente rehecho de la fatal desenvoltura de la Cava Florinda" (A Newly Fashioned Ballad of the Fatal Forwardness of La Cava Florinda) (*Flor nueva de romances viejos* [New Flowering of Old Ballads]):

> If they question which of the two
> has borne the greater guilt,
> let men declare, La Cava
> and women, Rodrigo. (54)[11]

La Cava's reputation becomes ever more tarnished as the centuries pass. In the *Penitencia de amor* she forms part of a concatenation of women who have brought great troubles to the world: "Consider the first of all women, Eve, and what she brought upon the world, consider La Cava, through whom Spain was lost, next consider Helen, through whom Troy was destroyed, and although there be not many examples of such great matters, still many other cases occur of which women are the cause" (18); in the *Quixote* she is alluded to as "the wicked Christian woman" (1.41.329).

That the motif of rape joins these three realms—myth, history, and politics—is not fortuitous. It corresponds to the same mythic plot, wherein the woman's body becomes the object of exchange—between kings, with national and international consequences, or simply between men, with merely domestic repercussions. As Claude Lévi-Strauss argued in *The Elementary Structures of Kinship,* if gift-giving is a fundamental transaction of social intercourse, marriage represents the most basic (and precious) form of this exchange. If "marriage is the archetype of [legitimate] exchange" (483), forming the basis of a bonding between the men involved, rape is then theft and can be expected to lead to an outbreak of hostility. A virgin's chastity, a husband's possession of his wife's body, cannot be transgressed without repercussions, not only to the individuals but to their societies, in much the same way that class and territorial boundaries cannot be transgressed with impunity.

An example of a betrayal of the marital exchange occurs in "The Outrage at Corpes" episode in the third *Cantar* of the *Poema de Mio Cid (The Poem of the Cid)*, where the Infantes de Carrión viciously beat and abandon their wives, the Cid's daughters (verses 2689–861) (see D. Puebla's eroticized nineteenth-century rendition of this scene [1871], fig. 2). Linked to the martyrological tradition (Walsh; Nepaulsingh) and so stated by doña Sol ("'Cut off our heads and make martyrs of us'" [2728]), in which sexual abuse of female victims was a common element,[12] this incident in all likelihood included, in addition to the beatings, denigrating and painful acts of a sexual nature. The lovemaking on the night before the incident ("On this spot they spent the night with all their company, and with their wives, to whom they showed signs of tender love" [2702–33) is the foreplay that in the text sets the erotic stage for the humiliation that follows.[13] The partial disrobing of the women ("There and then the young men took off their wives' cloaks and fur tunics and left them in nothing but their shifts and tunics of cloth of gold" [2720–21]), the paraphernalia ("spurs" and "strong, hard straps" [2722–23]) prepared for inflicting harm, the erotic overtones of doña Sol's focus on the sharpness of the Infantes' two swords (2726) in her plea for a less humiliating—and swifter—death by decapitation (2728),[14] the exhaustion of the Infantes after their rage is spent ("The two men struck till they were weary" [2745])—all point to the conflation of eroticism and hatred at the core of perverse sexuality (Stoller 8), as Thomas Hart has suggested in his remarks on the incident (22).

The implication of sexual sin is reinforced in the enactment of the bloody torture. There is a subtle difference from a scene of martyrdom, where blood gushes forth (as in St. Margaret's torture, when, bound and beaten, "the blood poured forth from her body as from a pure spring" [Voragine 352]). In the descriptions of Elvira and Sol, on the other hand, the blood is visualized as a stain on the undergarments ("the clear red

Figure 2. Dióscuro Teófilo de la Puebla Tolín, *Las hijas del Cid,* 1871. Courtesy of the Museo del Prado, Madrid

blood poured out over their golden tunics" [2739]; "their shifts and tunics all stained with blood" [2744]), creating a stark, contrasting image of red stains on a cloth background, a symbolic equivalent at the textual level of besmirched innocence.

In this complicated transaction between the baronet Ruy Díaz de Vivar—wealthy, successful, and redeemed in the eyes of his king—and the noble and steadfastly arrogant Infantes, the bodies of doña Elvira and doña Sol become the literal battleground of the symbolic competition between men. Of the two humiliating instances of their manifest cowardice (their conduct in the battle against Búcar and their flight from the lion), it is the public humiliation of the lion that the Infantes evoke as justification for their wife beating (Ulrich 296–97): "'rather than stay here to have the episode of the lion cast in our teeth'" (2548); "'rather than have any harping on what happened with the lion'" (2556); "'this is our vengeance for the dishonour with the lion'" (2719); "'we have our revenge for the dishonour we suffered in the episode of the lion'" (2762). In his discussion of the incident, Leo Ulrich points to the psychological motivation for such aggression:

> Why then, since they want revenge, do they not avenge themselves upon their alleged "offenders"? Because they are cowards who dare not challenge strong men, men hardened and seasoned in battle. The weak man, in order to feel powerful—and that is how the Infantes want to feel—seeks a weaker one. They will thus execute their vengeance on the only victims who cannot offer them resistance, on two frail women. (297)

Such a displacement mechanism is logical. There are, however, other—structural—factors at work in the decision of the Infantes, equally coherent though more hidden.

René Girard has delineated for us the mechanism of the surrogate sacrificial victim as the means by which a community avoids open warfare or struggle. He lists "prisoners of war, slaves, small children, unmarried adolescents, and the handicapped" (*Violence and the Sacred* 12) among the possible human victims for sacrificial substitution, suitable because of their marginality to the community, and notes that "women are never, or rarely, selected as sacrificial victims" (12). He continues: "There may be a simple explanation for this fact. The married woman retains her ties with her parents' clan even after she has become in some respects the property of her husband and his family. To kill her would be to run the risk of one of the two groups' interpreting her sacrifice as an act of murder committing it to a reciprocal act of revenge" (12–13). But women in their roles as "signs" to be communicated (*The Elementary Structures of Kinship* 496) can—and do—become the surrogate sacrificial victims. Patricia Klindienst Joplin argues convincingly that in instances in which the female victims are related to the main parties (Lucrece and Verginia in her discussion), it is precisely this relationship that determines them as targets ("Ritual Work" 52). Otherwise, they would have no symbolic value.

It is thus their link to the Cid that makes Elvira and Sol targets of violence, for by fatal synecdoche they function rhetorically as the *pars pro toto*. Upon their departure for Carrión, the Cid has referred to them as the most vital part of his own being: "For I give you my daughters, though it is like tearing my very heartstrings to do so" (2578). Literalization of trope leads to the grotesque conclusion that the way to the father's heart is through his daughters' bodies. Ritualistic aspects include the premeditated and carefully planned preparations ("'We shall take them away from Valencia out of the power of the Cid; afterwards, on the road home, we shall do as we like'" [2546–47]; "'we shall show our contempt for the daughters of the Cid'" [2551]; "'We shall make a mock of the Cid's daughters'" [2555] [Leo 295]), as well as the choice of a secluded location in the wilderness.[15] Whether the Infantes intended to actually kill their wives is a moot point, for "in the ethos of the times, such dishonoring by torment, marking and abandonment was just as great an offence as murder would have been" (Smith and Walker 5).[16]

What is surprising, in fact, is the nakedness of the issue among men. Here violence is not disguised as erotic passion but confessedly and blatantly a substitutive mechanism. When reported to the king, the focus is on dishonor ("'Entreat him [the king] to consider as a deep and serious grievance the dishonour done to me by the Infantes of Carrión'" [2906]; the king signals the cause of the legal proceedings as the wrong committed against the Cid ("'for we all know they have done him a great wrong'" [3134]). The fact that the women suffered and could have died is not a prominent feature in the arguments, as Colin Smith argues (Smith and Walker 4–5). But this may be less related to the question of intentionality than a clue to the substitutive mechanism at work. The king, repenting his role in the enactment of the marriage between the Cid's daughters and the Infantes, admits with feeling that "'I am as much grieved about it as the Cid, and I promise to do him justice, as I hope for salvation'"

(2959–60). The restitution of the Cid's honor is accomplished by the successful duel of the Cid's men against the Infantes; a full and perfect restoration is enabled by the prestigious marriage of the Cid's daughters to the Infantes of Aragon and Navarre, which, when requested by messengers, stuns the audience. The Infantes had predicted the daughters' permanent shame—"'for as long as they live what we did will be cast up to them'" (3358–59a). Instead Álvar Fáñez can taunt them with their repudiated wives' social betterment: "'Once you had them as wives and equals, but now you will kiss their hands and acknowledge them as your superiors. You will have to do them service, however unwillingly'" (3449–51). It is no wonder that this dramatic development pleases many, "but not the Infantes of Carrión, who found nothing pleasing in it" (3428). The king has already acceded to the marriage proposal; the duel enables the union to take place without stain: "'I can give them in marriage without let or hindrance'" (3716), claims the Cid, whose honor is aggrandized accordingly ("See what honour accrued to the Cid when his daughters became Queens of Navarre and Aragon" [3722–23]).

In an epic poem noteworthy for its fidelity to the history of the period and topography of the region, the ahistoricity of this portion is startling: "This is no mere reshuffling of historical facts but rather a complete fabrication lacking the slightest documentary or chronicled foundation" (Deyermond 22).[17] A poetic fiction it is, and a brilliant narrative ploy designed to ensure the vilification of these representatives of the upper nobility and, accordingly, to confirm resolutely the sympathies of the audience toward the lower-ranking men and their supporter, the king. In his discussion of the sociopolitical meaning of the poem, Alan Deyermond has stressed the magnitude of the political transition inscribed. There is, he suggests, "a decisive shift in the center of power. Power is passing from an old high nobility, day by day more venal and incompetent, to the new class of the 'infanzones' [new noblemen]; and there is an analogous transfer of power from the ancient crown of León to the new, and until recently subordinate, crown of

Castile. Such shifts, called *translatio imperii* in the Middle Ages, possessed great moral and religious overtones" (49).

Such a fundamental transition in codes and mores is legitimized by the invention of a personal affront of honor, which affects both the biological father—the Cid—and the symbolic father—the king, responsible for this ill-fated matrimony. The juridical resolution signals the replacement of the aristocratic code of private revenge by that of a public code of law, centered in royal authority (Lacarra 100–102). Glorification of the Cid (by poet and readers) tends to efface the fact that the political transition was not entirely blood free. The scapegoats are Elvira and Sol. It is they who make possible the resolution of the political crisis without open warfare: their bodies provide an alternative stage on which the rivalry between men is played out. They were beaten senseless ("The Infantes beat them so hard that they were benumbed with pain" [2743], and they "were left for dead in the oak forest of Corpes" [2748]). That they survived untouched by the wild beasts of the forest and recovered their pristine beauty without permanent bodily damage is miraculous, a function of the epic poem's hagiographic appropriation (Walsh 171–72).

Reciprocal violence characterizes Lope de Vega's play *El robo de Dina* (The Abduction of Dinah; 1615-1622),[18] based on the narrative in Genesis 34:1–31). The Old Testament account of the rape of Dinah by a Canaanite prince is preceded by an act of patriarchal land acquisition: Jacob had reentered the land of Canaan and purchased territory near the principal city of Shechem (33:18–20). What begins as a peaceful settlement by permission ends with the slaughter of the host tribe: King Hamor, his son Shechem, and other males are killed by Jacob's two sons Simeon and Levi (Dinah's full brothers), and the city and its inhabitants are plundered by Jacob's other sons. The cruelty, which Jacob reproaches (on pragmatic rather than moral grounds, fearing retribution [34:30–31]) is, in addition, a deceitful betrayal of an agreement. Jacob's sons, on learning of the rape, had assented to the proposed marriage between the prince and their sister, on condition that the Shechemites be circumcised.[19] This was but a ruse to debilitate the men and facilitate their revenge. In their response to the violation, the brothers evince a keen consciousness of the foreignness of Canaanite ways—"he had done what the Israelites held to be an outrage, an intolerable thing" (34:7), and their condition for the marriage—circumcision—again emphasizes differences in tribal customs. They explain that "we cannot give our sister to a man who is uncircumcised; for we look on that as a disgrace" (34:14). Hamor's vision was one of intermarriage and cohabitation: "Let us ally ourselves in marriage; you shall give us your daughters, and you shall take ours in exchange. You must settle among us. The country is open to you; make your home in it, move about freely and acquire land of your own" (34:10–11). The sons' persistence in reiterating the sexual wrong ("'Is our sister to be treated as a common whore?'" [34:31]), their refusal to countenance its legal rectification through marriage, and their stated perceptions of tribal differences point to a thinly disguised animosity toward the Canaanites as "Other."[20]

This Old Testament story is one of tribal rivalry in which the Israelites (the sons of Jacob) murder rulers and inhabitants and then destroy a city. The nakedness of such politics of power would be unbearable, I suggest, and requires an erotic subplot to mitigate its impact. The rape of Dinah provides her brothers with the motive for "justifiable homicide," and their despoiling of the city of Shechem is the symbolic equivalent of Dinah's despoiling. Violence is thus eroticized in order to legitimate it (Joplin). The prince is overcome by violent passion on seeing Dinah, and he takes her by force. Joseph had borne eleven sons but only one daughter; her illegitimate seizure necessarily provokes a political crisis. Only God's interference on behalf of the house of Jacob curtails the spiraling of a vicious cycle of revenge. He directs them to go to Bethel, where they arrive unharmed ("and the cities round about were panic-stricken, and the inhabitants dared not pursue the sons of Jacob" [35:5]).

While retaining the structure of a tragedy of revenge, Lope imbues his play with a lyrical quality that softens the harshness of the biblical narrative, as Jacob and his sons, a pastoral, rural people, voice their admiration of the Canaanite land in a poetry of praise. To the tribal differences marked in the Genesis account (Dinah is referred to as "an outsider" [31b] and the Canaanites as "barbarians" [38b; 39a,b] in the play), Lope in addition emphatically contrasts their religious practices (the Canaanites are presented as idolatrous worshipers of Astarte). According to the brothers, marriage cannot obtain here because—among other reasons—it would be "an infamous marriage" with "an idolatrous youth" (44b).

There is one surprising transformation in *El robo de Dina* that distinguishes it from the source. In the Genesis account, Dinah is a mute and passive victim, object of Shechem's lust and then, or so it is stated, of his love. Agency—and therefore blame—is ascribed to Shechem, and Shechem alone ("he took her, lay with her and dishonoured her" [34.2]). In the play, on the other hand, Jacob inculpates his daughter. Distraught and disheveled, she approaches her father and tells him of the rape, confessing to him that she went to the city without his knowledge or permission, driven by curiosity to see the local women ("I wanted to see them, I went out to see them" [38a]). Jacob replies:

> Going out was your ruin,
> for well you know, because of seeing,
> the most chaste risks
> her honor.
>
> . . . .
>
> You are party to deception
> nor are you free from guilt,
> for the one who grants the occasion,
> has caused the injury.
> And be not shocked at your own guilt,
> for you went to look at women,
> without considering that, being a woman,
> men then would look at you.
> I excuse not the aggressor

in this terrible crime;
but in part I do allow
that love is to blame. (39b)

Dinah continues to maintain her innocence, repudiates the proposed
marriage as a "cowardly remedy" (47b), and is impatient with her father's
advocacy of "prudence" and "equanimity" (qualities befitting his age).
She wants him to take revenge, not seek council: "Father, I am dishonored: / where a sword is wanted for slaying / there is no need for advice"
(40a). The bloody actions of her brothers she adjudges a "worthy undertaking" and cause for celebration: "I shall rejoice in his death" (48b). At the
end, Jacob addresses her as a murderess: "Ah, Dinah, you alone, alone /
assassin of a whole city!" (49a).

Dinah: from virgin to virago. This constitutes Lope's primary departure from the source narrative. Like the Old Testament authors, the Spanish
Golden Age dramatist holds virginity in the highest esteem; unlike them,
he portrays the postvirginal female as aggressive in her anger, pitiless and
revengeful. It is she who looks to the sword and implies that her father's
espousal of a peaceful resolution with honor is cowardly. The result is that,
along with the aging and reverent Jacob, the audience is swayed against
Dinah. Why the transformation? Traditions of blaming the victim and
strains of misogyny pertain. But embedded within these ideologies lies a fear
of female sexuality that emerges with particular intensity during the seventeenth century and is linked to the social and political crises.

Rojas Zorrilla's *Cada qual lo que le toca* (To Each His Own Concerns)
offers a provocative example for us to consider. According to a near-
contemporary commentator, Francisco Bances Cándamo (1661–1704),
informed by oral lore or an unknown written source, the play was a resounding failure:

The primary concern for the poet and a precept too for the
playwright should be that he not choose horrific topics nor

those that set evil examples; the public itself will not tolerate it. Francisco de Rojas's *Cada qual lo que le toca* was booed because he dared portray a gentleman who, upon marrying, found his wife to have been violated by another lover.[21]

Isabel had been seduced and abandoned by a previous lover but was forced into marriage by her father. She tried in vain to dissuade her husband-to-be from insisting on their union, explaining that it was not advisable "[f]or me to marry you / nor for you to marry me" (1.392–93).[22] He did not heed her advice, but the regret was immediate. According to his servant Beltrán, the master went to bed eagerly on his wedding night but woke up quite out of sorts the following morning, suffering from a "strange regret" (1.30). At the point that the play commences, the couple's miserable marriage is in its second year, and for various reasons the aggrieved husband is determined to learn the identity of the other man in Isabel's past and seek revenge.

In his study of the play, Américo Castro admits that the case of a compromised bride is unusual—but not unique—and alone is not sufficient to account for the audience's rejection.[23] He points to Ruiz de Alarcón's *La crueldad por el honor* (Cruelty for the Sake of Honor), which presents a similar situation but did not—apparently—provoke such a reaction.

Based loosely on a chapter in Aragonese history following the death of Alfonso I "el Batallador" (the Great in Battle) in 1134, the play's central character is an impressive young soldier, Sancho Aulaga, known as "the valiant" (1.110)[24] and considered "a new Cid" (1.108) for his military exploits. His father, Nuño, believed to have died in battle, reappears. Taking advantage of rumors that Alfonso I was still alive, he assumes the guise of the dead king. Nuño Aulaga is an imposter, a traitor to the legitimate heir, and, his son learns, pusillanimous regarding his marital honor. He confesses to his son that, on marrying his mother, he discovered to his great shame that "I was not the first / whom love set in her arms" (2.1419–20). Furthermore, although he learned the identity of the erstwhile lover and had the opportunity to take revenge, he was unable to do so: "I bared my sword / inflamed, but just cause could not / conquer might" (2.1449–51). His rival is too powerful, and he decides instead to depart for war. As the plot unfolds, the valiant Sancho is unwavering in his obedience to the law of revenge. Although it is none other than his beloved's father who is the responsible party in his mother's dishonor, he is willing to see him perish (3.5); he himself kills his own father, as a traitor and imposter (3.21), the act that gives the play its title *La crueldad por el honor.*

Critics fault Alarcón for the later denouement—the discovery that Nuño is not, in fact, Sancho's biological father—for it diminishes the tragic impact of a parricide in the cause of honor. Castro Leal judges that "the reader's reaction shrivels and ebbs" (qtd. 830) upon learning this outcome, for "the weak thread of a last-minute paternity only loosens the dramatic knots of the plot" (qtd. 831). The critic's metaphors of weakening imply an authorial laxness or feminization at the end that destroys the potency of the plot's climax.

Américo Castro in his edition of the play argues for another source of the discontent provoked by *Cada qual lo que le toca:* the unorthodox gender characterization in the play. The husband is presented as "a gentleman of vacillating character and feeble will who formulates designs he fails to carry out, being continually overwhelmed by the situation" (184). The conduct of the wife, on the other hand, "is clear and energetic throughout the play. . . . She is the center of the dramatic action and she provides the denouement, finishing off what don Luis could not or would not do" (184). The denouement referred to is Isabel's stabbing of her ex-lover, Fernando. His passion rekindled, he had penetrated her room at night determined to "attain my love," as he says (3.3276). Castro uses the word "usurpation" to characterize the wife's role in Rojas Zorrilla's play:

> In the end comes the explosion: she usurps don Luis's function, offering us a spectacle unheard of in our theater; a married woman, pursued by a former lover, who far from

suffering punishment proceeds to avenge herself, with the subsequent approval of don Luis, who exclaims: "Then should I not forgive you?" [3422] (185)

Although Rojas Zorrilla does not question the honor code per se, he does—and uniquely so—vindicate a woman's right to enact the code (197). And this is why the audience protested, Castro concludes.

But there is more at work here than the author's intellectual position on women's equality. The tearful and long-suffering Isabel undergoes a transformation that corresponds to the functioning of unconscious fantasy life. Upon seeing again the man who seduced and abandoned her, the man responsible for her deflowering, Isabel is represented as fiercely irate. In asides she expresses anger ("I cannot hide / the rage in my eyes" [1.1216–17]) and wishes Fernando were dead ("Oh, could someone but slay him!" [1.1223]). After she stabs him to death with her husband's dagger, her beautiful visage appears distorted: "What signs in your face / of cruelty" (3.3295–96), exclaims her husband. At this moment she not only wields a literal knife; in addition, as she herself warns, her words are metaphoric swords: "For my words are penetrating swords" (3.3299–300).

The portrayal of Isabel as a phallic female brandishing her fetishistic sword, deadly and threatening to the male, is the literary equivalent of Freud's theoretical construct of the postcoital female in "The Taboo of Virginity." Her contorted features acquire synecdochic value as the most obvious indication of the enormity of the change, here outwardly manifested.

In her reading of Freud's essay and its entangled argument whereby castration anxiety is construed as penis envy, Mary Jacobus suggests the following:

> If representations of castration can serve to protect the viewer against castration anxiety, it might by the same token be said that representations of the phallic woman protect

the viewer against doubts about his masculinity. Making her like a man conserves the small boy's narcissism, his belief in the universal possession of the phallus. One might expect, therefore, to find powerful representations of the phallic woman arising in the context of feminization. (127)

This "context of feminization" certainly corresponds to the gender transcription in *Cada qual lo que le toca.* In the opening scenes we find the husband, don Luis, in pain, haunted by "foolish ravings" (1.304), "grieved in soul" (2.1557), begging for a cure. His wife urges him to kill her and thus end their mutual agony ("Ah, why do you wait? / why not unsheathe the knife?" [1.463–64]). He wants to take revenge, but having been warned by her not to persist in his courtship for reasons of honor, he admits his own complicity and is irresolute. Isabel's past—her memories—torture him; finding a letter in her own hand to an unknown addressee inflames his resolve to discover the identity of the offender (who, unbeknownst to don Luis, is the very friend standing before him). Frustrated, he determines to kill Isabel ("My destiny is but / to give you death" [3.2548–49]). At Isabel's bidding he again delays, for a day. This stay allows her, rather than him, to wreak revenge. Fernando is indeed killed, but the wrong person commits the act. Phallic in deed and in word ("my words are penetrating swords" [3.3300–3301]), Isabel is the very embodiment of a castrating virago, the postcoital maiden turned monster.

Furthermore, it is not just one revenge plot that fails in this play. They all do. The play incorporates honor plots within the main honor plot, compulsively reiterating itself. Don Fernando had been insulted in a ball game and considered it necessary to kill the perpetrator of this offense. Inadvertently, the offender is killed by don Luis, who generously lets Fernando assume responsibility for the murder, thereby meriting his eternal gratitude: "before all men, because of you / do I have honor, life, and peace" (1.1093–94). The dead man's brother, through the intervention of don Luis, agrees to pardon Fernando's crime but remains apprehensive about how he will be perceived: "But, what shall I do / that all may know / that not slaying him / is not through want of valor?" (1.804–7). The subplot of two men vying for Fernando's sister's hand remains unresolved at the end. The comic inset of the servant Beltrán, whose wife's honor is at risk, includes his thrice-iterated phrase, "I with dagger in hand" (3.3128, 3140, 3148). But his weapon remains unused. A drawn sword "without issue" (used to describe Nuño's empty gesture in *La crueldad por el honor* [3.2855]) is cause for shame.

In other words, the social mandate to revenge is systematically resisted, questioned, delayed. The sword acquires a life of its own: it speaks ("Steel so articulate" [2.2152]); it lies quiet ("the languor of my steel" [3.2495]); it delays ("granting, since you plead, / brief respite to my steel" [3.2567–68]). Scandalously—for the male, too—the sword has become a fetishistic substitute. In this context the dagger proves mightier than the sword: when Isabel performs the bloody act, Fernando has his sword drawn and her husband's is unsheathed. The sword as phallic signifier is revealed as mere posturing and pretense: a sham.

Is this a "Christianization" of revenge? A brother is asked to forgive a revenge killing: "There is more courage needed / to conquer, pardoning, / than to pursue perhaps / a causeless vengeance" (1.812–15), argues don Luis. Later, don Luis is moved to forgive his wife, or at least he posits this as an option. But it is difficult to construe the play as an ethical message against the honor code, for revenge is taken. It just so happens that, in both of these cases, the wrong person is the avenger.

There is something confused and confusing about the code of honor in the play. Whether it be a question of insult or sexual possession, the scenario in which the conflict is played out pertains to the rivalry between men. Irresolution marks their behavior. The servant with dagger in hand— yet not taking action—can be dismissed as mere comic relief, but he, in fact, only mirrors the behavior of his master and the other nobles. The commandment to revenge demanded by the honor code is systematically undermined. Herein lies the radical difference between *Cada qual lo que le toca* and *La crueldad por el honor,* where unswerving compliance (even at great personal sacrifice) is lauded. There is too much doubt and vacillation in *Cada qual lo que le toca.*

"Doubt . . . is a sign of resistance" (Lacan 35). In a profound and radical way, the authority of the law ("Name-of-the-Father," in Lacanian terms), as expressed in its condensed and emblematic form in the honor code, is resisted, recast. Adherence is maintained, but it is disfigured (the wrong person does the deed). At some level, the audience intuited this collapse of authority signified in the irresolution and reacted accordingly: with displeasure, and, one assumes, discomfort. The political threat entailed in the questioning of the legitimacy of the law is expressed as a sexual threat, emblematized in the figure of a castrating female (Hertz). Though seemingly the cause of the unease, she is herself a symptom, as revealed in the unconscious of the text.

A dagger-wielding wife who bloodily revenges her dishonor by repeatedly stabbing her brother-in-law also describes the main character of María de Zayas's "Al fin se paga todo" ("Just Desserts"), the seventh novel (related by a man) in the *Novelas amorosas y ejemplares (The Enchantments of Love).* Like the wife in *Cada qual lo que le toca,* doña Hipólita is forgiven by her husband. Having knowledge both of her violation by his own brother (who, in don Juan–style, achieves illicit intercourse by fraud under the cover of darkness), as well as of her previous attempted trysts with a lover, don Pedro thus shows himself to be especially merciful toward his wife, whose adulterous intent alone qualifies her as sinful (according to the Fourth Lateran Council of 1215 [Williamsen 10]). One can safely assume that only the genre of "Al fin se paga todo" (a novel meant for private and aristocratic consumption) protected it from the rejection by an unforgiving general public that Rojas's play received.[25]

Furthermore, doña Hipólita's shattering of gender conventions extends beyond this act of murderous revenge. She is not only the stereotypical object of desire but also an actively desiring subject, the conniving wife of the comic tradition of the *entremés* (one-act play) who during her husband's absences plans adulterous assignations, only to have them all con-founded. Left wealthy and still young by the death of her husband, it is she who chooses the man who will be her second husband—the inter-locutor of her story, whose self-restraint and kindness merit him his good fortune. Most importantly (as Amy Williamsen stresses in her analysis), it is she who maintains discursive authority, narrating her own tale.

In burlesque juxtaposition with the comic prelude of obstructed desire and the romance resolution of second nuptials, the seriotragic implica-tions of the violation and revenge murder are considerably undermined—verging on parodic reversal. The comic resolution of a marital dishonor plot, coupled with the unconventional characterization and emplotting of the tale, mark a stance of resistance both toward the genre in which the tale is encoded and the gender ideology that subtends it. In such a context of "feminization" and concomitant threat to male authority, the emergence of a phallic female is to be expected.

A similar fantasmatic virago makes an appearance in a very different discourse and discipline—that of rhetoric. Elizabeth Patton has demon-strated the (seemingly paradoxical) ubiquitous metaphorical presence of women in this field that from ancient times was for and by men and from which women were excluded. Female personifications, in particular, are rampant, as seen in her quotations from Gabriel Harvey's *Rhetor* (1577). In the context of a discussion challenging Cicero's linking of *res* and *verba* (philosophical content and stylistic form), two hypothetical females are created. One is Tulliola (as Marcus Tullius Cicero's daughter); the other is Polyphemia (as the giant Polyphemus's offspring). Harvey argues against Eloquentia's being forced to "'wander outside the boundaries and limits of [her] estate' and to take on responsibilities more appropriate to her sisters *(Dialectica, Mathematica, Physica, Ethica, Oeconomica, Politica, and Iurisprudentia)*" (Patton 8). The "tender and delicate" Tulliola, once having entered the rhetorical field, is transformed into Polyphemia, described by Harvey as

mammoth and tall, and thick, and masculine, with a great
head, with heroic appearance, with stunning eyes, with a
rather long neck, broad shoulders, with powerful knots of
muscles, and an immense and muscular chest, and with a huge
and nearly Cyclops like body. (Patton 9, qtd. Gii)

Her dress and footwear are so inappropriately manly in terms of gender
decorum that they produce a visceral reaction, and "'turn your stomach'" (Patton 10, qtd. Gii–Gii^v).

Read symptomatically, this text reveals a process of representation
similar to that in Rojas's play. In the passage quoted above, boundaries—
deemed natural and necessary—are being conflated, here between the
fields of style (pertaining to rhetoric) and philosophy (pertaining to dialec-
tic).[26] The perceived threat of such an admixture is emblematized as a
hideous, albeit fascinating, woman in masculine attire. The anxiety occa-
sioned by a slippage from what is considered natural (as opposed to unnatural) and safe (as opposed to dangerous) is structured visually and discursively
as a castrating female. This coincidence is not attributable to an individual, authorial unconscious but can be interpreted, as Jacobus suggests,
"as a narrative of representation itself—that is, as an instance of the power
of representation to structure, and hence allay, the anxieties attending
indeterminacy" (128).

This excursus on rhetoric can provide further insights into a deeply
rooted gender ideology. The pseudo-Ciceronian *Ad Herennium* (first century
B.C.) illustrates the figure of digression with a tale of a girl who is lured
from her destination and then raped (qtd. Patton 16, n. 24). Thus is "wan-
dering from the point" duly castigated. Juan Luis Vives's foundational text
De institutione feminae Christianae (On the Education of the Christian Woman), written
in 1523 at the request of Catherine of Aragon for the education of her
daughter, is replete with the tensions inherent in the very concept of
rhetorical training for women, for whom public performance was unacceptable.[27] In this novel manual on the education of the maiden, wife,

and widow, the concept of *ducere* (to lead) had to be rigorously stressed in order to avoid any *digressus* by the female and the punitive consequences of such wanderings. He is quite explicit on the issue: "I am not at all concerned with eloquence. A woman has no need of that; she needs rectitude and wisdom" (1.4.§28.39).

"In his reconstruction of a tradition designed to train men in the art of effective communication *(bene dicendi),*" Patton writes, "women are given primary responsibility for the 'right living' *(recte vivendi)* of the entire household" (157–58). Vives specifies that men's studies will result in civic contributions, whereas women's studies exclude any possibility of public performance: "I wish the woman to be totally given over to that part of philosophy which has assumed as its task the formation and improvement of morals . . . for it is not fitting that a woman be in charge of schools or have dealings with or speak to men, and while teaching others, detract from her modesty and decorum either in whole or in great measure, and eventually lose these qualities little by little" (1.4.§29.41).[28]

It is in not speaking, and not being spoken about, that a woman best fulfills her paradigmatic role: "Theano of Metapontum, a most learned young woman and a prophetess, was of the opinion that silence was the greatest adornment of a woman. Sophocles was of the same opinion, and indeed silence is a sweet seasoning for chastity and prudence" (1.11.§105.141); "For that reason Thucydides expressed the opinion that in the end the best woman was the one of whom there was least talk, whether in praise or blame" (1.11.§93.127).[29] Modesty also demands that the maiden "should not desire to see or be seen" (1.11.§95.131); accordingly, Vives advises the maiden: "As far as you can, close your eyes and ears, which give entrance to the machinations the devil makes use of in his assaults upon us" (1.6.§39.57).

Predictably, Vives exalts virginity in the maiden and chastity in the wife; for these are characteristics that accord perfectly with the stipulations of silence and enclosure. Basing himself on sources in the English Renaissance (including Vives), Peter Stallybrass concludes that

> The surveillance of women concentrated upon three specific
> areas: the mouth, chastity, the threshold of the house. These
> three areas were frequently collapsed into each other. The
> connection between speaking and wantonness was com-
> mon to legal discourse and conduct books. . . . Silence, the
> closed mouth, is made a sign of chastity. And silence and
> chastity are, in turn, homologous to women's enclosure
> within the house. (126–27)

The semantic field all these qualities share is one of enclosure. Bodily ori-
fices must be guarded. The impermeability of the female body, in turn,
conjoins symbolically with the notion of the integrity and inviolability
of the state (Stallybrass 129–33). The effects of a violation on the part of a
married woman reverberate beyond the realm of the home. Church and
state are affected, argues Vives, tainted by her shame: "You contaminate
the immaculate Church, which sanctified your union. You destroy civil
society; you violate the laws of your country" (2.2.§8.11). The personal
and the political are one and the same; the female body as well as the body
politic are to be kept free of the stain and dishonor of foreign intrusion.
This symbolic imbrication and the ideology it expresses are not unique
to Vives's text, and they occur when the nation-state in question is
Elizabethan England, as Stallybrass's examples demonstrate.

We must turn to where Vives departs from the norms for information
specific to the cultural context of Spain. And here we find what can only
be characterized as an obsessive concern with chastity, as well as a strange
subtext of violence when dealing with the subject.

Patton makes a fine and subtle point when commenting on this issue,
having to do with the process of translation. Although in Latin two terms
are used—*castitas* and *pudicitia,* distinguishable as chastity and moral purity—
these terms in the first English translation by Richard Hyrde are conflated
into *chastity* (175–79). This flattening of meaning has occurred in the Spanish
translation also. But it is worthwhile noting that in a key phrase in the

preface rendered in English as "[a] woman's only care is chastity" (§3.5), the Spanish equivalent (in the Riber translation, though not in Beltrán Serra's) has remained faithful to the Latin: "el cuidado exclusivo de la mujer es la pudicicia" (986b). Even so, the overall effect of the Spanish version is excessive in its concern with chastity.

In his preface Vives distinguishes his text from eminent predecessors who have dedicated attention to the duties of women (such as Tertullian, St. Jerome, and St. Augustine): "They spend all their time singing the praises of chastity . . . but they gave very few precepts or rules of life, thinking it preferable to exhort their readers to the best conduct and to point the way to the highest examples rather than give instruction about more lowly matters" (§1.3). His purpose, on the other hand, is to "compile practical rules for living" (§1.5). Yet statements such as the following concerning all women are found throughout the text: "Above all she should be aware that the principal female virtue is chastity and it is equivalent to all others in moral worth" (1.10.§82.113). One chapter (6) is titled "On Virginity." The immaculateness discussed herein is total, of both mind and body: "I define virginity as integrity of the mind, which extends also to the body, an integrity free of all corruption and contamination" (1.6.§37.53).

Américo Castro first suggested a connection between the special historic circumstances of Spain and its cultural obsession with honor. It is the transformation from a medieval Spain of the three religions to a unified Christian Spain under the Catholic kings that marks the nation's entry into the modern period, accompanied by the nefarious statutes of purity of blood.[30] Legitimacy becomes more—much more—than an issue of property, for it is genealogy, as purity of blood line, that determines the essence of one's social identity: "The structure and pure-blooded ideal of Spanish life thus underlay the appearance on the stage of the themes of honor and hideous revenges" (28), and accordingly, "[t]he honor plays had as an invisible background the living drama of the laws concerning blood purity and the protracted polemics on whether or not these were desirable" (Castro, *De la edad conflictiva* 32). The political reality has been absorbed into Covarrubias's dictionary definition of *limpiar*: "'Limpieza' means stainlessness, or it means purity of lineage" (767). Even when class differences are collapsed, as occurs, for instance, in the projected marriage of the humble (but rich) Dorotea and the aristocratic don Fernando in part 1 of the *Quixote,* the caste boundary is maintained; her status as an old Christian is affirmed with vigor.[31]

The *Sentencia-Estatuto* (Statute of Purity of Blood) promulgated in 1449 in Toledo gave birth to the notion of "caste" (*Realidad* 30–31) and invented the Old Christian as a social category (*Realidad* 57). Though Castro states that "The term 'casta,' originating in Spain, was not used in the Hindu sense, although later on the Portuguese did apply it to the castes of India" (*Realidad* 30–31), the effect on social codes of behavior and values is similar. Commenting on a study of female purity in South India and Ceylon, Mary Douglas writes that:

> Here the purity of women is protected as the gate of entry to the castes. The mother is the decisive parent for establishing caste membership. Through women the blood and purity of the caste is perpetuated. Therefore their sexual purity is all-important, and every possible whisper of threat to it is anticipated and barred against. This should lead us to expect an intolerable life of restriction for women. Indeed this is what we find for the highest and purest caste of all. (144)

It is also what we find in Spain, as reflected in the literature of the Golden Age.

The mother is known; the father not always: such is the biological reality. Paternal uncertainty places the burden of blood line on the female, and her bodily purity is the guarantor of legitimacy, name, and reputation. Thus it is she who is indispensable to social purity. Stallybrass, in a discussion of the mapping of territorial boundaries in Elizabethan England, writes: "And as the nation-state was formed according to new canons of incorporation and exclusion, so was the female body refashioned" (130). If we apply these same canons to Spain, the external process of territorial incorporation and exclusion becomes aggravated and intensified. At the same time, a duplicative internal process is enacted whereby racial divisions are mapped and maintained. Legislation concerning purity of blood institutes a caste system, and with it a concomitant system of taboos against pollution (Douglas).

The reign of a politics of purity is revealed in the rhetoric of its opposite—the stain, which is insistent and pervasive, according to the caste system. Because only the blood of Old Christians is pure, "without stain," religious practices dictate that Christianity must defend itself against Jewish contagion, as Queen Isabella declares at the beginning of Lope's *El niño inocente de La Guardia* (The Innocent Child of La Guardia): "Religion cannot / grow with pure intent / when from this infamous stain / it takes its rise" (1.26–30). Theologically, Mary's conception was immaculate—thus the title of Lope's play on the subject, *La limpieza no manchada* (Purity without Stain). Rhetoric and social practice locate a man's honor in the body and being of the female, whose responsibility it is not to besmirch a family's reputation: "Through the adultery of a wife impure blood is introduced to the lineage," Douglas explains (126), which in Vives's discussion of the state of wifehood translates into warnings chastising the adultress: "'Then besides the defilement brought upon your family you transfer the heredity from its right owner to strangers'" (2.2§8.11). Her unfaithfulness "creates doubt about the offspring . . . and it ruins the domestic economy" (2.2§12.15).

The lexicon of purity/impurity is the nodal point at which, metaphorically, church, state, and family meet, enabling almost imperceptible gliding from the realm of one discourse to that of another. Such easy transferability can be seen in the following comments by Vives on a wife's chastity and love for her husband, in which the intact boundaries of church, state, and female body form one ideational cluster:

In each of these virtues she reflects the image of the Church, which is both most chaste and tenaciously preserves unshaken faith in its spouse Christ. Though harassed internally by suitors, which is to say, baptized heretics, and attacked externally by pagans, Moors and Jews, it has never been contaminated by the least stain and it believes and senses that all its good is found in its spouse, Christ. Chastity must be greater in a married woman than in an unmarried one, for if you pollute and violate it now (which may God forbid!), see the harm you do to many and how many avengers you incite against you by one wicked deed. (2.2.§7.11)

As we have seen, the same associative leap occurs when Vives inveighs against the adulteress who grievously endangers church, state, and family. The compulsive reiteration of the notion of purity in Vives's text acquires special poignancy when his own *punctum dolens* ([Fantazzi, *In pseudodialecticos* 5) is considered: his New Christian origins.[32]

Such is the manifest content of Vives's manual on the training of a Christian woman. In its tripartite structure (on the maiden, wife, and widow), division of topics, and didactic message it is a model of reason, control, discipline, and order. Castro makes an interesting observation in an early study of the concept of honor in the Spanish Golden Age. The observation is not about honor but its loss: "We may thus affirm that dishonor appears as an irrational thing that bursts upon a man. Gentlemen suddenly perceive that a world of darkness is wrestling with them and seeks to deprive them of their highest good" (24). The same irrational siege occurs in Vives's text when the subject of dishonor is treated. The readers are assaulted with a catalog of women who are killed—maimed, stabbed, drowned, even devoured by a starving horse: parents kill daughters, brothers kill sisters, friends drown a sullied female acquaintance.[33] Inevitably, there is a companion masochistic script, with overtones of martyrology: a catalog of exemplars who mutilate themselves to defend a man's cause (one bites out her tongue, another hangs herself to avoid revealing secrets under torture), who kill themselves to join a deceased husband (one swallows burning coals, another drinks her husband's ashes) or to avoid dishonor.[34]

Whether in praise or in blame, the women are hurt or hurt themselves, are murdered or commit suicide. Whence this subtext of violence? Antonio Maravall posits an "aesthetics of cruelty" (*Culture of the Baroque* 162) as part of baroque culture. These are socially sanctioned scenarios of violence—autos-da-fé, legends of martyrs (both religious and their secularized versions), replayed in stories, plays, and paintings. But Maravall's generalized formulation fails to take into account the specific gendering of violence that predominates in visual and discursive representations. It is precisely this aspect on which Ruth El Saffar focuses in her study of female visionary writing *(Rapture Encaged)*:

> Male dominance and female submission are gender-specific responses to a set of cultural conditions that create difference as a threat to be overcome. In periods when unification and a sense of the absolute are enforced as political and religious ideals, woman becomes the primary representative of otherness, and is therefore seen as a dangerous element that must be subdued. (35)

El Saffar characterizes the wife-murder plays as "dramas of ego anxiety, of a collective consciousness little at ease with its achievement of power and success, and driven to shore it up by further constricting and punishing the *other* to whom potential loss is attributed" (74).

At the risk of expanding still further the conceptual realm encompassed by the notion of the fetish,[35] I suggest that virginity and chastity are, in fact, fetishized: female purity is prized in and for itself; its value, institutionalized in strict behavioral codes, is both personal and social; its effect is irrational, in the sense that it is outside the legal system (Pietz

"Fetish II" 44–45) and excessive—its power is such that a transgression can destroy the health and well-being of an individual (44–45). Vives imbues virginity with magical powers:

> Chastity was always something sacred and venerable, espe-
> cially virginity, even among thieves, men of impiety, crim-
> inals and wicked men, and even among wild beasts it was
> safe and respected. "Thecla" says St. Ambrose, "transformed
> the nature of beasts through the veneration they paid to
> her virginity." So much admiration does virginity elicit that
> lions stand in awe of it. Of how much worth, therefore, is that
> quality which has so often freed and defended women from
> emperors, tyrants and mighty armies? We read that very
> often abducted women were released by arrogant soldiers,
> solely out of respect for the name of virgin, because, that
> is, they had declared themselves virgins. (*On the Education of the
> Christian Woman* 1.6.§40.57,59)

What is the function of such fetishization? The answer to this question within a psychoanalytic framework is found in Freud's 1927 essay on the subject, in which he traces fetishization in a man to a mechanism of protection, a defense against the traumatic fear of his own castration. Central to his discussion of the fetish as a misplaced or substitutive desire is the concept of ego splitting, wherein denial and recognition coexist. A compromise solution is arrived at between knowing and not knowing: fetishists have a "double attitude . . . to the question of the castration of women" (218).

By inserting the psychosexual logic of the individual fetish in a collective cultural logic (Freud offers the example of Chinese foot binding as a collective fetishism) and locating it within specific historical circumstances, we can arrive at the following application of the model. What is at stake in the fixation on female purity is control of reproduction. Virginity makes possible the belief in *limpieza,* which is the primordial fiction of Spanish history. But it is a belief that involves ego splitting, for knowledge exists that reproduction is uncontrollable (it is always already out of control). As the sexual fetish enables belief in the phallic mother, so this collective fetish enables belief in the logically impossible caste purity.[36] It acts as a screen protecting the collective consciousness from traumatic recognition. At the same time, both socially encoded and passionately personal, the fetish, as William Pietz writes, "might be identified as the site of both the formation and the revelation of ideology and value-consciousness" ("Fetish I" 13).

That an obsessive quest for female purity leads to a conundrum is evident: a society must devise compromises to avoid the reductio ad absurdum of barrenness as a collective ideal. But the boundaries between celibacy and indiscriminate fertility are perceived as dangerously close, requiring constant surveillance and control. Such measures entail a distortion of the human experience, as Douglas comments: "The final paradox of the search for purity is that it is an attempt to force experience into logical categories of non-contradiction. But experience is not amenable and those who make the attempt find themselves led into contradiction" (162). Into contradiction and, perchance, violence. Fetishization of necessity implies reification, and a fetish that has the female as its object involves a cruel act of dehumanization, a synecdochic reduction of a whole person to a part—the organ of reproduction.

Monitoring as a way of life exacerbates and radicalizes gender differentiation and separation. Vives's text discloses a system of male domination and female submission to father and husband that is absolute and incontrovertible, which sets the stage for a sadomasochistic dynamic, not erotic in its outlines but cultural. A revealing moment occurs during a personal recollection concerning child rearing:

> No mother loved her son more dearly than my mother loved me. But no son felt less loved by his mother than I.

She practically never smiled at me, was never lenient towards me, and yet when I was away from home for three or four days and she did not know where I was, she almost fell into a grave illness. When I returned I did not know how much she had missed me. There was no one I avoided more or shunned more as a child than my mother, but as a young man no one was more constantly in my thoughts than she. Her memory is most sacred to me even now and whenever she comes to mind, I embrace her if not physically, in mind and in thought. (2.10.§140.169)

The rejection of maternal nurture, coupled with idealization, reinforces individual isolation and coexists with socially sanctioned acts of violence. Vives's memory is prefaced by an anecdote:

Everyone knows the story of the young man, who when he was being led to torture, asked to speak to his mother and moving his mouth to her ear as if he were going to whisper something to her in secret, bit it off. When the bystanders reproached him for this act, that not only was he a thief but impious towards his mother, he replied that this was the reward for his upbringing. He said: "If she had punished me when as a boy I stole my companion's book, which was my first theft, I would not have reached this criminal state. But she was lenient and welcomed the thief with a kiss." (2.10.§138.167)

Subsequent tales of maternal praiseworthiness include examples of homicide: "Spartan women preferred that their children should die honorably for their country rather than save their lives in flight. Wherefore it is recorded that many of them slew their cowardly children with their own hands, adding this as a funeral inscription, 'He was never my son, nor a true Spartan'" (2.10.§141.169).

34

Vives both reflects and participates in the creation of the ideological under-pinnings of the early modern period in Spain, a time in which the nation and its empire are forged. He anticipates what the psychoanalyst Jessica Benjamin signals as the triumph of "male rationality" that characterizes modern society:

> The basic tendencies of Western rationality correspond to the male repudiation of the mother, in which the other is objectified and instrumentalized. In other words, that atti-tude toward maternal nurturance and recognition which infuses early male identity formation also infuses the ratio-nality that is dominant in our culture. It might be called "male rationality." Male hegemony in the culture is expressed by the generalization of rationality and the exclusion of nur-turance, the triumph of individualistic, instrumental val-ues in all forms of social interaction. (295)

Benjamin argues that the more differentiated and isolated individu-als become in a society, the greater the likelihood of the eruption of vio-lence, whether in reality or fantasy. The strains on the social fabric are too great: "The fantasy, as well as the playing out of rational violence, does offer a controlled form of transcendence, the promise of the real thing" (296). The conditions of vehement patriarchy as well as the exclu-sionary rigidity that characterizes the social and religious practices of early modern Spain provide fertile ground for the "return of the repressed" in the form of its cultural productions, much as today we witness an "increase of aestheticized and eroticized violence in our media" (296). This perverse choreography of dominance and submission characterizes the male/female interaction in María de Zayas's tales, particularly in the second volume, the *Desengaños amorosos (The Disenchantments of Love).*

The juxtaposition of piety and perversion in Vives's text is not only logical but also inevitable. And the representation of violence against women in the drama and narrative of the period may also be construed as inevitable; for the texts both reveal and conceal social meanings, condone and subvert the dominant ideology.

In the annals of myth and history, as in the plays and stories I will discuss, the motif of rape refers less to the obvious subject of sexuality than to the symbolic use to which it is put. Critical cultural and political issues are expressed through the male/female interactions both within marriage and outside its boundaries. The nubile virgins and lawfully wedded wives that emerge as dramatis personae from their silent and protected worlds do so only when thrust into a plot—against their will.

A gender-inflected rereading of various works of secular Spanish literature discloses a tradition of rape narratives in canonical works, from traditional ballads to contemporary novels. As in the mythological works, it is a literary inheritance that lives concealed. It is ensconced from immediate view by rhetorical stratagems of disguise and displacement, overwhelmed by the superseding conflicts that the act of violation unleashes. It is to the meaning of this tradition that this study is dedicated; its intent is to reinterpret gender relations as central rather than marginal and to make articulate the silenced private realm, not so much ignored as subsumed into the clamor of public, state interests and the politics of power.

My focus is on the various narrative functions of sexual violence—as a prelude to revolution (Lope de Vega's *Fuenteovejuna;* Rojas Zorrilla's *Lucrecia y Tarquino* [Lucretia and Tarquin]); as a corollary to war (Calderón's *El alcalde de Zalamea*); as a privilege of class (Cervantes's "La fuerza de la sangre" ["The Power of Blood"]; Lope's *Peribáñez y el Comendador de Ocaña* [*Peribáñez and the Comendador of Ocaña*]). Although order is established anew after the upheaval, these texts describe a dangerous crisis of authority. The disquieting political implications of the mob uprising in *Fuenteovejuna* are considerably mitigated in Tirso's *La dama del olivar* (*The Lady of the Olive Grove*), which closely follows the plot line of Lope's play, but then gives way to a miraculous apparition of the Virgin and successfully displaces attention from the terrestrial to the celestial. The issue of tyrannicide is even more delicate in Lope's *El príncipe despeñado* (The Prince Flung Down), based on an historical incident of eleventh-century Navarre in which the assailant is none other than the king himself (who tries to imitate the ploy of the biblical David who rids himself of Uriah to gain access to Bathsheba (2 Sam. 11). He is portrayed cautiously: first and foremost as a wrongful usurper of the throne, and only then as a rapist, thus mitigating the political impact of his homicide at the hands of the wronged husband.

Of special interest is the distortion that occurs in the translation of source materials, be they biblical (Tirso de Molina's *La venganza de Tamar* [*Tamar's Revenge*]; Calderón's *Los cabellos de Absalón* [Absalon's Hair]); mythological (Rojas Zorrilla's and Guillén de Castro's *Progne y Filomena* [Procne and Philomela]; Calderón's *El pintor de su deshonra* [*The Painter of His Dishonour*], in which Deianeira's rape by the centaur Nessus is the determinative intertext); historical (Rojas Zorrilla's *Lucrecia y Tarquino*). These works are shaped and limited by the fetishism of honor that so marks the literature of the period. By a process of domestication that enables the reigning aristocratic values to coincide with moral values, the narrations are uniformly deprived of their original force and ambiguity. Symptomatically, however, they provide insight into implicit, tacit assumptions in the social construct of seventeenth-century Spain and lend voice to the silent obsessions of the period. That these obsessions led to gender oppression and acts of cruelty is made explicit in relevant tales from María de Zayas's story collections on the "Enchantments" and "Disenchantments" of love (*Novelas amorosas y ejemplares; Desengaños amorosos*).

Though the theme may be continuous, its uses and resolutions change. The seventeenth-century texts define the issue in terms of socially constructed codes of honor and personal revenge. Not until the twentieth century does an overtly erotic language emerge—in Lorca's *romances* "Preciosa y el aire" ("Preciosa and the Wind") and "Thamar y Amnón" ("Thamar and Amnon"), for example. Not until then, with Ana María Moix's *Julia,* are the devastating psychological effects on the victim brought to the fore. The violation—unspoken, untold—becomes a particularly incapacitating kind of violence, for it is turned inward, against the self.

The works here considered are all canonical. They are discussed in terms of the class and gender issues underlying the struggles between power and powerlessness, particularly relevant to us today. The tools of traditional humanistic hermeneutics can disclose the sexual ideology that underlies the elisions and ambiguities in the representation of rape in these literary texts. Such a rereading will perforce entail returning violence to the language, which, with its brilliant strategies of circumlocution, so often seeks to disguise, rather than to express, pain.

ONE

Rape and the Resolution
of Class Conflict

Cervantes's "La fuerza de la sangre" *(Exemplary Stories)*

The phrase "a blood puzzle" is taken from Margaret Atwood's poem "Letter from Persephone" (134–35) and seems an apt characterization of this puzzling tale of rape and restitution. If we compare "La fuerza de la sangre" with Isabel Allende's disturbing story "Una venganza" ("Revenge") *(Cuentos de Eva Luna [The Stories of Eva Luna])*, we are confronted with a similar ethical and psychological conundrum of a victim falling in love with her rapist. But, as Allende's title indicates, the ending is not the Cervantine comic solution of marriage but the tragic one of death.

Readers' response to this particular "exemplary" tale is usually one of discomfort—and understandably so, for it is a story that begins with a brutal rape and ends with the blissful marriage of Leocadia, the victim, and Rodolfo, her imperfectly reformed rapist. Like the priest's reaction to "The Story of Ill-Advised Curiosity" in *Don Quixote* (1.35), the manner of its telling is deemed commendable. Critics have traditionally admired it as a "well wrought urn" of structural and metaphoric symmetry (Piluso; Selig; Levisi; Gitlitz) while deploring its lack of psychological verisimilitude.

In an effort, perhaps, to mitigate this unease, previous criticism has emphasized the allegorical level of narration and the symbolic nature of the rapist's redemption (Casalduero 121–34), deflecting attention away from Leocadia and her ally doña Estefanía. Although in her article Adriana Slaniceanu refocuses the issue by undertaking a reappraisal of the active role of the "calculating" woman (so designated in the title of her study), she then betrays her important revisionist impulse. She comes perilously close to valorizing the rape by once again subsuming the female into an overall symbolic design wherein, infelicitously, "the rape is symbolic of impotence" (103)—at the spiritual level, of course—and in an unprecedented twist of the *felix culpa* theme, "Leocadia's awakening after the rape, her act of 'volver en sí' [coming to her senses], represents the birth of her ethical identity, the beginning of the process of defining who she is" (103).

By concentrating on the beginning (the rape) rather than the end (the marriage), I propose to privilege the literal level of narration. More precisely, I mean to salvage from oblivion the body—the female body, to be exact—in two senses: literally, as the "character" of the story, Leocadia; and metaphorically, as the body politic. By reading the body into the text again, we can see how Cervantes has subverted not only the conventions of romance (as Edward Friedman has perceptively shown in his analysis[1]) but also, and more specifically, those of the typical rape narrative: he has transformed what is usually a man's story into a woman's story. This subversion, as is true of most reformulations, is not without its paradoxes and problems.

Two twentieth-century poems on rape, in this case the legendary rape of Leda, provide a frame for the discussion of "La fuerza de la sangre" and signal the transformations in Cervantes's treatment of the general theme. The beginning of the novella is analogous to Yeats's "Leda and the Swan" (1923), which opens with violence:

> A sudden blow: the great wings beating still
> Above the staggering girl, her thighs caressed

> By the dark webs, her nape caught in his bill,
>
> He holds her helpless breast upon his breast. (441)

Rodolfo, like Jupiter transformed into a beast, rapes the virginal Leocadia. In Yeats's poem, Jupiter, after the deed is accomplished, with an "indifferent beak," "let her [Leda] drop"; Rodolfo also drops Leocadia: after leaving her at the square to find her way home, he departs for Italy, displaying the same postcoital indifference as the avian god: "He ultimately went off with so scant a recollection of what had occurred between himself and Leocadia that it might never have happened" (138).[2]

In both cases, the act of violation is also one of procreation: from Leda's eggs are hatched Clytemnestra and Helen, the most beautiful of women; from Leocadia's fertilized egg is born the exquisite child Luis. In Yeats's poem, the human offspring are effaced, and only the catastrophic consequence of this intercourse—the Trojan War—is emphasized:

> A shudder in the loins engenders there
>
> The broken wall, the burning roof and tower
>
> And Agamemnon dead. (441)

The "shudder in the loins" in Cervantes's tale has less spectacular consequences, affecting not the cycles of Western history but merely Toledan historical records, as Leocadia and Rodolfo continue the family dynasty— "They enjoyed each other, their children, and their grandchildren for many happy years" (149).

Although Leocadia is also dropped by an equally "indifferent beak," the rape does not obliterate her. The unfolding of her life, significantly different from that of Yeats's Leda, makes her much more akin to the figure depicted in the revisionist poem "Leda" (1964) by the contemporary American poet Mona Van Duyn. "In men's stories her life ended with his loss," she writes. She provides a different resolution, not war but marriage:

She tried for a while to understand what it was
That had happened, but then decided to let it drop.
She married a smaller man with a beaky nose,
And melted away in the storm of everyday life. (129)

Instead of the brutal movement from creation to destruction that Yeats's poem engenders, the rape of Leocadia begets only tranquil domesticity (of happiness we cannot know). As occurs in Van Duyn's text, violence, wrested from the awe-inspiring beauty accorded to it by Yeats, is demythified.

In fact, the sexual nature of the violation is muted in Cervantes's narrative. Rather than depict the stark physicality of the encounter, Cervantes consistently excludes the brutal physical details of the invaded and invading bodies, saying only that "Rodolfo was able to satisfy his lust before Leocadia recovered from her faint" (132–33). Indications of the violence of male desire are projected onto the description of the initial act of seizing: "Rodolfo rushed at Leocadia and, snatching her up into his arms, he proceeded to run away with her" (132). And, consistent with the rhetorical strategies of dream language, the key that opens the locked doors becomes the metaphoric substitute for the penis: "he [Rodolfo] had a separate apartment in his father's house . . . and keys to this room and to the whole apartment" (132). All reference to the shedding of Leocadia's blood in the sexual act is suppressed. When we are later informed that an accident has left Luis "with blood pouring from his head" (140), the element of innocently spilled blood does indeed link mother and son (Calcraft 201–2; Gitlitz 118), but hers must be assumed in absentia by the reader; only his appears in praesentia. It is not the blood of Leocadia's ruptured hymen but that of the male heir's cracked skull that gives the story its title. The final words—"an enjoyment that was permitted by heaven and by the power of the blood which the brave, illustrious, and Christian grandfather of little Luis saw spilled on the ground" (149)—emphasize the second incident of male violence (the accidental trampling of Luis) as the origin of signification, for it results in the ensuing blood recognition of both nobility and patrilineal descent.[3]

The tale has a middle (Luis's accident) and an end (marriage), but the beginning is elided. The male transgression is not presented but represented, displaced onto the uncontrolled horse that treads on the child (Gitlitz 117): "a horse whose rider could not restrain him in the fury of his gallop. It ran over him and left him [little Luis] for dead" (140). Where is the beginning? What happened to it, both in the Cervantine text and in the critical interpretations of the tale?

Leocadia herself leads us to the answer. In this tale of mimetic reversals (repetitions, but with a difference), just as Rodolfo has stolen her treasure, her priceless virginity ("he robbed Leocadia of her most precious possession in the darkness" [133]), she in turn steals a treasure of his—the crucifix. The rape and the crucifix become inextricably bound, joined metonymically by their contiguity at the "scene of the crime"; the shedding of Leocadia's blood is conflated with the shedding of the blood on the crucifix and is subsequently suppressed. This imbrication of wounds has motivated an interpretive history of the tale.

The rhetorical movement, whereby the crucifix becomes the tangible emblem of Leocadia's own blood sacrifice, has authorized critical displacement onto a Christian system of meaning. Placed within the overarching story of the Fall and Redemption through Christ, "La fuerza de la sangre" becomes a tale of the sinner saved, a three-part symphonic movement of sin, guilt, and salvation (Casalduero 121–34; Piluso). The problem with this analogy is that the score of the novella is missing the second movement: Rodolfo sins and is saved, but there is no indication that he experiences a sense of guilt.

Rodolfo's culpability is minimized, and his consciousness of sin is, in fact, conspicuously absent, a textual silence that is especially noteworthy amid the luxuriant blooming in post-Tridentine Spain of stories of great and passionate saints and sinners. Some critics have adjudged this lack morally objectionable (Schevill and Bonilla 387–89; Gitlitz 121); others have considered it simply "in bad taste" (Hainsworth 20). By classifying the tale as a miracle narrative, albeit a secularized and conventional one, Alban

Forcione (chap. 4) dispels as generically irrelevant some old doubts about the story's lack of psychological verisimilitude. But his analysis also fosters new hesitations, especially if one compares the problematic "La fuerza de la sangre" with the unproblematic miracle recounted in this seventeenth-century Puritan fable of rape:

> On the fourteenth of November, 1642, *a young Virgine, daughter to Mr. Adam Fisher,* was hurrying along a country road in Devonshire *so darke that she could scarce discerne her hand,* when the figure of a *Gentleman, Mr. Ralph Ashley,* a debased Cavalier, approached on horseback. Inspired by the *Devill* himself, this gentleman told the trusting maiden that he knew her father well and would be pleased to escort her home in safety, for there were lustfull soldiers in those parts.

Of course, he tried to rape her, and she prayed: "Just then *a fearefull Comet burst out in the ayre* and *strucke* the rapacious Cavalier with a *streame of fire* so that he *fell downe staggering"* (Brownmiller 375; emphasis in the original).

A supernatural intervention achieves this ending; in "La fuerza de la sangre" a more modest anagnorisis, coupled with an entrapment scheme, leads to the resolution. It is not the action of divine grace but the enterprising resourcefulness of human (female, in this case) agents that effects a satisfactory ending. Forcione draws analogies between Cervantes's Leocadia and the legendary Leocadia of Toledo ("by echoing the legend of St. Leocadia, Cervantes elevates his suffering heroine and associates her restoration with the triumph of the martyr" [391]) and stresses the opposition between the saint's heavenly marriage to Christ and Leocadia's earthly version. But the significant difference between the two women both precedes the reward of marriage and is more fundamental: it is precisely Leocadia's refusal of martyrdom that distinguishes her from her saintly counterpart.

As a variation of the "miracle-from-without," another interpretive strategy posits a "miracle-from-within": a spiritual transformation (Braun 174–76;

Calcraft). R. P. Calcraft formulates the existence of a "new Rodolfo" (200) upon his return from Italy, whose "moral redemption" (203) has been secured. Proof of this metamorphosis is sought in his "reasoned argument" (200) to his mother concerning his desire for a beautiful (as opposed to ugly) wife. Yet his words—"I seek loveliness and I desire beauty" (145)—ominously echo the narrator's description of "the great beauty of the face which Rodolfo had seen, that of Leocadia" (131), which Rodolfo saw and sought that fateful summer night. Although the contemplation of beauty can have Platonic overtones (Slaniceanu 104; De Rentiis), the immediate context of the utterance is the "right and proper pleasure which a husband and wife enjoy" (145) in the marital state. Leocadia was, is, and will be apprehended by Rodolfo as a beautiful object, an incitement to his erotic fantasies.[4] By reading Rodolfo's speech for its omissions rather than for its admissions, Friedman notes its many lacks in terms of "a semiotics of change or of remorse" (149). There is no rhetoric of repentance.

Critical attention has focused almost exclusively (with the notable exception of Slaniceanu) on the male figure. The symbolic misreadings necessarily privilege the adversary in the plot, Rodolfo, as the sinner in need of redemption; in the interpretations that admit to the uneasy coexistence between human endeavor and Divine Providence (Forcione 383; El Saffar, *Novel to Romance* 134–36), gender considerations are absent: "human" is genderless. In its exploration of the assumptions about genre, Friedman's counterreading acknowledges the irony of the "rhetoric of power, of male authority" (151) at the conclusion of the tale but fails to address the assumptions about gender that inform the text from beginning to end.

A rereading of "La fuerza de la sangre" requires us to take into account the gender markings in the text. Annette Kolodny reminds us that reading and interpretation are activities that are "learned, historically determined, and thereby necessarily gender-inflected" (452). Have we, both male and female readers, accustomed to lending import to the male logos, emplotted the tale according to our expectations (both in terms of genre and gender), rather than according to Cervantes's actual practices?

It is as though the critics had performed the operation of Tereus, who cut out Philomela's tongue to assure her silence after he raped her. Leocadia is blindfolded and rendered mute by a fainting spell during the violation; it is precisely because she retains her tongue that the story continues. Rodolfo's only wish was to discard and disregard the victim: "Rodolfo immediately wished to be rid of her" (133); he subsequently left the country in a state of such forgetfulness about the act "that it might never have happened" (138). Yet seven years later his willed amnesia is cured, not by a miracle but by a reminder by his mother, who has called him home in order to restore honor and legitimacy to Leocadia and her child. It is thus doña Estefanía who denies him the right to forget what society might have allowed him to forget because of his privileged position.

If Leocadia had not regained her power of speech, Rodolfo's sin (and crime) would have remained undisclosed: her voice permits her to resist victimization and quite literally plot the ending. From the beginning her speech proves itself a powerful weapon, able to contain Rodolfo's sexual "instrument." Once she recovers her senses, Leocadia's verbal agility and sophisticated arguments confuse and silence Rodolfo, and "he did not know what to say or do" (133). A second series of "wise words" (135), coupled with physical opposition, render him impotent, at least temporarily, and save her from a second attack: "Tired and no longer aroused, Rodolfo left Leocadia lying in his bed" (135), and he returns to his male companions to seek advice. Then, years later, after the providential anagnorisis of grandfather and grandchild at the scene of the accident, the next, and decisive, stage of restoration occurs.

Leocadia is more fortunate than the tongueless Philomela, who must weave a tapestry to reveal her misfortune. Although her own mother remains a shadowy, silent figure, deferential to the father, Leocadia is able to tell her story to Rodolfo's mother, doña Estefanía, a wise, older female figure.[5] This maternal mediator actively assumes responsibility for weaving the text that will become known as "La fuerza de la sangre," and with infinite resourcefulness plots the ending. The result of her labor is a spectacular, live tapestry of a richly attired and beautiful Leocadia—an irresistible attraction to Rodolfo. If doña Estefanía's plan is artifice, the fine originality of its design and execution makes it literally an example of *ars facere.* As in the case of Philomela's tapestry, art becomes a means of resistance.[6]

If Leocadia was not at a loss for words at the crucial moment of the attack, neither was she at a loss for a remedy. Her theft of the crucifix was purposeful, done "not out of devotion or any conscious intention to steal it, but prompted by a clever plan of her own" (136): it serves both as icon and as the corroborating evidence of her rape, like that required by a court of law. She had intended to use the crucifix to identify the transgressor, if need be announcing its loss and possible restitution from the pulpits of Toledo, until her father counsels her to silence and passivity: "What you must do, daughter, is keep it and put your trust in it, for since it bore witness to your misfortune, it will also permit justice to be obtained on your behalf" (137–38). This advice, ostensibly a mark of discreet balancing of the conflicting claims of the spiritual and secular worlds (Forcione 385–86; Slaniceanu 103), also signals male compliance with sexual custom.[7] In contrast, and admittedly under very different circumstances, at the marriage doña Estefanía surprises both her son and his friends (erstwhile accomplices in Leocadia's kidnapping) by making a public statement: "Their sense of wonder increased when Estefanía announced in front of all those present that Leocadia was the young girl their son had abducted while in their company, a fact which left Rodolfo no less amazed than they" (148). Paternal suppression is thus countered by maternal expression; to the resolution doña Estefanía has achieved by theatrical persuasion she adds the binding ties of community pressure to social conformity.

The bonding between women (Leocadia and Estefanía) enables the plot to unfold, for they resist the cultural assumption of female passivity.[8] By breaking the silence of shame imposed by the male honor code, they risk a resolution. "La fuerza de la sangre" has a conventional denouement; what is not conventional is the women's role in achieving it. It is atypical within the *Exemplary Stories,* in which responsibility for resolving honor disputes falls on the brother, as occurs in "Las dos doncellas" ("The Two Damsels") and "La señora Cornelia" ("The Lady Cornelia") (Slaniceanu 197). Furthermore, Leocadia and Estefanía have avoided any repetition and reenactment of violence in their resolution of peace.[9] Herein lies a radical subversion of the typical rape sequence within the *comedia*.

Whether in Calderón's comedy *No hay cosa como callar* (There Is Nothing Like Silence) or in his tragedy *El alcalde de Zalamea,* the male codes dominate: in the first example only the threat of a bloody revenge can lead the rapist to the altar, and in the second instance, when negotiation efforts fail, the rapist is killed by the victim's father. In both cases it is the male culture of violence that determines the endings. Men instigate the action in rape narratives; men also cure the infraction. The female maintains her status as object—of desire and of exchange—throughout.

According to Sadie Trachman, a likely source for Cervantes's "La fuerza de la sangre" is Bandello's novella 15 (3:24–28). Reading the Italian tale reveals the dramatic nature of Cervantes's transformation of the model in terms of gender markings. The descriptive subheading outlines the plot: "Alessandro, duke of Florence, makes Pietro wed a woman he had ravished and supply her with a very rich dowry" (24). (The two male friends/accomplices are also required to contribute to the sizable dowry.) From this skeletal frame, Cervantes obviously produces a much more complex and multidimensional text; but what is interesting for our purposes is the male arrogation of power and control of all phases of Bandello's plot. In the Italian tale the men are the exclusive agents of the narrative sequence—the aggrieved father seeks justice by appealing directly to the duke, and the duke in turn exercises his authority by enforcing a marriage of distinct social inequality. The daughter remains a distraught and weeping victim, whose fate is in everyone's hands but her own: object of Pietro's desire; object of her father's grievance; object of the duke's justice.

Leocadia, in contrast, refuses victimization. Her first act of rebellion is to speak. Leocadia's shift from patient to agent (with the help of her ally, doña Estefanía) effectively changes her position "from object to subject of barter" (Wilson, "Cervantes's Last Romance" 117). Although she is inscribed within the external structure as an object of exchange between men (father and rapist/husband), the internal dynamics defy the sacrificial meaning. Leocadia enters the marriage union not as a martyr but as a desiring subject who gazes on Rodolfo with love—"now that she could see so close to her the man she already loved more than the light of her eyes" (146)—and literally faints at the thought that she might not achieve her goal (147). In Calderón's *No hay cosa como callar,* the resolution in marriage of Leonora to her rapist Juan is decidedly inauspicious (Mujica 43); in "La fuerza de la sangre," on the other hand, the narrator assures us that the outcome was felicitous (149).

In literature, as in society, politics and sexuality are connected intimately. Rape provides the most dramatic example of this association. Lucretia's rape, for example, motivates a rebellion against the rapist Tarquin and the government of his father, leading to the establishment of a republic; the attempted rape of Laurencia in Lope's *Fuenteovejuna* is a prelude to the townspeople's rebellion against the tyrannical Comendador, in favor of the rule of the Catholic kings. In "La fuerza de la sangre" violence threatens to explode, for once the family has identified Rodolfo as the rapist, closure is required: marriage or death. Because both parties are still single and both give their consent, marriage occurs instead of conflict, the bedroom replaces the dueling ground, and healing takes place both for Leocadia and for the body politic. A potentially dangerous social impasse—a confrontation between two families of unequal power and wealth—provoked by Rodolfo's abusive transgressions, sanctioned by male society, has been averted.

But the celebratory stance of what we may consider a final epithalamium is subtly undercut by the narrator, who at the crucial moment defers to another author—"it can be left to another pen and another wit more delicate than my own to recount the general rejoicing of all those present" (148)—and proceeds to describe the ritualized gestures of a theatrical spectacle, distant from the private and personal. Although the patriarchal family structure is seemingly intact at the end, the painstaking process by which it is pieced together after Rodolfo's initial assertion of power calls into question the politics of a corrupt aristocracy and the prerogatives of male sexuality. After all, Rodolfo has been exposed as a rich noble with "perverted inclinations, excessive liberty, and licentious companions" (131). Furthermore, his lack of restraint is seen as symptomatic and even canonized by his class: "For rich people who happen to be generous always find someone to applaud their excesses and call their foul deeds fair" (131–32). The formulaic, fairy-tale ending manages to sublimate political tension into an erotic resolution, but in the process the text has disclosed an insidious subtext of both gender and class conflicts—without overtly confronting them. The reigning ideology (conservative and hierarchical) is put into question but not overturned.

Considering the strictures within which she is functioning, as a woman and as a member of a class less distinguished than Rodolfo's, Leocadia emerges as a survivor. In a second revisionist poem on the subject of Leda ("Leda Reconsidered," 1964), Van Duyn envisions the maiden as curious and giving, not filled with fear and awe. Instead of the violence of the "sudden blow," the poem's final stanzas describe the action, as opposed to the reaction, of Leda:

> She [Leda] waited for him so quietly that
> he came on her quietly,
> almost with tenderness,
> not treading her.
> Her hand moved into the dense plumes
> on his breast to touch
> the utter stranger. (132)

As Leda here refuses the conventional passivity of brutal victimization by affirming her right to erotic fulfillment, so Leocadia has refused the passivity of silence, mutilation, and unwilling sacrifice and has actively negotiated a bond of mutual love (and pleasure) with her husband. She has indeed made this her story, not his/story, not Rodolfo's; she too, from a position of control, reaches out "to touch / the utter stranger."

TWO

Rape and Revolution

The Chaste Lucretia

Rojas Zorrilla's Lucrecia y Tarquino: *"The Taming of Lucretia"*

T he rape of Lucretia was well known by the time of Rojas's tragedy, which was probably composed between 1635 and 1640.[1] It had already entered the *romancero* canon, the opening lines of which are quoted—comically and anachronistically—at a moment of rising tension prior to the rape (3.1952–53).[2]

The story is as follows:[3] It occurs in Rome, still under the rule of kings (the traditional date given for the overthrow of the monarchy is 510 B.C.).[4] Already in possession of Rome, Tarquin "the Proud" orders the siege of Ardea. There Collatine, a member of the royal family, and two other noblemen (in Rojas's play also sons of the king) boast of the virtue of their respective wives in the presence of the king's son, Sextus Tarquinius (Tarquin). As a test, they return to Rome that night: two of the three women are found amusing themselves at a court party (in the sources, the other wives are the king's daughters); only Collatine's wife, Lucretia, is dutifully spinning wool at home. She, of course, wins the contest. Smitten, Tarquin later returns alone, and Lucretia is duty bound to offer him lodging. In the dead of night he enters her bedroom armed with a sword, and although Lucretia at first successfully repulses him (reminding him of the rules of

Figure 3. Lucas Cranach, the Elder, *The Suicide of Lucretia*, circa 1530.
Courtesy of the Alte Pinakotech, Munich

hospitality, his princely responsibilities, the family bonds), he then threatens her with public shame: unless she succumbs he will kill her and her
black slave and place them side by side, telling the world that he found
them flagrante delicto and killed them both. The next morning Lucretia
summons her father, her husband, and a trusted companion of each. She
confides in them, makes them vow her revenge, and kills herself with

Tarquin's sword. (In view of these circumstances, Lucas Cranach's austere depiction, in several of his many versions, of Lucretia as nude at this critical moment, though emphasizing the sacrificial exemplarity of her death, is startlingly unhistorical [fig. 3]). Brutus, until then a feigned madman, pulls the sword out of her body and swears to drive the hated Tarquins from Rome. They parade Lucretia's body in the public square, rallying the people's support to abolish the monarchy and inaugurate the Roman Republic.

This tale is a founding myth, as such, in which the personal and the political are tightly imbricated: Lucretia's violated body is one with that of the wrongfully usurped body politic of Rome; as Tarquin lies to the Gabii in order to enter their camp (1.639–744), so does he deceitfully gain entrance into the home of Lucretia, in both cases at first "without a sword," only later displaying the instrument of power (and sexual prowess). Lucretia dies in the cause of her honor and to retrieve the honor of the state, for her death signals the downfall of the tyrants.

The fame of the chaste Lucretia remained unblemished until St. Augustine, in the context of discussing the moral problem of suicide in *The City of God* (1.19), refocuses Lucretia's suicide in terms of guilt, rather than shame (Donaldson 33). He concludes: "and there is no escape from the dilemma, when you say: 'If she was made an adulteress, why has she been praised; if she was chaste, why was she slain?'" (1.19.89). The issue becomes one of spiritual chastity, which hinges on the question of consent. Augustine, writing in the immediate aftermath of Alaric's sack of Rome, adds another twist of logic when he considers the defilement of women in religious life (1.16) and differentiates between primary voluntary consent and secondary involuntary consent, given automatically when pleasure is experienced and described as "consent of the mind":

> But since it is not only the occasion of pain, but also the
> occasion of lust that can be inflicted on another's body by force,
> in the latter case, though shamefastness, to which a superla-
> tively steadfast mind holds fast, is not thrust out, yet shame

is thrust in, shame for fear that the mind too may be thought
to have consented to an act that could perhaps not have
taken place without some carnal pleasure. (75, 77)

According to St. Augustine, then, Lucretia is neither heroic (she gave her
consent to Tarquin) nor chaste (her body consented to pleasure) (Bryson
167). Augustine's decontextualization—in effect a radical depoliticiza-
tion—of the legend accounts for the Renaissance eroticization of Lucretia
in the visual arts: in Lucas Cranach the Elder's painting of the moment
of suicide, she is depicted alone and entirely nude while holding a knife to
her breast; in Titian's painting (1570), the sensuous flesh of the full, soft body
of Lucretia, semiprone amid bed linens, confronts the fully clothed Tarquin
(Bryson 167–71). Neither was Lucretia exempt from the general baroque
process of demythologizing: sixteenth-century Spanish poets enjoyed
rhyming *Lucrecia* with *necia* (foolish) and were equally at ease calling her a
whore (Gillet).[5]

It is against the background of these competing evaluations of Lucretia—
the pagan one concentrating on reputation; the Christian one on conscience—that we must perforce situate Rojas's glaring and apparently unique
departure from the plot (*L y T* 32, n. 20): Lucretia faints, and she is unconscious when the rape is consummated. First Tarquin ("Sexto" in Rojas's play)
informs us of this: "She swooned away, and in her swoon, / . . . guiltless was
she disgraced" (3.2030, 2033). Then Lucretia corroborates it:

> On account of no fault in me;
> for in a grievous swoon
> a corpse was I to his outrage,
> cold marble, motionless tree trunk. (3.2116–19)

A narrative hiatus mirrors the fainting. A blackout occurs. The rape is
recounted only in retrospect, the time lapse replaced by a nighttime view
of the suspicious husband, who in his distraught meanderings evokes the

image of the bloodied white dove wounded by an arrow (3.1982–89), the first symbolic presaging of the crime (1.541–46).

The loss of consciousness is crucial, for it obviates Augustine's sabotage of Lucretia's exemplarity. And, although they may seem strange bedfellows, it places Lucretia (literally and figuratively) beside her eighteenth-century descendant, Clarissa, who is drugged during her rape by Lovelace. Unconsciousness is equivalent to nonconsent: "For the law of rape specifically stipulates that unconsciousness (along with states like idiocy, insanity, and sleep) 'negatives' consent" (Ferguson 100). The result of this blankness is that neither the victim nor the reader experiences the rape as such; but neither does the rapist.

When Tarquin says, "I laid a dagger at her breast, / and she, her life in my arms " (3.2028–29), and Lucretia later describes herself as a corpse during the rape ("a corpse was I to his outrage"), the trope is one of lifelessness. Although the form of rape—its representation—has been accomplished, the substance of rape is missing, because there has been no possession (possession of the body is not equivalent to possession of the person). Because Lucretia's subjectivity has remained inviolate, her rapist is denied the satisfaction of complete domination of a humiliated and subjugated Other.[6] Rojas portrays Tarquin as immediately remorseful after the rape, hoping to be struck by a castigatory bolt of lightning (3.2038–41). In contrast to this, Rojas's principal source, the Spanish translation of Malvezzi's *Tarquino Superbo,* states that: "Tarquin departs both merry and triumphant" (qtd. *L y T* 33, n. 21). Raymond MacCurdy has tentatively interpreted this departure as Rojas's imbuing the character of Tarquin with the "recognition and self-knowledge" usually reserved for a tragic hero (*L y T* 33). But, except in the rare instances of necrophilia, how can there be either pleasure or a sense of victory when the body possessed is the equivalent of a corpse? Lovelace, too, feels cheated and dissatisfied after his rape of Clarissa. In a letter he describes himself as "gloomy," and he feels that the rape is incomplete: "And yet why say I, *completed?* when the *will,* the *consent,* is wanting—and I have still views before me of obtaining that?" (qtd. Ferguson

102; emphasis in the original). Tarquin persists in characterizing Lucretia as "the most chaste woman" (3.2037), even after he has performed the action of destroying said chastity.

By restoring Lucretia's pre-Augustinian purity (both voluntary and involuntary, as she neither gives consent nor experiences pleasure), Rojas effectively simplifies the story and Lucretia herself. She has lost her interiority as well as her adult responsibility for decision making. Although infantilized, she is unambiguous as a paradigm; she remains an unequivocally chaste wife rather than a possible adulteress. Why then, to return to Augustine's question, does she commit suicide?

Once again Rojas departs from the source materials (*L y T* 34, n. 23). According to the legend, before plunging the sword in her breast, Lucretia exacts from the men an oath of revenge against Tarquin, not just as her rapist but as a member of a family of tyrants. In addition, she wishes to preserve her model reputation for purity among Roman womanhood. The public and political concerns are uppermost. In Rojas, private and personal family motives determine her decision. Lucretia explicitly rejects the option of requiring male vengeance:

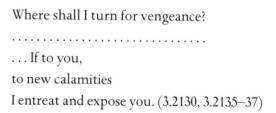

> Where shall I turn for vengeance?
> . . . .
> . . . If to you,
> to new calamities
> I entreat and expose you. (3.2130, 3.2135–37)

She replaces possible action against Tarquin ("vengeance must be exacted, / and from the offender, in vain" [3.2146–47]) with action against herself ("revenge against myself / will be the revenge of all" [3.2148–49]). Although the husband's revenge is promised in a second part (3.2163–65), the play ends with Lucretia's self-inflicted punishment for her shame, the stain of which only blood can cleanse ("May I cleanse this stain with blood" [3.2152]). It thus becomes an act of ritual purification—a rite of sacrifice to remove the stain and stigma of the sex pollution inflicted by Tarquin on Lucretia, but more importantly, on her husband and her father, on her lineage. The confessional nature of her declaration and her explicit assumption of blame provide the basis for a publicly sanctioned retribution.[7]

Throughout the play the pollution taboo located in a person's (Lucretia's) body is symbolically associated with the body politic (Douglas 128). Tarquin is a threat to the entire cultural system because he recklessly crosses boundaries, disrespecting designations of property, whether the ownership be of land or of females. As he deceives the Gabii for their land, so he betrays the bonds of kinship with Collatine for his wife. If doors mark boundaries between spaces, from his first appearance on stage Tarquin is defined by his violent opening of doors closed to him. Of the Roman senate he boasts: "They closed the doors on me, / but then did violence fling them open" (1.13–14); in the final act an improperly opened door is Collatine's first warning sign that the seclusion of his home has been violated: the visitors react with surprise when they see it: "The door ajar? The house / unlit? What is this, heavens above?" (3.2050–51). Both the sanctity of the home and that of the state have been trespassed, the rules of right order abused.

But rape is a private and largely invisible crime (an "unseen shame," an "invisible disgrace," a "private scar" in the words of Shakespeare's Lucrece [827–28]), which is why signs of harm (bruises, cuts, and so forth) are sought by courts as substantiating evidence of resistance to nonconsensual intercourse. The connection in the symbolic order between the physical body and the body politic needs to be made real—tangible and visible to the naked eye. Thus Lucretia's dead body provides the necessary proof that legitimizes political action. Her wound is the analogical equivalent to the wound of the state, and it is paraded for all to see in a way that the metaphorical wound to Lucretia's chastity could never be demonstrated. The final verses of Shakespeare's *The Rape of Lucrece* make this clear:

When they had sworn to this advisèd doom,
They did conclude to bear dead Lucrece thence,

To show her bleeding body through Rome,
And so to publish Tarquin's foul offence:
Which being done with speedy diligence,
The Romans plausibly did give consent
To Tarquin's everlasting banishment. (vv. 1849–55)

But for Rojas's Lucretia, her suicide is hardly the enactment of a trope, a stage setting to make symbolic wounds real. Her language is that of pollution, yet, although her rape entails bodily defilement, her spiritual chastity—we are assured—remains intact. Either we ascribe to her a secret guilt (and not that she inadvertently experienced pleasure, a possibility negated by the loss of consciousness) or she has failed to distinguish, as the Church did so assiduously, between body and soul. Or, these two possibilities are linked.

Pollution taboos center on sexual relations, which require strict enforcement to avoid their explosive, conflictive potential (Douglas 140–58). In a society's need for control, the quest for purity can become not a means but an end in itself. Although it is a worthy pursuit, Douglas warns, "It is another thing to try and make our existence into an unchanging lapidary form. Purity is the enemy of change, of ambiguity and compromise" (162). It is my contention that in Rojas's revisions of the Roman legend, his society's veneration of chastity—internalized by Lucretia and exemplified by her—constitutes a perverse scenario, wherein a usually normal and valid ideal of purity has run amok.

From the moment Lucretia appears on stage, she defines herself by deprivation—she rejects any but the plainest clothes, she rejects frivolous pastimes. She scorns the vanities of the world, paying exclusive attention to her household duties, a living example of Fray Luis de León's *La perfecta casada (The Perfect Wife)*. In the course of her first stage appearance, Lucretia's self-image is revealed as that of a "noble and chaste lady" (1.288), "prudent and honorable" (1.290), "prudent and chaste" (1.426). When her husband enters we learn that she is obedient to him (she is "a woman

58

who wisely obeys," according to Brutus [1.523]), entirely submissive to his will and desires. Later Collatine glories in the fact that his wife "possesses no more will / than I allow her" (2.885–86). She is exclusively—in fact fanatically—encoded in the language of female morality, understood as abnegation and chastity. And her reputation precedes her, for as her maid reassures her—"your reputation protects you" (1.282).

In her final speech, Lucretia seeks to blame herself: "Was it perchance / my virtue?" (3.2122–23). With this cue, the critic is quick to unmask her:

> But although as a wife Lucrecia has all the qualities enu-
> merated by Luis de León in *La perfecta casada,* she is a human
> being, and as such, is not faultless. She has about her a fault,
> a one-sidedness, that is to contribute to her tragedy—an
> excessive pride in her own virtue. (MacCurdy 44)

In a classic example of the victim victimized, Lucretia is here blamed for collusion with her rapist, albeit unintentionally. The accusation of exaggerated virtue is not invalid. Its formulation, however, is misdirected and too limited: it is the fault not of Lucretia personally but of a social mythology "that is to contribute to her tragedy." If she is guilty of any collusion, it is with the reigning gender ideology.

Lucretia asks if her virtue was the cause of her tragedy. To answer that, we must go back to the moment of origin of Tarquin's fascination that leads to the brutality. It begins not, as one might assume, with a tempting gaze at Lucretia's beauty but has instead "rhetorical origins" (Vickers 217). Let us recall that at a nocturnal evening gathering at their camp, Collatine (in the presence of Tarquin) boasts to his companions about the incomparable virtues of his wife (2.870–86), whereupon the men decide to ride back and see what each wife is doing. In Rojas's play, the horizons of competition are expanded intertextually, so to speak. Collatine is provoked into his competitive display by a song praising the unsurpassed fidelity of Dido (2.855–58), and the trial of the three wives is mirrored

humorously in the court performance of a *comedia de repente* (improvisation)
on the judgment of Paris. Its outcome—the Trojan War—known but not
represented, functions in anticipatory analogy to the nefarious result of the
seemingly innocuous wife-test among the three noble Roman soldiers.

The words spoken in praise of Lucretia fire Tarquin's imagination,
which Brutus fears and tries to warn against: "for praise awakens / the
most deeply sleeping lusts" (2.913–14); "for envy seeks / in just such high
repute / to practice theft and robbery" (2.932–34). Shakespeare had also understood praise as provocative: "For by our ears our hearts oft tainted be"
(38). When Brutus chastises the foolish husbands for giving free reign to
their imagination ("and do not laud lightheartedly / in your imaginings, /
that which is not for sale" [2.894–96]), he has intuited the central role of
fantasy in erotic psychology. Fantasy is at the very inception of sexuality
(as distinguished from the satisfaction of a basic need), and desire and pro-
scription go hand in hand.[8] The boastful praise has set in motion the desiring imagination and directed it toward an absent—and prohibited—good.
Collatine's evocation of his fantastic Lucretia has provided Tarquin with
his "stage-setting of desire" (Laplanche and Pontalis 28).

Although Lucretia is both beautiful and chaste, it is the latter quality that
most incites Tarquin (and, incidentally, distinguishes this foreground scenario from the background *comedia,* where only the beauty of the three god-
desses is at issue in the award of Paris's golden apple). Brutus notes in an aside:

(Either I am wholly mad
or Sextus Tarquin spies
the chastity of Lucretia
with envious eyes.) (2.1269–72)

Tarquin himself admits

That divine virtue
and that reserve seize

my soul; since beauty

increases with deprivation. (3.1583–86)

According to Livy, Lucretia's chastity was as much to blame as her beauty in arousing Tarquin's lust: "It was at that fatal supper that Lucretia's beauty, and proven chastity, kindled in Sextus Tarquinius the flame of lust, and determined him to debauch her" (98); in Dio Cassius's *Roman History* it is written that "Sextus, the son of Tarquin, set his heart upon outraging her, not so much because he was inspired with passion by her beauty as because he chose to plot against her chaste reputation" (1:89). The same is true of Malvezzi's version, where, among the incentives to lust, "the worst is virtue itself, and among the virtues, chastity, the most opposed to pleasure, is the one that most incites to lasciviousness: it is a virtue so attractive in itself that it makes even vice fall in love with it" (qtd. *L y T* 27, n. 18). Let us recall also that the full title of Juan Pastor's earlier play on the theme (1528) is *Farsa o Tragedia de la castidad de Lucrecia* (Farce or Tragedy of the Chastity of Lucretia).

The concatenation of desire and prohibition arouses Tarquin's imagination; the sight of Lucretia exacerbates his condition, for not only is she beautiful, she is also the perfect household nun. While the other wives are entertaining themselves, Lucretia, to a background song about the faithful Penelope (2.1133–36), is busy only with her embroidery work. The first meeting between the two is fraught with sexual tension: Tarquin refuses the sweets offered to him, for, as he informs us in an aside, Lucretia is the only *dulce* (sweetmeat) he requires ("He who has seen your eyes / requires no sweets" [2.1256–57]); he misplaces the glass he is returning to the tray—another proleptic symbol of broken honor, upon which Collatine immediately remarks, also in an aside: "If like glass / honor is in peril, before me lies a sign / that warns and prepares me" (2.1280–82).

To this portrait of Lucretia as the embodiment of a social gender stereotype of the feminine—pious and passive, obedient and subservient, and, above all else, pure—another quality must be stressed: she is devoid of sexual desires. Relegated exclusively to a domestic environment, protected within a confined space, she is "a pearl enclosed in a shell / a light protected within itself" (3.1581–82). In this encapsulated, rarefied space, sex is nonexistent: "Within marriage, within the 'asexual' domestic domain, intercourse itself loses its libidinous properties" (Stratton 43). As a wife, Lucretia lives a peculiarly disembodied existence, unbesmirched by the most elemental of biological ties: no children are mentioned, which further enhances her immaculacy.

If Lucretia is depicted as stereotypically feminine, so does her male counterpart, Tarquin, play the culturally defined role of the stereotypical male: he is violent, aggressive, authoritarian, and driven by an ungovernable lust, his virility symbolized by his ever-ready sword. This exaggerated and strictly maintained binary opposition of gender role identity is located spatially throughout the play in a contrast between inside and outside, or bedroom and battlefield. Tarquin's violent penetration of Lucretia's private locus of renunciation functions as a return of the repressed. He is the nightmarish monster of forbidden sexual desires ("this monster of cruelties, / this monster of gross deeds" [3.2096–97]). Rojas's use of exaggerated effects and inclination in the revenge plays to "cultivate horror for horror's sake" (MacCurdy 31) reflect, in addition to a Senecan legacy (MacCurdy 36), a proto-Gothic sensibility akin to María de Zayas's, whose cruel tales of chastity betrayed are fraught with erotic overtones.[9]

Because of the absence of an actively desiring subjectivity in Lucretia, and her self-proclaimed lack of will independent of her husband's, her existence as a passive object is assured. Her modesty in demeanor and dress is governed by her fear of being seen, which to her means activating the desiring male gaze ("she who dresses / in splendor desires to be seen" [1.311–12]). During the initial and fatal competition among the men concerning their wives, Brutus detected the commodification of women as though they were possessions with exchange value, and objected to it:

Are women horses,
to be praised for blood,
for bravery, for spirit,
for speed, for discipline,
that one may better sell them? (2.897–901)

Collatine's rhetorical excess, which merited his being characterized by Lucretia as "a foolish spouse" (2.1251), "an unwise husband" (3.1776), has endangered his most prized possession—his wife. As Catharine Stimpson has observed about Shakespeare's "Lucrece": "Because men rape what other men possess, rape becomes in part a disastrous element of male rivalry. The woman's body is a prize in a zero-sum game that men play" (58).[10]

Lucretia's body is, paradoxically, desexualized yet the very locus of desire, as though the site of the primal maternal prohibition. It is both revered and feared, invested with an aura, surrounded by an invisible magic circle that makes of it a fetish object. The etymological origin of the word, through the Portuguese *feitiço* from the Latin passive form *facticius (facere)* "meaning made by art, artificial, was probably first applied to images, idols or amulets made by hand, and later included *all objects possessing magical potency, i.e.* bewitched or 'faked'" (Haddon 67; emphasis in the original). It was appropriated by Marx for his concept of "commodity fetishism" and by Freud for his analysis of "erotic fetishism."[11] In both cases there is confusion between the power an object represents and the object itself: for Marx the commodity itself is confused with the value assigned to it in the system of exchange, and it is worshiped falsely; for Freud the object associated with sex is itself desired. In both instances desire is, therefore, misdirected and misplaced.

Rojas's elision of any description of Lucretia's specifically sexual attributes is noteworthy in comparison with Shakespeare's text. As he admires Lucretia asleep in bed, Rojas's Tarquin restricts himself to the cosmetic cosmos of her face, the "heaven of her eyes" (3.2003), the "sleeping . . .

sun" (3.2008–9); Shakespeare's Tarquin allows himself to gaze downward onto "[h]er breasts, like ivory globes circlèd with blue, / A pair of maiden worlds unconquerèd" (407–8). National differences as well as generic differences between poetry and theater account, in part, for the greater modesty of the Spaniard. It is also related, however, to the Spanish Lucretia's special sacralization as a fetish object, a process that always entails "aversion from the real female genitals" (Freud 216). There is a refusal to confront the sexuality of this "earthly saint," as Shakespeare describes her (85).

In the deranged movement of desire enacted in this play, chastity, embodied in the person of Lucretia, has been invested with erotic value and is accordingly venerated. It is, of course, an impossible and doomed scenario, above all for Lucretia: for her to function successfully as the object of desire, her subjectivity must be annihilated. To quote from Louise Kaplan:

> In its narrowest meaning, the fetishism in a male perversion
> entails a displacement of sexual desire away from the whole
> identity of a woman to some accessory or garment, some
> object ancillary to her being. . . . By virtue of its fantasized or
> actual isolation from the woman's breathing, responding,
> sensing, pulsating, experiencing body, the fetish object, unlike
> the woman herself, can be controlled and manipulated. (34)

Lucretia's loss of consciousness during the rape further reinforces her reification.

Let us return to the scene of the crime—really the two crimes, if we take into account the Christian condemnation of suicide. The exaggeration of gender role identity has extended beyond the bounds of normalcy and moved into the pathological. The socially sanctioned ideals of masculinity and femininity have turned on themselves, so to speak, and provided the script for a perverse and dangerous scenario, in this case with sadomasochistic motifs. If rape is one of the manifestations of sexual sadism in males (Kaplan 26–28), self-mutilation is one of the manifestations of perverse masochism in women.[12] The erotic connotations of Lucretia's stabbing herself with Tarquin's sword are clear: "Self-mutilation is the pornography of the mute," according to Kaplan (360). Lucretia—whose very being is defined by its lack of spoken desire—is acting out this statement.

In her final speech, Lucretia refers to herself in the third person:

> . . . you see here
> the glass of her honor shattered,
> the chaste bed defiled,
> the ermine, guardian
> of her snowy white coat when pure,
> besmirched with mud. (3.2078–83)

When she adds in the following verse that "Lucretia is no longer Lucretia," it is clear that she, too, has confused the sign with the thing, her personhood with her value as the object of others' erotic interest. Her existence and her meaning are her chastity; but her fetishistic power has been broken, and she has lost her magic potency. She is the nexus where patriarchal values (woman as possession) and Christian values (woman as pure) meet. Although Rojas's Lucretia has escaped from Augustine's terrible logic concerning involuntary consent, even this cannot save her. She commits suicide in spite of her continued spiritual chastity, and in so doing exposes the distortions in the social imaginary of her culture. Ideology, not the Church, has condemned her.

We cannot yet take our leave of Lucretia. Virtue and victimization may not be the last word. Critics have, after all, remarked on Rojas's "unwonted feminism," especially in matters of revenge (MacCurdy x).

In *Lucrecia y Tarquino* the suicide weapon—Tarquin's sword—is double-edged. In contrast to his sources, Rojas explicitly rejects Lucretia's exhortation to the men to seek vengeance, as well as the appeal to her posthumous status as an example among women. Instead, she takes revenge on herself. In so doing, she usurps the traditional role of the male (which Shakespeare's Lucrece affirms: "Knights, by their oaths, should right poor ladies' harms" [1694]). In an ecstatic moment when victimization and recuperation meet, the masochistic fantasy of feminine annihilation is unveiled as a masculine striving. Here she ends her caricature of a female masquerade (Rivière; Kaplan 267–83) and appropriates the male role, for which historians bequeathed her heroic status. In the version of Dionysius of Halicarnassus, during his peroration from the tribunal Brutus stresses the significance of the role change (like Lope's heroine in *Fuenteovejuna,* Lucretia both inspires and shames the men to action): "After this, Lucretia, when you, who were formed a woman, have shewn the resolution of a brave man, shall we, who were born men, shew less courage than women?" (2:290). In Rojas, the onlookers praise her unique valor (2.2156).

Like Lope's *Fuenteovejuna,* rape as a prelude to revolution is the main plot of *Lucrecia y Tarquino.* By reading in Rojas's play a subtext of the enactment of perverse desire, I do not mean to divest the main script of its powerful political significance. But, as the body is central to Freud's deliberations on the psyche, so is the body central to political discourse. This is the language we use to describe and delimit what we can and cannot do to another's body, whether it be providing pleasure or inflicting pain (as Elaine Scarry has so aptly demonstrated).

It so happens that "sexual politics" (Kahn) are poignantly clear in the legend of Lucretia. By focusing on the difference in Rojas's Lucretia—her unique immaculateness—and reading it symptomatically—implicit, tacit assumptions in the social construct of seventeenth-century Spain become explicit. The text of *Lucrecia y Tarquino* lends voice to the silent obsessions—and oppressions—of the period.

Lope's El príncipe despeñado: *"Lucretia Interrupta"*

In his cannibalization of salient portions of the Lucretia myth in *El príncipe despeñado* (The Prince Flung Down) (1602; published 1617),[13] Lope unwittingly unmasks the structural principle of the classical tale: the eroticization of violence. In an article on Livy's Lucretia, Patricia Klindienst Joplin asserts that "In Ovid, as in Livy, spontaneous erotic desire, 'passion' or 'lust,' is a cover story for violent political rivalry among princes, a rivalry acknowledged only in its effacement. Its meaning passes unseen" (53). Lope's dramatization of a historical incident in *El príncipe despeñado* bears the hallmark of such a "cover story."

The oldest chronicles are laconic on the subject of the death of Sancho IV of Navarre: they agree on the date (1076) and the place (Peñalén), and they agree that he was killed. They do not name the "alleged perpetrators" of the murder, whom most modern sources have identified as the king's siblings, don Ramón and doña Ermesenda. According to Father Juan de Mariana's history of Spain, the king, a virtuous though elderly man whose young son was to succeed him, becomes the target of his brother Ramón's ambitious and unlawful pretensions to the throne. The rivalry breaks out in the open, and opposing alliances are formed. Publicly condemned to death, Ramón treacherously kills his brother, King Sancho, a fact silenced, conjectures Mariana—"Perhaps to avoid sullying his nation by the recollection of so odious a case" (qtd. *Obras* xxix, n. 2).

This version was known to Lope; he chose, however, to follow another source, the chronicle of the prince of Viana (ca. 1450), more doubtful as history, more compelling as romantic intrigue, which imitates features of the David and Bathsheba story: at war with Castile, King Sancho deliberately sent one of his warriors, the señor de Funes (the Uriah of this triangle), to the front "and enjoyed this noble's wife" (qtd. *Obras* xxviii). The noble returned and, in revenge, pushed the king from the top of the mountain, saying "For a malicious king, a treacherous vassal" (qtd. *Obras* xxviii). In this version, the rawness of naked power politics is obviated altogether as the political is displaced by the personal: the struggle for the throne is turned into a struggle for the female. The king's reputation is besmirched, but only slightly: the comparison to David palliates the blame ("and wishing to emulate King

David's dealings with Uriah, this measure failed"); the rival husband, the warrior, is not killed; as occurs in the story of David and Bathsheba, King Sancho is guilty of adultery, rather than rape.

Lope takes the plot back to the death of King García of Navarre and to the battle for succession between the supporters of Sancho, the king's brother (the illegitimate pretender), and the supporters of García's child, still in utero (the legitimate heir). The main representatives of the contending factions are the brothers Martín and Remón [sic] García, who in this civil war find themselves in opposite camps: don Martín backs Sancho; don Remón supports Queen Elvira's plea for the birthright of her unborn child. Up to a critical point, Lope follows his chronicle source: Sancho, who has declared himself king, develops a passion for Martín's wife, doña Blanca, and fraudulently invents a war front to which the deceived husband is sent. Martín, like Uriah, is a faithful servant.

Here the biblical paradigm is superseded by the Lucretia legend. The motif of rivalry between men asserts itself: as Tarquin wants what the worthy Collatine possesses, so Sancho wants what the worthy Martín possesses. Reason and passion contend for Sancho's soul: briefly inhibited by recognition of his rival's loyalty, anger against any curtailment of his power quickly resolves the dilemma in favor of his will:

> Do I hesitate to enjoy
> This renowned wife?
> If I am a king without power,
> Of what use is it to me to reign? (2.139)

He gains entrance into the house, and what ensues is rape, not adultery. Determined to overcome Blanca's resistance, he invokes his role model: "Let me be Tarquin now, / And later you Lucretia!" (2.145). And, greeting her returning husband with herself and her household in mourning, Blanca is determined to finish the play in her prescribed role as Lucretia; but she faints as she is about to stab herself with King Sancho's dagger. Her husband's words effect a stunning reversal of the ending:

> Hold!
> She fainted to the ground,
> But the blow never fell.
> Oh wife chaste and honored
> Above all others born,
> This is excuse enough!
> Heaven forbid you be
> The new Lucretia of Spain;
> For I have honor fit
> For a more just revenge. (3.150)

The visual rhetoric of the scene, dominated by the black of mourning, retains the meaning of rape as murder, which the literary model elides, instead of recognizing, by displacement onto suicide. This has the insidious effect of equating rape with self-murder, making them metaphorically equivalent. The result, according to Mieke Bal, is that "the metaphor displaces the rape itself. Thus its very occurrence conveys the idea that the victim is responsible for her own destruction. As far as the subject of action is concerned, the act of killing herself shifts attention from the rapist to the victim" (*Reading Rembrandt* 68).

By undoing the connection of cause and effect between rape and suicide, Lope tacitly acknowledges St. Augustine's criticism of the Roman heroine—"if she was chaste, why was she slain?" Her spiritual chastity is maintained, as Remón later states:

> And this is truth most plain;
> There cannot be dishonor

Where honor cries aloud
And the will is lacking. (3.158)

The female body is not subjected to the sacrificial knife. Instead, on stage
appears the corpse of the dead King Sancho, whose seemingly accidental
fall Martín and Remón, newly reconciled, have accomplished in collusion. The death of the king both avenges the dishonor and vacates the
throne for the legitimate heir, the newly born son of Queen Elvira. The
murder of King Sancho thus restores order to the personal and political
realms.

Lope's distortion of his chosen source serves the ideological purpose of
whitewashing national history: the murder of King Sancho II at Peñalén
in 1076 is no longer a regicide, a nasty business at best. According to *El
príncipe despeñado,* Sancho from the beginning was a usurper. Martín, who
supported him, suffers as a result of his error and begs the wronged queen
and her child, if alive, forgiveness for his sin:

Forgive me, doña Elvira,
Forgive me, saintly Queen;
I know that God avenges
Your sorrows on my honor.
Forgive me, saintly Abel,
Innocent one of my soul;
For if you live, I swear
By Heaven, by its lofty lights,
By sea, by earth, by fire,
By men, grasses, birds, and plants,
To see you hailed as King
Once I have taken revenge
On the treacherous, cruel wolf
Who soiled the snowy coat
Of my white lamb. (3.150)

The queen has fled the court in disguise, fearing for her life. Her son's birth at the end of the first act is an entirely fictional elaboration of Lope's, and it has been criticized as an irrelevant "childish story" that the playwright might well have excluded (*Obras* xxxii). The iconography of the scene explains its inclusion, however. The birth in the wilderness of the child in seeming poverty bears obvious analogies to the birth of the Christ Child, an association made explicit in Elvira's cry for help at the onset of labor:

> Virgin of Childbed! Remember
> That night in Bethlehem
> You likewise found no
> Shelter, nor host nor charity!
> Lady, take pity on me! (1.12)

In the final scene, the protagonists kneel before mother and child as they recognize their new king (3.159). The contrast between illegitimate usurper and divinely appointed legitimate heir is thus starkly marked. The murder of Sancho, instead of being a national disgrace, becomes a matter of patriotic obligation, even pride. Lope's version achieves a feat of semantic reversal, which has the effect of legitimizing a regicide by calling it, in effect, another name: tyrannicide. And, of course, the king is not the real king. His literary imagination manages to purify the polluted waters of history.

Blanca, the Lucretia *in potentia* of the drama, does not lose her life, but she nevertheless retains the status of sacrificial victim, the innocent "white lamb" mauled by the "cruel wolf" (3.150); like Lucretia, she is a mere pawn in this tale of political rivalry used to legitimize revolt and murder (Joplin 61–62). The difference is that it is not the mob that must be aroused to rebel but only her husband. Her rape marks the turning point in the political crisis; thereafter, Martín joins forces with his brother against King Sancho, and order is restored to the kingdom of Navarre. The secrecy of the crime and the punishment save Blanca from the fears of Lucretia, who feels she must preserve her reputation and set an example for other women. Nevertheless, Blanca must work hard to disguise her pain, lying to conceal the real cause of her distress:

> For so fierce is the sorrow
> Of that misfortune past,
> That even the meanest folk
> Have cause to suspect me;
> And I through this deception
> Must hide away my woe;
> For any harm to honor,
> Concealed, will be less harm. (3.154)

A secondary plot involving a love triangle among the peasants (Danteo and Elisa love one another, but she is promised to Fileno) complicates matters, to the distraction of the main argument, according to Menéndez y Pelayo's prefatory comments to the play: Lope should have restricted himself to the main plot, "instead of uselessly complicating things with another episode, in itself romantic and interesting, but presenting a capital defect: it breaks the unity of the play and for quite some time distracts from what should be the main theme" (*Obras* xxix). As in the case of the incorporation of childbirth in the theatrical spectacle, if we read for the details the seemingly marginal in *El príncipe despeñado* is not necessarily so. A playful lover's quarrel between Danteo and Elisa mirrors—with parodic distortion—a key issue in the Christian scrutiny of Lucretia's suicide: the divisibility of body and soul.

Elisa, betrothed against her will to Fileno, insists that she can continue to love Danteo: "Though my body belongs to my husband, / My soul is ever yours" (1.127). Danteo dismisses her simplistic reasoning as idiotic and unabashedly adds sexual innuendo to her literal (mis)understanding of the body/soul division:

I want you to open your eyes,
And let this be understood:
Men give all they have for the body,
And for the soul they give words.

. . . .

But why do I haggle with you
Over these chimeras,
When you plan to give me flowers
And your new husband the fruit? (1.127)

The comic distortion of the body /soul division is a prelude to the serious moral dilemma that will ensue with Blanca's rape.

Blanca expresses the psychological effects of loss of worth ("My worth is less!" [3.149]) and loss of identity ("I used to be yours" [3.149]; "I transformed both life and fate, / Everything is changed for me" [3.153]) that follow the assault on her chastity, the exclusive possession of her husband, whose honor resides in her body ("Your honor is dead!" [3.149], she cries in anguish). The only visible sign of this wound is the blackness of mourning, by convention the symbol of death. Blanca, "imitating the Roman matron, / With a dagger" (3.156), intends both to reiterate and complete the symbolic death with her bodily death. But she does not kill herself (her fainting and her husband's restraint prevent the fatal thrust); nor does her husband kill her—"I spared her life / With just compassion for her innocence" (3.156).

Lope has taken seriously St. Augustine's casuistry concerning the noble Roman lady: "If she was made an adulteress, why has she been praised; if she was chaste, why was she slain?" (1.19.89). Without consent, argues St. Augustine, spiritual purity remains inviolate, and suicide implies guilt. Thus, he continues:

This is not what the Christian women who had the same experience and still survive did. They did not avenge a crime

not their own upon themselves, but feared to add crimes of
their own to those of others, which they would have done,
if, because foes lusting had committed rape upon them, they
blushing had committed murder upon themselves. For
indeed they have within themselves the glory of chastity,
the witness of their conscience. They have it also in the presence of their God and need nothing more. (1.19.89, 90)

It is not Blanca who rewrites Lucretia's script according to Augustine—
her loss of consciousness deprives her of any decision-making power. In
his recounting of the fearful moment to his brother, Martín assumes full
responsibility for staying her hand: "Her hand I restrained, Count, and /
I spared her life / With just compassion for her innocence" (3.156).
Significantly, he omits the fact that she fainted, which deflected the course
of the knife thrust. Martín's "more just revenge" (3.150) requires only
her silence: her consent to the new script is assumed.

What, we may ask, is the impact of this new plot of "Lucretia Interrupta"?
In the gentler world of the Christian resolution delineated by Augustine,
the raped wife's life is saved (because Augustine's subject is suicide, he
does not enter into the ethics of the blood revenge against the rapist).
But the saving of her life in the text has condemned doña Blanca to post-
textual oblivion (her rapist, too, is forgotten). Despite the quibbles of St.
Augustine, Christian authors such as Juan Luis Vives recall Lucretia as a
model to be emulated: "Not that I should propose this act as an example
to be imitated, but her mentality, so that you will believe that nothing
remains to a woman who has cast away her chastity" (*On the Education of
the Christian Woman* 1.6.§44.63). Nowhere does Blanca appear in the lists of literary heroines; nowhere is she praised for her valor and resolution.

St. Augustine would have commended, it seems to me, this erasure
from memory. Among his criticisms of Lucretia is that, as a Roman lady,
she was "too greedy of praise" (1.19.89). And fame—being talked about,
being on the tongues of men—is hardly an appropriate goal for a good Christian

woman. As delineated by Vives, the Renaissance ideal of conduct becoming to a woman is lack of renown, even for her goodness: "Thucydides does not even allow that a good woman be praised amongst the populace; although far from suggesting that she be slandered, he nevertheless wishes her to remain totally unknown to the outside world and wants her reputation in no way to proclaim her doings" (2.9.§3.292–93). Neither a woman nor her name should circulate, for "silk, which is delicate and fragile, should not be touched by too many hands" (2.9.§2.291–92).

Blanca's acquiescence to the conceptual distinction between body and soul and to the soul's priority allows her to continue living. But her persistence has the paradoxical effect of unmasking her for what she is—a mere pretext. She is literally a fictitious pre–text invented by Lope to justify the ways of men in the text of Spanish history.

THREE

The Gendering of Violence

Women in the Peasant Honor
Plays: A Diversionary Tactic

Within the western European literary tradition, Lope's *Peribáñez y el Comendador de Ocaña* (*Peribáñez and the Comendador of Ocaña;* 1605–1613); *Fuenteovejuna* (1611–1618); *El mejor alcalde, el Rey* (*The King the Greatest Alcalde;* written in 1620–1623 [Morley and Bruerton], published in 1635);[1] and Calderón's *El alcalde de Zalamea* (*The Mayor of Zalamea;* 1636–1642)[2] have been singled out by Noël Salomon as exceptional examples of the unique Spanish exaltation of peasant dignity and honor, a conclusion both questioned and modified by Dian Fox in her revisionist readings of these *comedias* of peasant honor: "None of these works can be said unequivocally to exalt the peasant. Nor do any of these plays, excepting *Fuenteovejuna* and *The Greatest Alcalde* but including *The Villano in His Corner*, applaud their stage kings' final dispositions of the peasants with respect to their agricultural callings" (172).

My intent is neither to blame nor to praise, neither to justify nor to vilify the actions of violent redress for grievances sought by commoners against nobles. I will not focus on the political struggle, on the theory that subtends it, or on its theatrical representation. Instead, I wish to redirect attention away from the master discourse to the underlying secondary stories, which, in all instances, are commonly (and paradoxically) classified as "love stories": a virginal maiden or chaste wife is sexually assaulted by a man of superior rank, wealth, and authority, who is in turn killed by an avenging father, husband, or enraged community. Although the women themselves are the objects, rather than the subjects, of action, the event of their violation triggers the main plot development.

For the significance of their role we must turn to Lévi-Strauss's *Elementary Structures of Kinship,* in which he delineates a conceptual framework of exchange as the basis of social organizations, and marriage as the most basic form of gift exchange:

> The total relationship of exchange which constitutes marriage is not established between a man and a woman, where each owes and receives something, but between two groups of men, and the woman figures only as one of the objects in the exchange, not as one of the partners between whom the exchange takes place. (115)

If gift-giving as rightful exchange (marriage) is construed as fundamental to social discourse and the means of achieving and maintaining peace,[3] wrongful exchange (rape as theft) logically leads to war. Laurencia's famous tirade against her father and the assembly of men in *Fuenteovejuna* (3.1723–93) is predicated on this underlying principle. Her wrongful abduction occurs during the wedding festivities celebrated with music in the public square. This constitutes a ritual scenario, in which

> the father hands over his daughter to the husband, who takes her to his house. The religious ceremony, enacted midway in this process, serves to ratify it. "The woman does not marry," Beneviste adds, "she is married. She does not accomplish an act, she undergoes a change of condition." She is like an object that is handed from one owner to another. . . . In any case, given the essential purpose of mar-

riage, which was to convey a woman from one house to another, the circulation of objects throughout the ritual was designed to facilitate symbolically the circulation of the woman herself. (Belmont 2)[4]

The transfer of property is not completed until the marriage is consummated. Not protected from wrongful abduction by her current owner (her father), Laurencia can rightfully claim that the social system has failed her. Her exchange value depends on an intact hymen, which is thus her most valuable possession, her precious jewel. She draws an analogy that reveals her awareness of commodification: "for even though I buy a jewel, / until I take possession / it isn't up to me to see / it's safe from rogues and robbers" (3.1736–39). When Lévi-Strauss returns to the subject of the role of women as objects of exchange in a later book, *Structural Anthropology,* he notes that words were once values as well as signs:

However, one should keep in mind that the processes by which phonemes and words have lost—even though in an illusory manner—their character of value, to become reduced to pure signs, will never lead to the same results in matters concerning women. For words do not speak, while women do; as producers of signs, women can never be reduced to the status of symbols or tokens. (1.61)

A dubious distinction, argues Christine Brooke-Rose. For the system to work properly, it is imperative for women to remain silent, and throughout the ages their speaking has been castigated, meriting their marginalization as witches and hysterics (308).

If we return to the *comedia,* we see that the women's lack of any speaking position of authority is thus not at all commensurate with their crucial role as value-objects in the social structure. The part they play is akin to that of the main character in an acclaimed film by Jane Campion, *The*

Piano (1993). The female protagonist is mute. Yet from her position of seeming powerlessness she triggers the male rivalry that leads to violence. In this instance the husband and lover do not harm one another; it is she who is mutilated, doubly so, in fact: already without voice, her husband eventually hacks off one of her fingers with an ax. As a gifted musician whose only means of expression is the piano, her maimed hand is the symbolic equivalent of castration. She is—predictably, according to Brooke-Rose—punished for speaking through her music. (I will later address the question of the fate of speaking women in the *comedia*.)

The use and purpose of the secondary plots are most evident in the *comedias* that are expressly based on a discrete historical incident, as are *Fuenteovejuna* and *El mejor alcalde, el Rey*. Fray Francisco de Rades y Andrade's *Crónica de las tres Ordenes y Cavallerías de Santiago, Calatrava y Alcántara* (Chronicle of the Three Military Orders of Santiago, Calatrava, and Alcántara; Toledo, 1572) served as Lope's source both for the Fuenteovejuna rebellion and tyrannicide (in 1476) and the incident of the taking of Ciudad Real by don Rodrigo Téllez Girón, the young master of Calatrava. Lope did not consult other available sources, which would have yielded a different picture, in particular of Comendador Fernán Gómez de Guzmán, villainized in all aspects of his life, both personal and political, in the play.[5] Although the sources may disagree in their characterization of the comendador and in their assessment of the behavior of the mob, the Laurencia/Frondoso subplot is in its entirety an imaginative supplement to the historical record. No incidents of sexual profligacy by the comendador are mentioned by the historian Alonso Fernández de Palencia, who states unequivocally that "[t]he only complaint of the inhabitants seemed to be the increase of tributes because of the annual income" (qtd. Anibal 694); even in the Rades account, the motives given are primarily political and economic, with one mention of sexual misconduct:

> That Lord had treated his vassals ill, keeping many soldiers
> in the town to support there the authority of the King of

Portugal, who sought to be King of Castile: and he allowed that rabble to commit great injuries and offences against the inhabitants of Fuente-ovejuna, above and beyond devouring their goods. In addition, this same principal Comendador had wrought great wrongs and dishonor upon the townspeople, seizing by force their wives and daughters, and stealing their possessions to sustain these soldiers of his, ostensibly because his lord, Maestre don Rodrigo Téllez Girón, had ordered him to do so, since at that time he supported the cause of the King of Portugal. (qtd. Anibal 660, n. 13)

Lope concentrates on the sexual aspects, to the exclusion of the many other affronts (except for the mention of the burning of the peasants' houses and vineyards [3.1710]). And he does so in spite of the fact that: "Judged by standards of 1476, the Comendador's alleged profligacy, even if true, could at most have been considered little more than 'minor morals,' a weakness which mediaeval tradition gave him a perfect seigniorial right to indulge" (Anibal 693, n. 94).

In terms of theatrical effectiveness, the answer, it seems, is obvious. As stated by Anibal: "With fine sense of dramatic economy, he [Lope] has contented himself with emotions far more compelling than those which mere property damage or town rights could be expected to arouse" (661). But is this so self-evident? What, exactly, are these emotions? Why, specifically, does the abduction of Laurencia during her marriage ceremony elicit such a response? How could the playwright depend on similar reactions from commoners and nobles alike, especially during the representation of a play interrogating the use and abuse of authority by the dominant group on the subservient one?

Let us recall briefly the case of rape and revolution that resulted in the overthrow of the Tarquins and the establishment of the Roman Republic around 510 B.C. Livy's *Early History of Rome* posits the chaste Lucretia's rape by Tarquin and her subsequent suicide as the cause of the political upheaval, and this is the story that has been handed down through the generations. Nevertheless, the historicity of Lucretia's rape and subsequent suicide is doubtful: R. M. Ogilvie, in his introduction to Livy's work, opines that "The story in Livy is a melodrama (I.57–60) of a charming Hellenistic kind" (23). It is a romance, in other words, that distracts us. It diverts our attention from the real story, which is one of political rivalry among men. In the words of Patricia Klindienst Joplin, "Tarquin and Lucretia may both be read properly as pawns in a struggle to legitimize revolution, insurrection, expulsion, and murder" (61–62).

Mutatis mutandis, we can recover the same underlying structural principle discerned by Joplin in Livy's history in Lope's dramatization of the Fuenteovejuna incident. René Girard distinguishes between the "scapegoat *of* the text (the hidden structural principle)" and the "scapegoat *in* the text (the clearly visible theme)" (*The Scapegoat* 119). The Laurencia motif provides the hidden dynamics—she is both innocent of any wrongdoing and unique in terms of her physical beauty and moral purity, singled out among her peers, other women in the village who have capitulated to the comendador's attentions ("Didn't Redondo's wife, young Sebastiana, / though they were married, readily accede? / And what about Martín del Pozo's bride, / a bare two days from when they'd been betrothed?" [2.799–804]). Extremes are thus pitted against one another: both Laurencia and the comendador are thus exceptional—he a monster of depravity, she an angel of light. The mechanisms of romance are at work here (as Donald Larson has noted, including Fernán Gómez among the "monster-like antagonists of the 'pure' forms of romance" [94]). Because Laurencia is rigorously unhistorical, her role as dazzling cover story that overpowers the ugly tale of mob violence is all the more conspicuous.

The play is situated at a time of great unrest: at the national level, there is a civil war in process as Isabella contends for the crown of Castile against the claims of Henry IV's allegedly illegitimate daughter, Juana "la Beltraneja," who is betrothed to the king of Portugal; at the local level, the rightful jurisdiction of the town of Fuenteovejuna is in dispute—the royal city of Córdoba claimed as her own what Henry IV had granted (illegally, according to the townspeople) to the master of the powerful military order of Calatrava. That Fernán Gómez de Guzmán, comendador of the order, had set up his headquarters in the town (1468–1469) added insult to injury.

The sixteenth-century sources, as we have seen, differ in their views. Although he does not formally classify him as a "tyrant," Rades implies this justification by stressing the comendador's "treating his vassals ill" and his support of the forces opposing the Catholic kings. Alonso de Palencia, on the other hand, refers to the "iniquitous conspiracy of the people of Fuenteovejuna" and the "furious mob," the "savage peasants" who are "thirsting after the Comendador's blood" (qtd. Anibal 694). Twentieth-century critics of the play continue the disagreement: Robin Carter's theoretical overview of Spanish treatises dealing with tyranni-cide concludes that

> The attempt to establish relationships between the theories and Lope's *Fuenteovejuna* presents further difficulties. In the first place, theoretical analyses of tyranny seem to be totally irrel-evant in one sense, namely, that they are concerned with the tyrannical government of a city-state or nation-state rather than with tiny communities such as Fuenteovejuna, and with perversions of monarchy rather than with local despotism such as the comendador's. Secondly, there is no evidence in the text that the characters (with the possible exception of Leonelo) are aware of the complexity of the arguments sur-rounding the issue. . . . In conjunction with this second point, the text is almost devoid of references which might give the spectator some hint of the theoretical concepts Lope might want us to bear in mind. (*"Fuenteovejuna* and Tyranny" 320)

Angus MacKay and Geraldine McKendrick argue to the contrary, using as evidence contractual law rather than theoretical political treatises.

According to a Valladolid Cortes proceeding of 1442, the royal privilege of alienation of towns was to cease; both the current king, John II, and his successors were to be bound by this solemn contract. The pact included the right to armed resistance by the inhabitants of a town illegally dispossessed. They could rise "'on their own authority and without any punishment'" against the recipient of said royal privilege (130). In terms of the history of the Fuenteovejuna rebellion, therefore, "All the circumstantial evidence suggests that some of the rebels of 1476 were probably aware of this right to resort to arms" (130). The language of MacKay and McKendrick's conclusion is hesitant (evidence that is "circumstantial"; not "all" or even "most" but merely "some" of the participants; not "were aware" but only "were probably aware"); nevertheless, their claim is that in history as well as in fiction the crowd's recall to violence was legitimate. The townspeople's manner of killing the comendador, their behavior following the murder, and their joint bearing of responsibility point to a ritualistic and symbolic rite of violence.[6]

Whatever the legitimizing reasons may have been, a discomfort with the mob action remains, as evidenced by the conspicuous absence of unambiguous royal approbation (Salomon 857–60; Carter "*Fuenteovejuna and Tyranny*" 329–31; Fox 133–34). How unacceptable the notion was is further revealed in a subsequent reworking of the play by Cristóbal de Monroy, in which the massacre by the crowd is effectively censored. The odious comendador is indeed killed—but this time not by commoners but by other nobles (Salomon 862, n. 37).

As we know from his *El arte nuevo de hacer comedias (The New Art of Writing Plays)*, audience reception was of utmost importance to Lope ("for, since the crowd pays for the comedies, it is fitting to talk foolishly to it to satisfy its taste" [25]). The question perforce arises as to how Lope makes reparation for the discomfort of an audience's (and reader's) ambivalent reactions to a massacre, which in addition entails a violent breach of social decorum. Salomon looks outward to historical context, to the ever-diminishing prestige of the military orders ("Military orders at the start of the seventeenth century were nothing more than great dead trees, half uprooted" [863]), to a new, more liberal ideology governing seigniorial-vassal relationships (863–64) that makes the negative dramatic presentation understandable and acceptable. He furthermore notes the female's role in precipitating the conflict in Lope's (and Tirso's) "Comendador" plays, which he attributes to an archaic collective sentiment against the medieval feudal privilege of *jus primae noctis,* which never acquired legal recognition in Castile and León (in contrast to central France and Piedmont, for example) (883–84). We may also look inward, to the text itself and its rhetorical strategies.

The movement from event to history to fiction entails a complex process of filtering, as Catherine Larson explains: "The seventeenth-century drama deconstructs its primary sixteenth-century source, Francisco de Rades y Andrade's *Crónica de las tres Ordenes y Cavallerías de Santiago, Calatrava y Alcántara* (Toledo 1572), which, in a very real sense, deconstructs its source: the historical events surrounding Fuenteovejuna's murder of the Comendador, Fernán Gómez de Guzmán, in April, 1476" (113). In particular, Lope alters his chronicle source concerning both the catalyst of the violence and its subsequent developments. The Rades account stipulates that the incendiary agent was a group of gathered men: "upon an April night in 1476 there met together the mayors, regents, judges, and councilmen, together with other citizens, and with armed force they entered the lodgings of the Encomienda Mayor, where the said Comendador was found" (qtd. *FO* 36).

Let us now recall the scene in *Fuenteovejuna.* At the beginning of act 3, in response to the escalating crisis of abuse by the comendador, the men call an emergency session of the town council. Frondoso has been taken prisoner; Laurencia has been abducted. The situation is clearly an emergency. Yet the men, with controlled anger, deliberate, weighing the alternatives, considering an appeal to the monarchs, whose arrival in Córdoba is imminent. Some call for armed action; others resist it, reacting with shocked disbelief ("You mean, take arms against our overlord?" [3.1699]), urging cautious restraint ("Be careful, sirs, / and mind you move with caution in such matters" [1703–4]). The turning point is provided by the entry of Laurencia. Carter's analysis of this scene is revealing: the catalyst for action is "Not words, but the entry of a disheveled and demented girl. . . . The massacre, then, is not the result of an orderly reasoning process, but of the opposite: the complete breakdown of reason and order. Lope is offering an *imitatio vitae,* rather than an *imitatio libri*" (326). Salomon makes the same observation about Laurencia's role, which "becomes the active, determining factor of the revolt, which would not have taken place without the heroine's dynamism" (856, n. 28).

But something else is happening, too. The breakdown of one order (that of reason) and its supplantation by another (that of unreason) is marked by a dramatic shift in gender: in *Fuenteovejuna* violence is gendered as female.

To continue: in the Rades account the women participate only after the men have beaten the comendador almost to death, defenestrated him, and then caught his body on the heads of their lances and swords. It is at this point that they enter: "In the midst of this, before he had entirely expired, the townswomen arrived with tambourines and timbrels to celebrate their liege lord's death; they had made a banner for the purpose and appointed a captain and standard-bearer" (qtd. *FO* 37). They continue to act alongside the men and children in the dismembering of the body in the square: "They have only a secondary role," concludes Salomon (856, n. 28). In the play, on the other hand, the women mobilize immediately alongside the men, and it is they who catch the comendador on the points of their weapons, according to the report to the monarchs: "Then from his highest balconies / they fling him to the ground, / where women wait to raise his corpse / on lances, pikes and swords" (3.1980–83). They are not content to wait outside while the men do the killing ("Pascuala, I'm going in; swords shouldn't stay / so unemployed and useless in their scabbards" [3.1902–3]). They insist that they, rather than the men, should do the final killing of the comendador's despised lackey, Flores ("Give

him to us now, Mengo; you lay off, / and let us women have him" [3.1908]);
Pascuala vows, "I'll kill till I can't stand" (3.1918). In their self-proclaimed
quasi-military organization, it is the women who most clearly identify
the common enemy to extirpate, calling themselves "valiant men-at-
arms" rather than women (3.1889).

Lope adds another supplementary detail of violence: the pulling out
of the comendador's hair and beard functions as a symbolic attack on his
virility, and it has been suggested that the other acts of cruelty alluded
to may have included castration (MacKay and McKendrick 137), which
remains censored—neither stated nor staged. The Rades account, however, makes no explicit mention of decapitation, which acquires special
theatrical prominence in the play, as the villagers celebrate with music
and song while carrying the comendador's head on a lance. A note explains
that wax or cardboard heads would have been utilized for the scene (314).

Let us return to Freud's equation in the essay on "Medusa's Head":
"To decapitate=to castrate" (212). Articulated by means of upward displacement, the mutilation of the comendador is thus rendered repre-
sentable by Lope, and the horrifying effects of the knife are made palpable.
If, as has been argued, bodily mutilation is appropriate punishment for a
traitor as sanctioned by the *Siete Partidas* (MacKay and McKendrick 138),
Lope's supplementary detail of decapitation is an especially fitting punishment
for a tyrant whose sexual crimes he has emphasized. It can be argued, furthermore, that it is congruent with the particularized feminine revenge
depicted by Lope, whose sword-wielding women seek remedy for rape in
castration.

In the Rades account, the only objects the women wield are music-
making instruments, tambourines and timbrels. They all, women and
children, tear the body to bits. No weapons are mentioned. The women
and children enter at the point where murder and ritual celebration are
conjoined in a festival of slaughter that reenacts the *sparagmos* of Euripides'
Bacchae, where, according to Dionysiac practice, the women dismember the
body with their bare hands. Pentheus's mother, Agave, takes the lead in

this ritual: "Ignoring his cries of pity, / she seized his left arm at the wrist; then, planting / her foot upon his chest, she pulled, wrenching away / the arm at the shoulder." Then the other Bacchae join in: "One tore off an arm, / another a foot still warm in its shoe. His ribs / were clawed clean of flesh and every hand / was smeared with blood as they played ball with scraps / of Pentheus' body" (1124–27, 1133–37) (Girard, *Violence and the Sacred* 131).

In her study of religious riots in sixteenth-century France, Natalie Zemon Davis notes the coincidence "between the rites of violence and the realm of comedy," which mimic carnivalesque inversions and parodies (84). In the *Fuenteovejuna* scene, hierarchy is dislodged, all rules of stable order challenged, and gender identification confused, effectively inscribing the play within "a carnivalesque theatre of terror" (Fischer, "*Fuenteovejuna* on the Rack" 61). There are no rituals of religious parody, but the festal atmosphere functions in much the same way:

> As with the "games" of Christ's tormentors, which hide from them the full knowledge of what they do, so these charades and ceremonies hide from sixteenth-century rioters a full knowledge of what they are doing. . . . [T]hey are part of the "conditions for guilt-free massacre". . . . The crucial fact that the killers must forget is that their victims are human beings. These harmful people in the community— the evil priest or hateful heretic—have already been transformed for the crowd into "vermin" or "devils." The rites of religious violence complete the process of dehumanization. (Davis 85)

In *Fuenteovejuna* the peasants express no regret. Rightly or wrongly, their legitimizing strategies work, and they manage to achieve a "guilt-free massacre" (an issue separate and apart from the king's exemption from punishment).[7]

Lope distorts his source here also, and in a very curious way. Offered in the *Crónica de las tres Ordenes y Cavallerías de Santiago, Calatrava y Alcántara* a dazzling opportunity for a scene of female frenzy of music and dancing, he opts instead for a very attenuated, male-dominated version. The procession with the beheaded comendador is accompanied by music, but the celebration is politically marked by the musicians' song recognizing the legitimacy of the Catholic monarchs and the demise of the "traitor," Fernán Gómez de Guzmán: "May Isabella and Ferdinand / ever rule our happy land, / and all tyrants be dead and damned!" (3.2028–30). The new order is suggested symbolically: "A shining sun, that shows / a brighter day's begun to dawn for us!" (3.2076–77), but the potentially subversive meaning is immediately curtailed by its delimitation to the monarchy. The spirit is "The King is dead. Long live the King!" No pause is allowed between the two chronological moments that might allow an alternative political structure to emerge. With further insistence on a legitimate transfer of power, Lope includes a reference to the effacing of the insignia of the comendador and their replacement by royal emblems ("They rend his coat-of-arms with pikes / and shout that they intend / to raise your coat-of-arms instead, / for his is an offence" [1992–95]), a detail of official ritual not included in Rades.[8]

Lope hastens the cathartic process to a closure; the return to order is marked within the theatrical space by the return of the men as central actors. The women's ceremony of celebration in the chronicle, the joy they express, the explicit association of women and song—these are removed from the drama. The return to reason is swift and sure; instead of the ceremony of misrule, the political rule of reason is expressed. In accordance with the mirroring technique that structures the play (the national and local, macrocosm and microcosm reflect one another throughout), at the level of the secondary plot—the so-called love story—the chaos of inversion ceases: the weapon-wielding Laurencia makes a solitary appearance on stage and in an elegant sonnet declares her love for Frondoso ("I adore my husband, seek his good alone" [3.2169]). Proper hierarchy is reasserted at all levels. Her virginity intact owing to her valiant efforts of defense (her virtue remains "unsullied" [3.2411]), the marriage with Frondoso ensures an ending appropriate to the paradigm of comedy and the mythos of romance.[9]

At the end of *Fuenteovejuna,* then, a conservative ideology asserts itself, which Anthony Cascardi has analyzed in terms of Frederic Jameson's concept of "strategies of containment": "in this case as strategies for the containment of the modernizing threats to the traditional caste structure of Spanish society" (8). In terms of the culturally defined sex/gender system represented in the play, the outcome is also conservative. In spite of the challenge voiced and enacted against the established hierarchies by the brief resurrection of "the age of Amazons" (3.1792), the traditional structures reassert themselves. How are we to understand this? Are we to see this as yet another example of the marginalization of women, the invalidation of their cultural role?

I think not. In her study of the role of the feminine in Greek drama, Froma Zeitlin concludes:

> In the end, tragedy arrives at closures that generally reassert male, often paternal, structures of authority, but before that the work of the drama is to open up the masculine view of the universe. It typically does so, as we have seen, through energizing the theatrical resources of the female and concomitantly enervating the male as the price of initiating actor and spectator into new and unsettling modes of feeling, seeing, and knowing. ("Playing the Other" 81)

In *Fuenteovejuna,* as we have seen, violence is gendered feminine. The male effort at a rule of reason collapses after the onslaught of Laurencia, and it is the irrational fury of the women that provides the catalyst for the slaughter. Laurencia derides the men as useless and effeminate, and she and her squadron of women take up arms. This period of sexual inversion does not last long—just long enough for the murder to be committed by the townspeople. Before the entry of the female, the men are unable to act, restricted by their remembrance of the law, and this version of the revenge play is blocked, as it were, by the paternal metaphor of prohibition. In the scene of their debate, each and every man has suffered grave injury. Like Hamlet they can say "How all occasions do inform against me, / And spur my dull revenge!" (4.4.34–35), yet they quibble and are irresolute, inhibited by "some craven scruple / Of thinking too precisely on the event" (4.4.41–42). Hamlet's speech could be theirs:

> Thus conscience does make cowards of us all,
> And thus the native hue of resolution
> Is sicklied o'er with the pale cast of thought,
> And enterprises of great pith and moment
> With this regard their currents turn awry
> And lose the name of action. (3.1.91–96)

It is perhaps the most memorable theatrical moment in the play. Laurencia interrupts the men's deliberations, or more precisely, erupts into them through barriers—of closed doors and of gender restrictions: "Let me come in, for well I may, / when men are met in council" (3.1712–13). The stage directions use only one word to describe her appearance: "dishevelled" *(desmelenada)*. If we read this detail synecdochically, as *pars pro toto,* it represents the entire process of disordering that Laurencia's appearance heralds, of things being out of place and out of control.[10] The men have been talking about the comendador's hurt to the body politic. Then Laurencia displays her bleeding and bruised body before them ("Does this my hair not tell the tale? / Can you not see these scars, / these signs of savage blows, this blood?" [3.1750–52]). At this point the conventional metaphor linking the human body and the body politic becomes revitalized and acquires the necessary rhetorical persuasion to provoke action. Like the witch before her audience of inquisitors, or the hysteric surrounded by doctors, Laurencia makes a spectacle of herself before the eyes of men. She is scandalous: she is offensive (in the usual sense of the word), and (in the other meaning of the word), creates a stumbling block, causing the men's reasoning process to trip, allowing the rage to emerge and vent its fury. It is this mechanism of splitting off, of projecting aggression against an authority figure onto the feminine, that enables masculine action. Although gender coded according to the most stereotypical societal expectations, equating the feminine, as it does, with irrationality, with passion verging on madness, and with inattention to the law, without the participation of the feminine there story would not exist.

To be precise, there was, of course, a story, a his/story as told in the sources, an event in which men, women, and children participated. But there was no Laurencia, not even a remote model on which to base her. Other characters in the play, the peasants and Frondoso, for example, are also fictional. But it is Laurencia's decisive role in the central action of the play—the decision to rebel—that makes her exceptional. Laurencia is, therefore, not a woman (a real person who acted in the historical rebellion) but Woman: an imaginary projection, a representation, an image constructed according to deeply rooted cultural systems of differentiation between the sexes, which are both reiterated and reproduced. In terms of plot narrative Laurencia's behavior might be shocking and unexpected; in terms of spectator reception she is profoundly recognizable, familiar in fact. This is not without political consequences. Laurencia as imaginary construct provides crucial ideological support for the main text of *Fuenteovejuna*—the power struggle against the feudal aristocracy. I would argue that the gendering of violence in the play permits the "pleasure of the text" to be experienced by the spectators. The strategy of displacement onto Woman as catalytic agent of violence circumvents the legal, moral, and psychological consequences for the men of actually having decided to kill the "father," albeit the bad father (Girard reminds us that the Latin root of "decision" is *decidere,* "to cut the victim's throat" [*The Scapegoat* 114]).[11] The consequences are also considerably mitigated by the splitting mechanism at work in the authority figures, where polarization occurs between the bad comendador and good monarch(s). The meanings produced allow for spectator identification by both female and male subjects, and the pleasure of the public is assured.

The gendering of violence points to distortion, in the psychoanalytic sense of distortion as a mechanism of censorship in dream work. The sword-wielding, blood-thirsty women are, then, politically useful. But this female fantasy construct is not entirely risk free. Their actions are not in response to an ideological cause but a direct result of sexual penetration or the threat thereof. Sexual knowledge, apparently, changes everything. The *virgo intacta* is portrayed as a submissive daughter and innocent bride-to-be, obedient and respectful; the postcoital female (whether in fact or intent) has become abusive and demanding, dangerous in fact. In "The Taboo of Virginity," Freud offers the example of Judith's decapitation (castration) of Holofernes as corroborating poetic evidence of the psychological reality of woman's hostility toward man following defloration. Lope's examples are Laurencia and others, who seek their revenge on the comendador. He, too, is beheaded.

Any rootedness in female psychic reality (if, indeed, there be any at all) is not here the issue.[12] The coincidence between Freud's theoretical discourse and Lope's dramatic representation points, rather, to the rootedness of the phantasm of castration in our culture. It is a question of ideology, not psychology. This becomes even more evident when the contextual setting of such representations is taken into account: the situation is one of revolutionary violence.

Fuenteovejuna is our best-known example; but the combination of rape and revolution in Tirso de Molina's *La dama del olivar* (The Lady of the Olive Grove; 1614 or 1615), set in thirteenth-century Aragon at the time of King Jaime's conquest of Valencia, serves to reiterate the thematics of the homicidal female. Obviously derived from the *Fuenteovejuna* model for the secular portion of the plot dynamics (Salomon 874–76), the play portrays an abusive comendador who abducts, rapes, and then discards a betrothed village maiden, provoking a reaction from the local population. The victim, Laurencia, determines to take revenge against Guillén de Montalbán—"Then, since I am dishonored, / changing attire and name, / let Aragon see me as a man, / my spindle transformed into a sword" (2.8.249)—and in a speech closely resembling her model's (Laurencia in *Fuenteovejuna*) insults the men into taking some action (2.11.250–51), restricted to the burning of the comendador's headquarters. In *La dama del olivar,* Laurencia's aggression is a solitary gesture, separate and apart from the men's action, in which neither she nor other females participate. She seeks recourse outside the established channels, in banditry, dressed as a man (Laurencio), and vows that, "No man shall be left alive / of those who fall into our hands / be they but commoners / or be they of noble blood" (2.15.254). When she encounters don Guillén, she threatens to hang him and swears: "Your heart, praise God! / I shall tear out and eat" (2.16.255). She has him and his lackey tied to tree trunks, relishing her power over them: "I shall devise torments / newfound and bloody" (2.16.256). Then the rustic to whom she had been promised in marriage, the innocent and rather simple Maroto, comes her way. Having witnessed and deliberately interrupted an assignation between his betrothed and the comendador, he had reneged on his promise to wed (1.13.243–44). Declaring herself offended by his recusancy, she orders him hanged from an olive tree (2.18.257–58).

The subversiveness of the political project in *La dama del olivar* is considerably attenuated: the bad comendador (don Guillén) is disciplined—albeit ever so gently—by the good comendador (don Gastón). According to Salomon, Tirso's avoidance of mob violence dictates a conformist solution to the conflict that "emasculates" the vigor of *Fuenteovejuna*'s antifeudalism.[13] Nevertheless, the potential for sedition is sufficient for the eruption of the fierce and armed female as emblematic representation of revolution.

The phallic rhetoric of potency in Noël Salomon's critical discourse contrasting *Fuenteovejuna* and *La dama del olivar* unwittingly relates to the inscription of revolutionary violence as feminine. Following the insights of Neil Hertz in his study of the "hideous and fierce but not exactly sex-less woman" (27) that dominated representation of the 1848 revolution in France, we can turn to a remark by Freud that links the sexual and the political. It occurs in the essay on "Fetishism." Reconstructing the narcissistic panic experienced by the young boy when he perceives the female geni-tals as "lack" and fears a similar mutilation, Freud adds: "In later life grown men may experience a similar panic, perhaps when the cry goes up that throne and altar are in danger, and similar illogical consequences will also follow them" (215). The sequence is formulated by Hertz as a "litany of nervous questions,"

> questions that give expression to epistemological anxiety (can I trust my eyes?), to narcissism (can I hold myself together?), to sexual anxiety (can I hold on to my penis?), to—beyond that—social and economic fears about prop-erty and status (can I hold onto anything, including repre-sentations of myself?) or—put more grandly by one of this century's grand hysterics—Can the center hold? or is mere anarchy to be loosed upon the world? (31–32)

As visual representation, the image of the unruly woman embodies all that is freakish and disordered in a societal upheaval, when the world is turned upside down. At the psychosexual level, in a political context the activated castration anxiety gives rise to the Medusa fantasy, ambivalent in its double capacity of terrifying and reassuring at the same time.[14]

A return to sociopolitical order is marked in the plays by a return to a normative gender economy—to marriage and domesticity in *Fuenteovejuna;* to a life of religious dedication in *La dama del olivar.* Secular marriage is not an option for Tirso's protagonist, for she is not the heroine of chastity that defines Lope's Laurencia. The complicity between her and her assailant prior to the abduction makes her a guilty accomplice in her sexual sullying, which is then reinforced when she hands herself over to the bandit chieftain, in exchange for help with her revenge:

> Don Guillén has slain my honor;
> avenge me, and collect,
> if duty be a debt,
> from me payment
> in the treasure of my will.
> I am yours from this day;
> . . . .
> and if my love inflames you,
> I shall pay you in such guise
> that no further debt be owed you;
> if you loved me as a peasant,
> as a bandit you shall love me more. (2.15.253)

Laurencia is no longer viable as merchandise. As a nonvirgin, she is variously compared to leftovers of a meal that the master shares with the pages (2.3.247), a worn-out shoe given to the servants (2.8.249), a melon without its seeds (1.9.241). To excuse his call of alarm that interfered with the comendador's nocturnal meeting with Laurencia, Maroto fabricates a dream that reveals, in code, the amorous triangle. His symbolic equivalent for Laurencia is the beehive, filled with virgin honey. This must be protected, "for hives without virgin honey / are not worth even half" (1.13.243). Her retrieval into acceptable societal codes requires miraculous intervention—the apparition and beneficent power of the Virgin Mary (dubbed the *Dea ex machina* by Salomon for her rapid-fire resolution of all personal and political conflicts in the play [883]). Comparing herself to Mary Magdalene, Laurencia vows to consecrate herself to the Virgin (3.19.272). With earthly nuptials broken, marriage to God is still an option for this repentant sinner. The cross-dressing of Laurencia/Laurencio should have pleased the audience, if we can rely on Lope's testimony that "male disguise usually is very pleasing" (34). But Lope also implies awareness of its generic risks and recommends caution: "Let not ladies disregard their character, and if they change costumes, let it be in suchwise that it may be excused" (34). The anxieties aroused by Laurencia's male costume should be assuaged, one assumes, by its projected replacement with a nun's habit.

Tirso's thematic conflation of a miracle play and a drama of social conflict has definite ideological consequences, as Salomon has documented with contextual reference to the stubborn entrenchment of feudal conditions in Aragon, in marked contrast to Castile (879–81). The *comedia*'s general tendency in closure to the "erasure of power relations" or to their "euphemization" (Cascardi 16) is unmistakable in this particular example, as it is in the other *comendador* play of Tirso's Aragonese cycle, the second part of the hagiographic trilogy *La Santa Juana* (Saint Joan; 1613–1614), set in the reign of Charles V. Here the bad comendador, don Jorge de Cubas, who pursues and finally seduces the peasant girl Mari Pascuala, experiences a spiritual awakening and, dying a repentant sinner, is saved from damnation at the request of Mari Pascuala by special intercession of the Saint (Christ says to Juana: "He is dead / and for love of you, Juana, / he is suffering in Purgatory" [3.17.864]). His subsequent incarnation, don Guillén of *La dama del olivar,* is redeemed by the miraculous appearance of the Virgin, who, in addition, quells the lingering need for revenge voiced by Laurencia's father, Niso ("If he does not kill Don Guillén / and avenge me on Don Gastón, / I shall have just cause against him" (3.16.1089). Whereas Lope's plot fashions historical events into a moral meaning for his dramatic closure, Tirso's transcends the workings of history and depends on providential intervention to accomplish the positive reconciliation of comedy.

Tirso's transcendent emplotment has a decided impact on the representation of woman in the plays, which reiterates ascetic Christianity's familiar gestures of misogyny. The devout Maroto, who is sought after by Laurencia's father rather than himself seeking, is a reluctant bridegroom from the beginning, voicing Quevedesque satiric common-places against women and marriage and from the first act declaring his allegiance to a divine Bride: "Virgin, the best of wives / were you for me" (1.8.238). As anticipated, he determines to join an order (of the Mercedarians, one assumes): "From now on the Virgin's shepherd / I shall be, and She my wife" (3.19.272).

Where Mary is, resplendent in her immaculacy, there too lurks Eve as interpreted by later Christian tradition—the lustful woman who yields to temptation.[15] Marriage is represented to Maroto with a maternal image that reiterates Christian iconography of Mother and Child: "Is there any glory like seeing the cherished children / at the tender side of their chaste mother / who emerges to greet them rejoicing" (1.5.236), but the shadow of the female's inheritance from Eve remains dominant for him. The peace and purity of the Marian vision collapses in the face of the reality of child-bearing and becomes an image of squalor, for both the male and the female: Maroto asks, "Is there anything more annoying / than a child laid in the cradle / when he is bawling?" (1.8.238); Laurencia complains of woman's lot, "encumbered with children, now soothing, now rocking / a thousand pains suffering / nine months of pregnancy, / always in terror lest childbirth surprise us, / while men leave us the torment / and enjoy the pleasure?" (2.2.246). The response is an invocation of Eve's responsibility for the Fall and her punishment for disobedience:

> Had gluttonous Eve not enjoyed
> the apple's taste
> She would bear painlessly. (2.2.246)

The rustic setting justifies a more earthy portrayal of women, and the father's parodic blazon of his daughter's charms can be construed as a mockery of Petrarchan clichés (1.1.229–30). But in these verses, as in other passages, the references to physical excrescence in the imagery cluster point beyond the familiar literary topoi, moving into the realm of abjection. Niso's burlesque praises include "Concerning the nose not a few / have remarked: 'I'd be happy, / Laurencia, if love made me / part of your nostrils' snot'" and "Teats are heavy cheeses / and bodices moulds / and love would suckle them / were the nipples not hidden" (1.1.229). The servant Gallardo describes the purge administered to him in revenge as "[a]n aggravating malady / mother's malady from behind" (3.15.269).[16] Lactation, dignified by its association with Marian imagery, is here debased to a bovine function through the word choice of "teats" and "udders" (instead of "breasts"); menstruation, associated with ritual uncleanliness,[17] is further denigrated by its analogy with defecation.

Only by repudiating her body, by renouncing that part of her feminine self, can woman aspire to wholeness and cleanliness. In Tirso's logic, woman and defilement become inextricably linked; only the impossible paradox of the seamless body of the Mother of God is worthy. Mari Pascuala *(La Santa Juana, Parte II)* is saved from suicide by the miraculous intervention of the saint, who invokes the example of Mary Magdalene as a reminder of God's infinite mercy toward a penitent sinner ("He who forgave the Magdalene / will pardon you, Mary / for His compassion is / as then it was, infinite" [2.15.854]). Mari Pascuala resolves to enter the order and feels herself born again into a second life: "Heaven has given me two lives / one of the soul and one of the body" (2.16.854). Santa Juana and Mary Magdalene effectively serve to repress female sexual desire. The abjection of the female/maternal body is contained by sealing off the body and its loathsome apertures, making it self-contained and seamless. In *La dama del olivar,* immediately after the repentant Laurencia consecrates herself to a life of chaste devotion, the lackey Gallardo follows suit ("I shall be a holy steward"), feeling himself cleansed of bodily waste: "I come so thoroughly purged / that no ill humor lurks / in my body nor in my soul" (3.20.272). The clean and proper body is not only a gendered concept (male versus female) but also a class concept (noble versus ignoble or plebeian). The purging of the female's bodily desires and the closing of the vaginal aperture (foreclosing entrance), the purging of

waste products and the closing of anal apertures (foreclosing unruly /
excessive excremental discharge) become associated in Tirso's world by
contiguity and are an equivalent precondition for entrance into a life of
the spirit.

I have already noted that the conflict provoking the emergence of
the castrating female achieves a different and conservative resolution in
Tirso's *comendador* plays. What about the phallic female? In *Fuenteovejuna,*
male mastery is reaffirmed when the political order is stabilized and
women resume their secular, societal roles as wife and mother—distaffs
will replace swords. In *La dama del olivar* a more radical resolution is offered:
the obliteration of female sexuality. Although linked, as in *Fuenteovejuna,*
with a class conflict between *comendador* and *villano,* in *La dama del olivar* the
female in dispute is not resolutely chaste. The phantasmatic projection
as castrating female is not dignified by its catalytic role in a political struggle that is successful. Instead, Tirso's Laurencia is marginalized as a bandit, another sign of disorder yet external to the specific conflict at hand,
and again there is an sexual relationship with the band's leader. It is this
evidence of sexual desire that makes her unmarriageable and requires a
more rigorous control than marriage could ever provide (even if she
were adjudged marriageable). And, although Mari Pascuala in *La Santa
Juana, Parte II* is not projected as a castrating female, her desiring, therefore sinful, nature leads to a similar plot unfolding: withdrawal to the convent—in these instances not perceived, as in so many of María de Zayas's
tales, as havens of protection from the enemy without (the male) but
rather as places of refuge from the enemy within—one's own lust at the
mercy of a weak will. Seduced and abandoned by don Jorge, Mari Pascuala
is tarnished in both mind and body and resolves to commit suicide:
"While sane, kill then a mad woman / desperate and damned / for she
who has lost honor / should rightly lose her life" (2.14.854). The miraculous intervention of the saint, her own repentance and pardon, effect
a restoration of the soul. The body's stain requires negation of the flesh.
The divisibility of body and soul, the priority of soul over body, allows

her to continue to live. The decision to enter the convent is, in effect, a repudiation of the body.[18]

Lope's *El mejor alcalde, el rey* offers a clear example of what we may call the politics of substitution. As indicated in the last verses of the play, the plot is based on an historical event: "Here ends the comedy 'The Greatest Alcalde,' / A history the Chronicle of Spain / Records as true, the Fourth Part of the tale" (187). According to both the chronicle (the *Primera Crónica General* of Alfonso X [2.§980.659b–660a,b]) and the ensuing Lorenzo de Sepúlveda ballad on the subject, the dispute in which Alfonso VII (1124–1157) intervened between the nobleman don Fernando and a peasant involved property *(heredad)*. In the play it is the feudal lord's (don Tello) abduction of Sancho's betrothed, the beautiful Elvira, on the eve of the nuptials, his willful disobedience of the king's written command to restore her to her rightful owner, and his subsequent rape of her that provoke the personal intervention of the king. Commentators explain the replacement of female for land as a function of the entertainment requisite for successful (popular) theater: according to Sainz de Robles, in his edition,

> With prodigious dramatic instinct, Lope alters the anecdote from the *Chronicle.* In the latter, land is wrested from the commoner by a noble, a plunder of very little interest to the imaginative and passionate Spanish theater goers of the sixteenth century. A woman's honor was quite another story. (451–52)

Salomon notes, "But Lope shifts the conflict to the emotional and amorous level, thereby rendering it more passionate: instead of land, it is the peasant's betrothed that the lord steals; the struggle between the lord and the vassal becomes so much the more bitter and violent" (887); Fox comments that "no *comedia* can do without a romantic complication, and the love story is Lope's most important modification. In the earlier accounts, the nobleman is executed solely for his defiance of and disrespect for the King" (79).

The metaphoric assimilation of woman and land in the literary imagination has been so naturalized through rhetoric that it is hardly noticeable, much less worthy of comment. Land is plowed; so is woman (in the *Antigone* of Sophocles, Creon trivializes the impact of Antigone's death on his son, to whom she is betrothed, with the words "Oh, there are other furrows for his plough" [569]); land and woman are fertilized and render produce or children (the comendador of Ocaña, his lust excited by Casilda's beauty, expresses his envy of Peribáñez by exclaiming, "Oh lucky man, to keep, / Garnered in bed, such plenty as you sleep!" [1.2.556–57]. And land is raped, as is woman. Inherent in the feminization of land is its position as object rather than subject—it is acted upon. Thus is the representation of violence "gendered": the active agent assumes the masculine position; the passive object the feminine position (de Lauretis 42).[19] The verbal formulation of the injured Elvira's plea to the king for justice reveals her own utter lack of subject position: the action is exclusively don Tello's:

> He saw me, he craved me
> And foul plot he brewed.
> He put off the wedding,
> He came to my door
> With men bearing weapons
> And black masks before.
> I was borne to his dwelling,
> With treacherous art
> He sought to destroy me,
> My chaste firmness of heart.
> And then from that dwelling
> I was haled to a wood,
> A farm house adjacent,
> A fourth league removed. (3.184)

Even at this moment of telling, her disempowerment as a subject is evident:

> My locks tell the story,
> What struggles I bent
> Against his offending,
> And all the flowers know
> How I left on their blooming
> Fond tresses of woe;
> My eyes tell the story,
> What tears there I shed
> That the hard rock might soften
> Like down to the head. (3.184–85)

Her body is on display, an object of the king's vision. Because her tale may not be believed, her bodily distress must speak for her, assuming the role of the telltale. The king's justice is swift and sure: don Tello is beheaded, but not before being married to Elvira, which restitutes her honor so that, widowed, she may marry Sancho. She is also an heiress.

A happy ending. But a nagging question remains about the play's unfolding. Why does the king delay the execution of his justice, eating a hearty meal with wine, allowing enough additional time for Tello to actually rape Elvira? In other words, were Tello's wrongful abduction and disobedience of the king's written order not sufficient to warrant the noble's execution? In the source materials, the issue of disobedience is the only one to emerge, and that warrants a punishment of death by hanging: "And the emperor then ordered him hanged from his own doorway" according to the *Primera Crónica General* (660a); "The King ordered him hanged / In the doorway where he lived," according to Lorenzo de Sepúlveda's historical ballad in the *Romancero General* (3). In the play, we recall, the guilty party is beheaded, not hanged ("But yet I may do justice, and strike off / The head from Tello" [3.185]; "when they strike off your head / Then she shall marry Sancho" [3.186], says King Alfonso).

This constitutes yet another modification in the source materials, certainly not as glaring as the substitution of female for land, but politically significant. Since Roman times, decapitation was the punishment reserved for the upper classes, whereas hanging, among other methods, was used for the lower classes (Edgerton 87). In *El mejor alcalde, el rey*, therefore, the noble dies in a manner suitable to his station; the punishment specified in the historical source, in contrast, is an insulting one (the decorum of death emerges as a salient issue in Calderón's *El alcalde de Zalamea*).

The characterization of the King Alfonso VII is at issue. Comparing historical source with dramatic text, Carter concludes that "the faintly hagiographical simplicities of the historical accounts" are rendered more complicated and ambiguous in *El mejor alcalde, el rey* ("History and Poetry" 210). Lope lays bare the wellspring of the raw drive to power that the histories submerge under the guise of the king's consuming passion for justice. The chronicle, Carter suggests, "is a eulogistic account of an essentially political ploy on the part of Alfonso VII, the aim of which would have been to consolidate the King's power in a peripheral part of his realm" (194). Time is of the essence when the crime is an abduction, as opposed to wrongful dispossession of land. Therefore, argues Carter, the failure of Lope's Alfonso "to effect timely restitution" (197) is the most obvious symptom of Lope's critical stance toward the source.

Is Lope's interpretation, in fact, critical? Carter notes the uncertainty of the operative legal codes. One of the sources cited is the *Siete Partidas*, which, though it dates from a century after the events in question, is contemporaneous with the historians' accounts and, like the *Primera Crónica General*, also written at the behest of Alfonso X (211, n. 6). A clause from the *Siete Partidas* relevant to the historical don Fernando is cited,[20] and the punishment stipulated for such disobedience was forfeiture of property and exile (211, n. 6): not death, and certainly not an ignoble death by hanging. The *Siete Partidas* (VII-20-iii) does, on the other hand, prescribe the death penalty for rape as well as for abduction (Carter 212 n. 17). Lope's rendition of the king is, if anything, less harsh than the chronicler's, who stresses people's reaction of fear: "and so great was the fear of all in the land who heard of this event that none in all the land dared harm another. And this act of justice and others like it were carried out by the emperor, so that people feared him, and all minded their own affairs and lived in peace" (660a), rendered in the *romance* as "Greatly they feared him!"; "Very much feared is he by all / All lived in great peace" (3). The fact that, in contrast to the historical account, Lope's king acts in an unorthodox manner without judicial formalities ("No local officials are involved, and no formal charges are made" [Carter 199]) reveals less about the characterization of the king than about the nature of the crime: a crime of honor rather than of property requires much greater discretion for the protection of the family. It is Lope, I would contend, who disguises the nakedness of the power struggle between men (the *infanzón* and the king) by anchoring his story in violence against a female. The political closure is reached at her expense. Lope's king kills the offending noble with more cause and (a not insignificant detail) with the decorum appropriate to his class. Fox makes the point that "Lope sacrifices Elvira's honor—with every intention of making up for it afterwards—to an artistic good. In order to justify poetically a marriage between Tello and Elvira, the former must actually have carried out the grave offense against her" (89). It also justifies partial forfeiture of his property (as a dowry the king bequeaths to her half of don Tello's sizable estate). In the chronicle and in the *romance* it is the peasant who experiences pain, who complains of the grave wrong committed, and who has tears streaming from his eyes. His plea becomes Elvira's in *El mejor alcalde, el rey*. Lope's distortion of the historical source has gendered this pain and turned psychic hurt into physical assault.

The distance traversed from chronicle to play is one of legitimization of violence. By transforming the conflictual dynamics at work, Lope's play casts the monarchy in a distinctly favorable light. Whereas the king of the chronicle publicizes his action, taking advantage of the punitive example to consolidate his power in Galicia ("Then the emperor went openly and publicly throughout all Galicia and pacified the whole land" [660a]), the discretion of the king's dramatic incarnation curtails the propaganda of fear.

El mejor alcalde, el rey emphasizes the power of the monarch in yet another way. The royal letter ordering immediate restitution of the stolen property (land or female) is central to the conflict between the king and his subject; Lope has the contents read aloud.[21] The strange force of this written document and the implications of its disobedience are felt in all versions, but Lope makes explicit its implicit assumption as a commandment: "Upon two tables God set down his law. / Does he not break those tables who doth fail / To keep that law? Such is the law of Kings" (3.163). The evocation of the Mosaic stone tables, "written with the finger of God" (Exod. 31:18), takes us back to the foundation of the Law, to the analogue between God and king, Last Judgment and earthly justice, human judge as "vicar of Christ" (Edgerton 88). Is it the aura of a sacred writ that restrains don Tello from tearing the letter ("He read but did not tear it" [3.163], reports Sancho to the king)?

Disobedience may be "like" breaking the God-given stone table or royal mandate, but the next step is to blur the distinction between literal and figurative, collapsing similitude into identity. Don Tello finds substitutive satisfaction in another tearing: not of a piece of paper, but of Elvira's hymen. And here the tearing is literal. Enacting an Oedipal melodrama, defiant against paternal prohibition, don Tello usurps the place of the rightful owner, takes possession—not of the mother, here as elsewhere erased—but of a prohibited female (whose virginity makes her taboo), and suffers the punishment of decapitation at the behest of the castrating father figure. Law and Death stand side by side.

In the gentler world of Lope's *Peribáñez y el Comendador de Ocaña,* a lord's abduction of a vassal's most precious possession assumes a novel form. In this play, the role of gifts in establishing relations among men is very much in evidence. The comendador don Fadrique gives to Peribáñez a pair of mules and to his wife Casilda a pair of earrings, ostensibly a token of appreciation for their having tended to him after he fell from his horse at their wedding celebration. His real motivation is access to the beautiful Casilda; the purpose of the gifts is to distract the husband from his usual vigilance and to establish a sense of indebtedness. As don Fadrique's lackey explains: "Once husbands stand obliged by favours done / They watch their honour with less close concern, / Since obligation, as the saying goes, / Makes the most careful careless of his trust" (1.2.588–92). Peribáñez, in turn, recognizing the comendador's indebtedness to them, requests a "panel-cloth and tapestry / With which to decorate the cart" (1.4.871–72) for the Feast of the Assumption in Toledo. The comendador happily supplies these. Peribáñez thus establishes a tie that binds; as Carter states, "it is not unfair to suggest that he really ought to know better" ("*Peribáñez:* Disorder Restored" 18). These tapestries acquire an erotic life of their own. In a state of jealousy, Peribáñez acts quickly to remove the hangings from his home: "I think it's better for us if our house / Displays no cloths sewn with another's arms; / The gossips of Ocaña must not say / That a plain farmer hangs his guiltless bed / With hangings of his lord Comendador, / Blazoned with his manorial coat of arms" (2.7.2038–45). The sexual overtones are made explicit by the location of the hangings— originally for public display on the cart, they have now made their way into the secret quarters of marital intimacy.

Another object passes from hand to hand in *Peribáñez y el Comendador de Ocaña:* Casilda's portrait, which, unbeknownst to the subject, don Fadrique has had painted on a small card and then enlarged. The shock of seeing this picture of his wife in the artist's studio is the occasion for Peribáñez's jealousy and instant resolve to kill the comendador (whose responsibility for the commission he correctly surmises): "I am his vassal, he's my lord; his hand / Should shelter us, but if he means instead / To take my honour, I will take his life" (2.4.1750–52). The effect (murder) seems hyperbolic in relation to the cause (portrait). Why does the portrait warrant such panic?

At one level, the disturbance it occasions pertains to the laws of artistic decorum. In the semiotics of class in the play, a portrait of a peasant woman is as inappropriate as the plumed hat that Peribáñez spurns (1.3.783–85). It is, in fact, transgressive in the extreme. The seventeenth-century "passion for portraiture" (Davies 299) was an aristocratic court obsession. A character in Antonio de Mendoza's *Querer por sólo querer* (Love for Love's Sake; in *El Fénix castellano*) states: "Simple rustic women / neither lie nor pose for portraits, / for these hard tasks pertain but / to the very grand ladies" (qtd. Davies 299, n. 49). In his entry for *retrato* (portrait), Covarrubias incorporates the category of social rank in the definition, assuming it to be a necessary precondition for the genre: "The imitation of some distinguished and important person, whose form and visage should justly remain for the memory of centuries to come" (908b).

The artistic impropriety betokens the grave moral infraction contemplated by the comendador; for the portrait is evidence of his illicit interest in Casilda. It is also, in the context of the plot and ploys of the nobleman's designs, theft of another man's property—a symbolic act that preludes the real theft.

The painting was the result not of a consensual arrangement between artist and sitter but of secrecy and spying. Gareth Alban Davies reminds us in a discussion of seventeenth-century portraiture: "In the period before the advent of photography the portrait had a magical quality, so that comparison between it and the human original was a source of bafflement and *admiratio*" (301). A poem by José de Valdivieso on the painter Juan de Van der Hamen's wonderful likeness of him speaks of a transfer of identity—body and soul—to the canvas: "And when I see myself so very much myself because of you, / As if you moved my soul into the copy, / Although I touch my living self, I doubt it's me" (qtd. Davies 301).

The capture of Casilda's image is, therefore, a serious matter, involving not merely a reproduction, an icon, but a dangerous act of robbing and despoiling: a rape, in the archaic sense of the word. Once transformed into an object, Casilda becomes a commodity in a system of exchange (the painter mentions that he has not yet been paid [2.4.1723]), and she is available for viewing by everyone's eyes. The trafficking of his wife means that she no longer belongs exclusively to Peribáñez. Through no fault of her own, Casilda runs the risk of being common property and, as such, unchaste.

Contrast is established in the play between this portrait and images both religious (in particular San Roque, the patron saint of Peribáñez's brotherhood) and monarchical (Güntert). The king, a public persona ruling by divine right, provides a spectacle for adoration and respect; the saint is also worshiped in public, displayed in processions. Religious and monarchical imagery are linked by sacredness and, as such, correspond to an allegorical imagination with its inherent doubleness of concrete and abstract, matter and meaning. Casilda's portrait lacks this dual structure—its materiality does not provoke a transcendent signified, and Platonic theories of particular beauty as a reflection of divine beauty are not invoked. Peribáñez himself says about the portrait that "You'll see an angel's face" (2.4.1671), which is the first time such language is used by the peasant, reiterating the comendador's lexicon of love (Randel 156). But Casilda is not an angel, for angels are sexless. The sin of the portrait lies in its potential as an erotic object that will satisfy the fantasies and obsessions of the comendador. He is explicit about his need and use of the canvas, "which I want to keep / Where it will always stand before my eyes, / And show me pity which her heart's denied" (2.2.1264–65). Scopophilic pleasure, if not "voyeuristic phantasy" (Mulvey 9), characterizes the comendador's looking at his unwitting prey.[22]

When Peribáñez rejects all but religious imagery—"Since portraits are like ghosts – they haunt our walls. . . ." (2.7.2063)—he alludes to portraiture's function of inscribing the image in memory ("Insofar as images are effigies of men, you will see the word 'portrait,'" notes Covarrubias [732b]), but as *fantasmas* (ghosts) they are false images, a "fantastic vision or false imagination" (Covarrubias 584b). The usual meaning of *imagen* is a religious figure "among devout Catholics," the function of which is also to commit to memory—"so that we may freshen our memory in them and so that for common folk, who cannot read, they serve as books, like history for those who can" (Covarrubias 732a). Christian figurative art is justified for its anagogic usefulness, a dimension absent in secular figurative art. And the remembering it triggers is ghostly in its frightfulness, forcing to consciousness the knowledge of impending dishonor.

Peribáñez's agony on seeing his wife's portrait is not unwarranted. It is at once sign and signifier of a robbery in progress. He rightly recognizes the portrait as a fetish object: "The truth of the fetish resides in its status as a material embodiment; its truth is not that of the idol, for the idol's truth lies in its relation of iconic resemblance to some immaterial model or entity" (Pietz "Fetish, I" 7). It is not the sacrilege of idolatry that he fears but the scandal of fetishism.

A different but intimately related problematics of power is at work in Calderón's play about peasant honor, *El alcalde de Zalamea*. In this work (as in an earlier version [before 1610, according to Sloman 218] attributed to Lope and in Vélez de Guevara's *La serrana de la Vera* [The Mountain-Maid of La Vera]), military men of noble birth are pitted against peasants, who, unlike the nobles, were not exempt from the obligation to quarter the troops. This system subjected them and their villages to multiple abuses by unsupervised soldiers and imposed on them a heavy financial burden they could ill afford to bear. A litany of plaintive complaints are registered in the records of the Cortes proceedings from the late sixteenth century on (Salomon 893–97), with ample evidence of continuing military delinquency throughout the realm during the early 1640s (Diez Borque 64–66), the time of Calderón's writing of the play. When the peasant Pedro Crespo's daughter Isabel is abducted and raped by the captain don Alvaro, and Crespo, newly named to the position of mayor, has legal authority in the town of Zalamea, two issues emerge: the jurisdictional conflict between civil and military law, and the manner of execution imposed on the captain—death by hanging. There is no doubt that Pedro Crespo has proceeded incorrectly in both matters: the military court alone had proper jurisdiction, and decapitation alone would have been the appropriate manner of executing the death sentence. The reactions of the captain don Alvaro, the outraged general don Lope de Figueroa, and King Philip II himself leave no room to doubt that the mayor has usurped powers that do not belong to him.[23] The king objects on both counts, criticizing Crespo both for the fact of the punishment ("you have no authority / to execute it; that's a matter for another court's decision / and jurisdiction" [3.212]) and for its manner ("But how is it you did not behead / the prisoner as he deserved, / being a captain and a nobleman?" [3.213]). His subsequent assertion to his general that "the deed is done. / The execution was fully / justified" (3.213) is hardly a resounding approbation; it is a tepid, formal approval of a fait accompli. The importance of both these issues is minimized, even trivialized, by Pedro Crespo in his invocation of the legal principle of *De minimis non curat lex* (qtd. Diez Borque 312, n. 924), which the king reiterates: "What harm's been done / if some detail is slighted / in accomplishing the broader / purpose which justice must serve?" (3.213). In the enunciation of this principle, Crespo exercises authority over the king: "Here, in *El alcalde,* Philip II is challenged and must bow to Crespo" (Sobré 221). Morality takes precedence over legalities, or, as Sloman states: "Justice has been done, even if the law of the state has been broken" (244).

Paradoxically, in the process of breaking the law to achieve justice, Pedro Crespo insists on procedural correctness in the details (reminiscent of the convert Paul, whose exaltation of the spirit to the detriment of the law is couched in the most legalistic language of the New Testament). Isabel is, of course, the key witness of Crespo's zealous paper trail of the case, for which the king will commend him. The request that she sign the written complaint of the crime against her elicits the one and only protest that Isabel utters. She actually reprimands her father:

> You who wished to keep that grievous
> insult secret, how can you now
> persuade yourself to publish it?
> If you cannot manage

> to avenge it, at least try
> to say nothing more about it. (3.207)

His new position, he answers, prevents him from an act of revenge. But let us look more closely at his reply:

> No, I cannot treat the matter now
> in any other way. As Mayor
> I can no longer satisfy,
> as I might wish to do
> in private, an attack
> against my honor. (3.207)

He does not, in fact, explain why silence cannot be maintained (Fox interprets Crespo's stratagem as the means whereby he can protect his son, who has wounded the captain, from arraignment: "Pedro Crespo proceeds to distract attention from his son's case by drawing attention to that of his daughter, even though Isabel would rather let the matter drop than face the shame that publicity will bring" [162]). Something even more fundamental happens. There is a revealing shift in the possessive pronoun used to characterize the harm: Crespo speaks of "my honor." For Isabel, father and daughter are separate, though a unit; for Crespo, either the daughter is erased or he has incorporated her into his paternal identity. Either way, she ceases to have independent existence—or feeling. Her brother Juan, whose volatile temper and imprudence so differentiate him from his father in terms of actual behavior, mirrors the paternal ideology in his attempt to kill his sister in order to "[a]venge the life and honor / which you compromised today" (3.206). Henceforth the battle is defined as one between the competing authority of men and their respective realms of power: civil authority coupled with peasant honor (Pedro Crespo); military authority coupled with the prerogatives of nobles (don Lope de Figueroa; don Alvaro).

A question emerges: Do the performative centrality of the victim at the beginning of act 3 and the subsequent dialogue with the father disturb and undercut the males' narcissistic narrative? Does the theatrical representation, with its focus on the body and voice of Isabel, serve to dislodge the ideological underpinnings of the social discourse of honor? Because of the unusual length and complexity of the recounting of her rape, Isabel affords the reader a unique opportunity to view her speeches as a "survivor's narrative," albeit it an artificial fabrication far removed in meaning (and time) from the oral testimony that this term currently designates.[24]

Although linked by theme and speaking voice, the soliloquy and dialogue are contoured differently. The narration of the soliloquy is contained within a poetic frame (an apostrophe to the sun to detain its rising) patterned on the overall opposition darkness/light, night/day (later expressed as a moon "white and chaste" now "totally eclipsed" [3.191]), which by convention and context functions as the objective correlative of the oppositional concepts honor/dishonor or innocence/sin. It also reiterates by intratexual allusion the captain's earlier rhetoric of spontaneous and swift passion ("Within a day the sun sheds light / and fades away" [2.168]; "And so within a day my love, / like a planet, may come to know / both dark and light" [2.168]) (Evans 53). With Isabel's questions—"What am I to do? Where shall I go?" (3.190)—and the alternative actions considered in response, a reflective consciousness emerges, not now a protagonist of a past event but a thinking being in the present, acutely aware of her responsibility for her own actions and decisions. Isabel reveals awareness of the cultural stereotypes involved in rape stories and weighs her options accordingly: if she does not return home, the risk is that "I thereby invite the world / to name me as accomplice / to my own disgrace, and by so blind / an inadvertency let / innocence attest to slander" (3.191).

This concern prepares us for Isabel's recounting of the assault to her father (and, of course, to the audience). Unlike the first speech, a plot narrative unfolds, which repeats information already known (the when, where, and how of the abduction) and specifies details about the time (a particularly dark night, with the moon covered by clouds) and geographical locale of the rape ("this dense dark forest" [3.193]). The protagonist of her own tale, Isabel recalls her implorations ("How I pled with him and wept—at first / spoke humbly, then cold and cuttingly" [3.194]). As a narrator, Isabel has carefully constructed her plotline in order to ensure her credibility in the minds of her listeners as a completely innocent victim. Her control of the details selected for telling reveals her full awareness of cultural stereotypes about the victim's complicity, against which she must establish her own integrity. Her narration must be read as "double-voiced" (in Bakhtin's sense), for stereotype is implicit in her recounting. As Jane Bennett states in her study of the oral testimony of rape survivors: "In other words, to be in a 'rape story' at all as the victim places a narrator in direct confrontation with stereotypes about gender and sexuality whose implications may eviscerate both her credibility as an innocent sufferer of a crime and her pragmatic right to authority over her experience" (202). Another strategic deployment of language occurs during the recounting of the actual rape, in which the very failure of language serves to enhance the veracity of the account:

> But all in vain. And then
> (now let my voice grow dumb),
> the arrogance (and grieving cease),
> the insolence (let my heart moan),
> the impudence (let my eyes shed tears),
> brutality (rumor shut its ears),
> cruelty (and breath fail to tell it),
> and shamelessness (and I wear mourning) . . . (3.194)

In the comparisons between the earlier *El alcalde de Zalamea* and Calderón's play, Isabel's unquestionable lack of culpability emerges as a salient difference from her precursors, Inés and Leonor, who "flirt shamelessly with the captains of the companies, Don Juan and Don Diego, and at the end of the first act prepare to elope with them" (Sloman 218). Their fate is to be seduced and abandoned, rather than raped (Isabel's encounter is decidedly not a "seduction," as Sloman characterizes it at one point in his discussion [245]). What is the effect and purpose of Isabel's spiritual immaculacy, which the author has gone to great lengths to prove in Isabel's reporting, so carefully constructed in order to elicit her audience's belief in her?

Moral justification of Crespo's illegal action is one effect. When the mayor of Lope's play confronts the king's hesitation with the question, "Is raping maidens not just cause / for death?" (3.1434a), the answer is in the affirmative, although the language of force pertains to Calderón's rather than to Lope's plot version. The honor of Lope's female protagonists is technically redeemed, because the marriage ceremony was performed before the execution: "It was / in order that they remain widows / and not harlots," explains the mayor to his king (3.1434a). Is it against this intertext that Calderón scripts Isabel's narrative choreography of blamelessness? Lest, denied marriage "as the Church requires" in Lope's play (3.1434a), she be perceived, in keeping with the reigning cultural assumptions, as a "harlot"?

The ending is the same for all these protagonists: the convent, chosen on their behalf, though not at their behest. The symbolic meaning of this space is, however, different. In Lope's *El alcalde de Zalamea,* Crespo, having decided that his daughters will become nuns, answers the question, "Are they to be nuns?" with a dismissive "Or may the Devil take them" (3.1434b). Safekeeping for the otherwise ungovernable seems to be the operative reasoning. The king himself offers to provide the daughters' dowry for their cloister of choice, which suggests the likelihood of an environment both prestigious and comfortable. For Calderón's mayor, on the other hand, the convent (or the church) is a social institution. As such, in his imagination (and the audience's) it reflects, through "negative reiteration" (Bennett 224) the social drama of the play. Its principles and priorities are the opposite of those of worldly society. His daughter has been refused as the captain's bride; she will instead be the bride of Christ, "who cares nothing for the differences / in social origin among us" (3.214). And Isabel? She had expected to be killed by Crespo, having narrowly escaped her brother's sword. But her initial surprise at her father's merciful response is so great that it gives way not to immediate gratitude but to suspicion, as her aside indicates: "Oh, stars above, does this show / true concern or simply caution?" (3.196). She is described by her cousin as being in a state of extreme affliction: "You grieve and sigh so heavily, / my dear, your suffering / is like a living death" (3.205). Isabel replies, "Inés, who told you I find my life / anything but odious?" (3.205).

Considerations of a "poetics of space" have characterized the closure of the play as an enclosure: Gwynne Edwards comments that "[t]he end of the play is dominated by the convent, the physical imprisonment that awaits Isabel but which is equally a symbol of the imprisonment of Crespo in the dark world of his own anguish" ("The Closed World" 65); Antonio Carreño indicates that "[r]ead from its closure, *El alcalde de Zalamea* becomes a metaphorical social and historical prison of seventeenth-century Spain" (35). Because her life is spared, the word "tragic" is rarely used to describe Isabel's fate. There are exceptions, however. Louise Fothergill-Payne concludes that: "Compared with Juan's punishment, his sister's fate is more tragic. She will waste the rest of her life locked up in a convent, not through religious vocation but as the result of an 'enorme maldad' [great wickedness]" (226). Isabel survives. To the eye she appears intact—not even scratches, bruises, or disarray of clothing are provided in the text as evidence of violence. Yet in the exchange between the cousins, death, not life, is the theme. The effect of her defilement is social death; an unclean being, she is jettisoned from the father's house. The convent, which removes the female from the economy of desire, is also the resting place for the abject, the culturally constituted "non-object of desire" (Kristeva 65).

Isabel's rape is, for all intents and purposes, murder.[25]

FOUR

Text and Transformation

Mythology and Bible as Source

"The Rape of Deianeira" in Calderón's El pintor de su deshonra

A
rt historians have recently noted the need to return to textual sources in order to follow narratives correctly (Bryson 162). By the same token, it seems to me that, as students of literature, we have undervalued the visual sources available to us in a text. Because of its incorporation of a mythological painting in a secular drama, *El pintor de su deshonra (The Painter of His Dishonor)* offers us a unique opportunity to study the interrelationship between the arts, as well as to appreciate the transformative power of myth. Yet, except for Susan L. Fischer's brief and thoughtful essay on the meaning of the Hercules painting ("Art-within-Art"), little critical attention has been dedicated to the topic. Further exploration at this time is, therefore, justified.

In 1982 a judge at the Cambridge Crown Court summarized his opinion on a rape case to the jury thus:

> Women who say no do not always mean no. It is not just a question of saying no, it is a question of how she says it, how she shows and makes it clear. (qtd. Temkin 19)

Whether this particular judge was aware of it or not, concentration on the issue of female consent harkens back to St. Augustine, who in the *City of God* introduced the subtle yet deadly distinction between actual and "internal consent." Rape ceases to be an event that is definable in terms of public actions or statements; sexuality exists in the realm of "privacy and inward specificity" (Bryson 169), in the shadowy regions of "consent of the mind" known only to God according to the Church fathers, or, in our modern world, to the psychiatrist—perhaps. A woman can betray herself, however, in the involuntary manifestations of her body; the merest smile or unguarded gesture reveals her desire and becomes a certain sign of her "secondary" consent. In the betrayal of the body, the soul is revealed, as it were.

In *El pintor de su deshonra* the abducted Seraphine is doomed when she responds, involuntarily after a nightmare, to the embrace of don Alvaro, her rapist in intent, if not in fact: "Never have your arms / a greater comfort been" (3.3068–69).[1] All equivocations stilled "when I see her in his arms" (3.3080), the aggrieved husband shoots them both, asking afterward for his own death: "Now killing me is all they've left to do / for life's no longer worth a thing" (3.3085–86). If language is the sign of the conscious, rational mind, the body is the sign of the irrational, unconscious self: the sexual sign. In an early article on this play, Bruce Wardropper noticed that "it is only in the critical moments of dream, swoon, confidence, and *turbación* that it [the unconscious life of the mind] stands revealed in its true nature" (289), which led him to conclude that Seraphine "was not the victim of an heartless code, but of her own repressed sin" (300).

There is no doubt that the "rape" (in the Latin sense of "carrying off by force") of Seraphine constitutes the nucleus of the action of the play. Although the abduction does not result in sexual consummation, this technicality cannot offset the general effect of contamination that determines the tragic outcome. The obvious unlawfulness of don Alvaro's act of seizure has encouraged us to approach the text in the spirit of a prosecuting attorney, called to pass judgment on the guilt or innocence of

Seraphine according to the Augustinian concern with "consent." Whatever judicial opinion is handed down determines an attitude of praise or blame for the husband's revenge, which in turn determines our interpretation of the author's opinion of the so-called honor code—approval or denial through irony. Does don Juan's act of murder invalidate his stated repudiation of the honor code? Does the playwright mean "pardon" when the prince and fathers exonerate the murderer? To return to the beginning, does Seraphine mean "no" when she says "no"? Is Seraphine guilty of secret desires, or is she "a victimized woman who is only to be esteemed for her steadfastness and virtue" (Fischer, "Art-within-Art" 76–77)? The text lends itself to multiple interpretations because of the gaps between intention and utterance, utterance and performance.

In order to move beyond the intricacies of "words, words, words" (2.2.194), Hamlet sought another source of evidence: "The play's the thing / Wherein I'll catch the conscience of the King" (2.2.616–17). There is not a "play-within-a-play" in *El pintor de su deshonra,* but there is a painting described, "The Rape of Deianeira," where we can look to catch the conscience of don Juan, "conscience" being used here in its obsolete but etymologically valid sense of "inmost thought or sense: knowledge of inner self." An example of ekphrasis, but by no means a mere rhetorical ornamentation, the painting functions as an "iconic enclave" (qtd. Bergmann 124), which, by conveying information about the play and its players, helps clarify some of the ambiguities and determine a meaning. I recognize that by focusing on the painting I am committing a double act of displacement: I begin at the end of the play instead of at the beginning (the description appears in act 3), and I move the painting from its background position into the foreground. My justification is that the *historia* of the myth provides a narrative allegory mirroring in miniature the action of the play, which it infuses with moral energy.

The rape of Hercules' bride, Deianeira, by the centaur Nessus falls unequivocally into the category of the "bestial" (as opposed to "heroic") rape. This is the moment chosen for depiction by don Juan, who, disguised as a painter, asks the Prince of Orsino to look at his fable of Hercules and see "beauty and ferocity combined" (3.2685):

> Since his dire wrath
> is painted in its fullness
> as he sees the Centaur Nessus
> carry the stolen Deianira off;
> so vigorously, so zealously
> he enters in pursuit, I do maintain
> that no one seeing him can then refrain
> from saying, "This man is overcome by jealousy."
> He's placed on the edge of the composition,
> and if, in the middle, did not appear the creature
> after whom he goes, then Hercules would feature
> even further from the centre of our vision.
> This forms the major part
> of the canvas, and in the boscage, in darker hues,
> forming shadows and distant views,
> made smaller by perspective art,
> you see him set himself ablaze upon his pyre;
> this motto I would on him bestow,
> "He who first was jealous, go
> and perish after in the fire." (3.2686–705)

The plot analogies are evident: the bride Seraphine/Deianeira is abducted by Alvaro /Nessus, who is killed by the husband don Juan/Hercules. The patterns of interaction and symbolic meanings of this ancient mythic discourse impinge on the problematic areas of Calderón's society in ways that he obviously thought relevant to explore.

The characterization of the centaur is particularly relevant. These monstrous creatures, fathered by the transgressor Ixion, are noted by the mythographer Pérez de Moya for being, in addition to "very swift and invincible," "very lustful" (2:123). In his "moral application" the commentator elaborates further:

> In saying that these animals were lustful, they meant that
> there are men who are half beasts, given over to their vices
> and sensualities, governed by appetite and not reason, who
> having the form of men live like animals, having surren-
> dered to filthy lust, which all the other vices accompany in
> a mad rush. (2:125)

Hybrids who inhabit the mountains of Thessaly, centaurs live removed from the civilized society of the polis. One of their most celebrated outrages recounted in the *Metamorphoses* (2:12.210ff.) occurs when they try to carry off the women at the wedding of Pirithous, Theseus's companion, to a Lapith princess, Hippodameia (Zeitlin "Configurations of Rape" 131–36).

In the case of Nessus, too, the affront is associated with the marriage rite—Hercules is returning to his homeland with his new bride. The motif of violence marks the vulnerable moment of transition for the female as she moves from virginal childhood to married adulthood. If, according to Lévi-Strauss *(The Elementary Structures of Kinship)*, legal marriage as an "exchange of women" epitomizes the rules of "right exchange" of gifts, governing the relations between the sexes and serving to integrate society (Rubin 171–77), so the centaurs show themselves hostile to this order, which they subvert (duBois 27–29). Thus is established the line of demarcation between culture and nature, between the "bestial sexuality of untamed instincts and the structures of marriage exchange" (Zeitlin, "Configurations of Rape" 134). If marriage involves a gift, rape is theft: don Alvaro, violator of the marriage rules, is called a "thieving pirate" (3.2118–19). He himself recognizes the power of legitimate possession after his first secret visit to Seraphine, which leaves him intimidated,

> Afraid at having found
> it's true there's nothing like a husband's pluck
> when he's standing on his own home ground. (2.1486–88)

In the Greek myths the acts of violence, allied as they are with instinct, are perpetrated by other-than-adult Greek males—gods, hybrids (centaurs, satyrs), barbarian enemies, or even adolescent males (Zeitlin, "Configurations of Rape" 125–26). In the play, don Alvaro, defended by his sister because of his youth ("the irresponsibility of youth" [3.2157]; "active young fellow" [3.2160]), a kind of sea creature miraculously resuscitated after he was assumed dead, a Protean being of disguises, acquires the status of a demonic hybrid. Like the centaurs excluded from the city center (duBois 66–71), he inhabits the outskirts of civilization, the sea and the woods (Edwards, *The Prison and the Labyrinth* 126–27; Paterson, "Comic and Tragic Melancholy" 254, n. 12).

In the final act we find him and the distraught Seraphine in the environs of Naples in the family lodge, which provides a respite from hunting, fittingly the traditional metaphor of male pursuit of the female (Parry 270–72). This provides the perfect locus for the conflation of venatic and erotic hunts, involving not only the primary action but also the secondary characters, the prince and his lady Portia, dressed for hunting and armed with an arquebus. In the final ironic twist of fate, the place of refuge and rest from the exertions of the chase becomes the place where violence occurs. Although it is expected that a hunt will end with a killing (Parry 274–75), here not animal but human prey is trapped and subjected to a literal and ritual death when don Juan exacts his revenge.

If Alvaro's youth provides the stimulus, the enabling circumstances provide the occasion for the transgression. It is carnival time, "Carnestolendas," the privileged time preceding Lent marked by laughter and confusion, gaiety and license, and a general relaxation in sexual and social mores, facilitated by the use of disguises (Caro Baroja; Bakhtin, *Rabelais and His World*). Don Alvaro plans to take full advantage of the disequilibrium:

The introduction
of those days was a matter of some note,
for despite the fact the lady's father
or her husband may attend her,
Fabio, permission to pay her court
has been given. (2.1807–12)

The lackey Fabio, aware of those very passions normally unacknowledged by the refined upper classes, makes an observation about carnival festivities that has been termed an "ironic prophecy" (Parker 340; Hernández-Araico 60):

And so organised
that though this is a warlike nation
and jealous, too, by inclination,
there hasn't been a case of homicide. (2.1812–15)

In an atmosphere so different from the serious formality and hierarchical strictures that usually governed, vigilance is relaxed. The occasion presented itself to Alvaro, as it did to the centaur Nessus, who offered his help across the swollen river to Hercules' bride: "The Theban accordingly entrusted to Nessus' care the Calydonian maid, pale and trembling, fearing the river and the centaur himself" (*Met.* 2:9.111–12). So, too, does don Juan entrust to the care of a stranger his own bride, who, had she been conscious, would have been even more "pale and trembling," more fearful of her caretaker, than was Deianeira. In both instances the females find themselves unprotected, outside rather than inside the home. The "moral declaration" of Pérez the Moya is just as applicable to don Juan as it is to Hercules: "This tale warns us that we should exercise great caution when we entrust to others what we dearly love, as Hercules wrongly entrusted his beloved Deianeira to Nessus" (2:126). In the words of don Juan, "It was my trust that brought my ruination!" (2.2077). Like Nessus, don Alvaro will suffer the consequences of his action: as the centaur is pierced by Hercules' poisoned arrow, so is don Alvaro pierced by don Juan's bullet. Theirs have been acts of defilement; their deaths mark the expulsion of disruptive and alien elements and constitute the cleansing necessary to the reintegration of society, the restitution of the "right rules" governing the exchange of women (duBois 105).

Another version of the moral explicitly connects the breaking of sacred boundaries with the role of women in society. Of the same incident the commentary of Sánchez de Viana draws the following conclusion: "From this tale we can note how cautiously men should trust in others, however friendly what they love may be, especially in the case of women, who are generally a cause for scandal to the very wise, for lack of which caution we have seen and see every day very ugly incidents" (173v). There is no possible doubt about Deianeira's innocence in the matter of her seizure; questions have been raised regarding her counterpart, Seraphine, who, unlike Deianeira, had known and loved her abductor. Questions of culpability may not, in fact, be entirely relevant. The fault is not individual but generic.

It is not the particular woman (Deianeira or Seraphine here) but the symbolic force of the female sex that is acknowledged by the commentator. Her power does not lie in her position in society, where she does not acquire importance; on the contrary, it has been noted that, within myth, woman is associated "with the wild and the sacred, with what is outside the limits of ordered civilisation, and with the forces of life" (Gould 52). The source of her power is beauty: of Deianeira it is said that she "was once a most beautiful maiden and the envied hope of many suitors" (*Met.* 2:9.9–10); Nessus also desired her. Seraphine's beauty is such that all the suitable men, young and old, are drawn to her—don Alvaro, don Juan, the prince. In fact, when don Alvaro learns that the prince, too, is smitten, he utters a despairing aside that is almost comical: "This surely is the final straw" (1.830).

Her physical perfection and her female alignment with nature impede don Juan's ability to paint his wife: like nature, she exceeds the powers of human understanding and control: "yet I have realised / that I cannot, for all my diligence, / ever have imagined them to be / such as you have proved them in reality" (2.1136–40), the artist says of her flawless proportions. The critic Alan Paterson has written convincingly on the theme of painting in the play. He points to relevant passages in the "aesthetic excursus" of Albrecht Dürer that comment on the intractable mystery of nature and concludes that, in the plight of Juan Roca, Calderón "caught, with precision, the central preoccupation of the 'excursus' and the engraving: reason's defeat in the face of what lies beyond reason" ("Juan Roca's Northern Ancestry" 208). Like Apollo pursuing the wild Daphne whose hair is in disarray (*Met.* 1:1.477) and imagining, "What if it were arranged?" (*Met.* 1:1.498), only in death can he impose on her the desired control. The *deus artifex* topos is a prominent feature of the play and has merited much critical attention (Curtius; Paterson, "Juan Roca's Northern Ancestry"; Ter Horst). Art theory turns into parody when, in a travesty of this motif that he himself presents (2.1130–56), don Juan cannot paint Seraphine in life (2.1163–69), only in death, as a still life. As Daphne is immobilized only when transformed into a laurel tree, so is Seraphine's image captured only as a statue, as her sleeping, soon-to-be lifeless body is described ("art itself conspires to spite, / for it has made a statue in the place / where I had come to paint a face" [3.3029–31]).

Woman's position in a patriarchal culture is inherently ambiguous: she is necessary at all levels of society for the purpose of reproduction; among the moneyed and noble classes she is required for the assurance of legitimate succession and inheritance. Don Juan marries late in life, finally succumbing to concern about "an inheritance which I believe to be / of credit and importance, / and of no little substance" (1.61–63). In spite of the warnings of his lackey, Juanete ("Bunion"), against marrying so young and irresistible a woman, he is not mistaken in terms of settling his estate, for according to the humoral psychology of the day: "The procreative faculty has as the indication of fecundity woman's beauty; and, if she is ugly, it abandons her" (Huarte de San Juan 323). Yet she is by nature excluded from the governing force of that culture—the Logos. To quote again from Juan Huarte de San Juan, all women are "cold and humid" (318), and, the good doctor adds, "coldness and humidity ruin the rational part (319).

Woman, necessary to but different from the standard point of reference, the adult male, was as alien and threatening as that hybrid creature, the centaur, with the result that: "They came to represent a potentially dangerous, even poisonous force which was both within the city and outside it" (duBois 5). Their effect is to destabilize, to drive the settled don Juan to say, "I can / hardly tell if I'm the same man" (1.82–83), to drive the prince wild (2.1595), to derange don Alvaro, to whom Seraphine says: "forgetful of your proper role, / you don't remember where your true self lies" (2.1403–4). Although Seraphine seems to have adjusted gracefully and with pleasure to her state of adulthood, for she has matured from a "sunflower" (2.1334) to a "sturdy oak" (2.1320), she has nevertheless unintentionally created chaos around her. She has unleashed that dangerous force, eros (played out metaphorically in the fire imagery [Wilson 72–77]), which is quite unlike her peaceable state of contentment. Juanete, by class and upbringing less discreet about bodily urges, alludes quite explicitly to the sexual drives (to be aroused or quieted, as the case may be) that propel the action of the play: "so he, grey hair'd and she a girl / will either bring the one down off the boil, / or put the other on to heat" (1.234–36), he warns of the May/December marriage of his master.

Thus Seraphine, who was to bring order to don Juan's life as guarantor of legitimate succession, brings only destruction. She plays the role of *pharmakon,* both cure and poison—like Deianeira, in fact. It has been noted that "in the mythical theme of the 'don fatal,' it is commonly a garment of death that is the woman's gift: we have only to remember Eriphyle, Deianeira, Medea" (qtd. Gould 52). Woman's weaving—one of her main role functions—is shrouded in paradox: "The contribution to society has become the source of its destruction" (Gould 52). In Calderón's mythological fiesta, *Los tres mayores prodigios* (The Three Greatest Prodigies; 1636), in which the same abduction by Nessus is portrayed, all three women characters (Deianeira, Medea, and Phaedra) bring ruin to their heroic counterparts.

The representations of Hercules in the mythological play and in *El pintor de su deshonra* are similar. Don Juan characterizes the Hercules of his painting as the man "in whom I think my skill conveys / beauty and ferocity combined" (3.2684–85). From this multifaceted hero Calderón chooses not the exemplar of virtue of the allegorical tradition that persisted in painting, an example of which is Zurbarán's "Labors of Hercules" series for the Buen Retiro Palace (Brown and Elliott 156–61). Instead, Calderón's Hercules is "demythified" (O'Conner, "Hércules y el mito masculino"): the playwright develops a salient facet of the classical literary tradition, which includes Euripides' *Heracles* and Seneca's *Hercules furens,* according to which the hero, overcome by an attack of madness, mistakenly kills his first wife, Megara, and children.[2] In these classical tragedies, as in Sophocles' *Women of Trachis,* the finality of the hero's death further emphasizes his human, as opposed to godly, stature. The final sequel in the *Metamorphoses,* the apotheosis—Hercules' reward by Zeus for his labors and ascent to heaven (9.242–72)—is, therefore, significantly absent, as it is from both *El pintor de su deshonra* and *Los tres mayores prodigios* (de Armas 162–63). This focus on the hero's lack of control directly contradicts, in fact, the standard iconography, according to which one of his virtues, represented by a golden apple, is "never to get angry" (Pérez de Moya 2:102).

This rage or madness of Hercules was eventually attributed to medical causes, and Hercules (as well as other Greek heroes) is cited as an example of "melancholy" by the pseudo-Aristotelian *Problemata* (30.i), a common source for the Renaissance books on humoral psychology: the characterization in standard reference works is as "Herculanus morbus" (Babb 59; Galinsky 232). As Teresa Scott Soufas has shown in her work on the subject, Calderón's wife-murderers are also figures of melancholy, as well as of distinction, as befits the fascinating question posed in the *Problemata:* "Why is it that all those who have become eminent in philosophy or politics or poetry or the arts are clearly of an atrabilious temperament?" (qtd. Babb 59). Calderón uses the source material freely, imposing a curious role reversal. In the myth the direct cause of Hercules' fiery and agonizing death is not his own, but Deianeira's, jealousy, which has prompted her to use the alleged "love potion" given to her by the dying Nessus. The complexities of her emotions are vividly portrayed in the classical sources; the earlier event, Hercules' killing of the centaur, is a minor incident—an uncomplicated, instinctive reaction of justified outrage, the serious consequences of which only become clear with the passage of time.

Calderón has conflated the sources; more importantly, he has deviated from them by attributing the hero's notorious rage to jealous passion, a state of irrationality reserved for the female by Sophocles *(Women of Trachis)* and Ovid (both in the *Metamorphoses* account and in Deianeira's letter [9] in the *Heroides,* concerning her jealousy of Omphale). Thus if don Juan is the "painter of his dishonor," he is also the "writer of his madness." The inscription of the painting—"He who first was jealous, go / and perish after the fire'" (3.2704–5)—deviates from the standard allegorical interpretation of this portion of the myth and serves to reveal don Juan's pathology— his "conscience," as it were. Like the Hercules "furens," however, don Juan commits a terrible act when "out of his mind." If Juan Roca's act of revenge due to love is forgiven with uncomfortable readiness (in this and other such revenge plays), it is perhaps due to an implicit defense of "not guilty by reason of temporary insanity." Like Hercules after the slaying of his wife and children, he also remains alive after the act, but condemned to a state of suffering.

The abduction has contaminated all involved, and purification requires a catharsis (duBois 100)—as Deianeira is sacrificed, so is Seraphine, and don Juan is also expelled from the communal scene at the end. Society is indeed reconstituted; however, the ending of the play is not harmonious but unsettling, with fathers staring at dead children and a less-than-desirable

marriage in the offing between the prince and Portia. The cost of maintaining such pristine integrity has been too great, Calderón appears to
suggest.

In her analysis of Sophocles' *Women of Trachis*, Page duBois states: "The
tragedy shows the attempt of civilizations to construct a circle within
which culture exists, from which all elements of otherness, of difference,
are excluded" (103–4). In part, as the critic suggests, this effort is doomed
to failure because of the liminal position of women, outsiders needed
within (104); in part, we should add, this attempt is also doomed because
such efforts at perfect control are bound to fail.

If the mythological painting mirrors the play, so does the play mirror
the society beyond it. The play interprets the myth in terms of sexual
codes relevant to Calderón's era: in spite of the efforts of reason, the "beast"
of sexuality has wreaked havoc. But sexual mores do not exist as a discrete element in a society; they too are a social artifact and coincide with
other societal norms and preoccupations. Lawrence Stone has noted that
periods of sexual repression (of adultery or homosexuality, for instance)
are generally marked also by intolerance of racial, religious, and political
deviance. This is certainly true in the Spain of the Habsburgs, where neither Jew nor Arab nor Protestant was countenanced.

Calderón had written a play to celebrate Spínola's triumphant taking
of Breda in 1625 (*El sitio de Bredá* [The Siege of Breda]), only to see the city
lost again in 1637. Of another time and place, William Butler Yeats wrote:
"Things fall apart; the centre cannot hold" ("The Second Coming" 402).
How can Calderón not have perceived the futile sacrifice in lives and
resources of Spain's mighty efforts to preserve a center that history no
longer made viable? If the wasteland at the end of *El pintor de su deshonra* was
the price exacted for the preservation of this particular culture, the cost
was indeed too great.

Alexander Pope wrote: "To Err is *Humane,* to Forgive *Divine*" ("An Essay
on Criticism" [v. 525, p. 297]). In the *auto* by the same name written shortly
after the *comedia,* Roca's allegorical counterpart Painter (God) forgives

Human Nature, Seraphine's allegorical counterpart, killing only the actively guilty party, the Devil ("Lucero"/Alvaro) as well as Sin/Guilt ("Culpa"). The "logical progression" posited from the secular world of the *comedia* to the *auto*'s realm of the sacred (Mitchell 360) may be less a progression than a rupture. The divine order is utopic (God and Law are one and the same); society, bound by ideological constraints, exacts its own violence. It demands from the individual the sacrifice of the personal to the sociosymbolic totality, the subordination of the desires of the self to the law (of the code of honor, of the state, of religion). What remains after the fulfillment of duty, and the profound alienation and conflict it entails, is a void. Calderón does not leave us with a sense of glory, or exultation; only with the sadness that we inhabit the human world of error, not the divine world of forgiveness.

A Tale of Two Sisters: Procne and Philomela

The *Progne y Filomena* plays of Guillén de Castro (1608–1612?)[3] and Rojas Zorrilla (first performed in 1636)[4] are based on one of the most memorable legends in Ovid's *Metamorphoses:* the tale of the sisters Procne and Philomela, daughters of Pandion, king of Greece (6.412–674). Procne is given in marriage to Tereus, king of Thrace; Philomela, who follows the couple to Thrace at her sister's request, is raped by her brother-in-law. Sexual violence, adultery, incest: a concatenation of shocking and reprehensible acts worthy of committing this myth, above others, to the annals of cultural history? Yes—and no. They are not sufficient to explain the emblematic status of this particular rape story. For more powerful, more fascinating is Tereus's atrocious act of mutilation. To silence his victim, he cuts out her tongue. Visually riveting, the image of the mute Philomela with blood gushing from her mouth is particularly horrific in Ovid's rendition: "The mangled root quivers, while the severed tongue lies palpitating on the dark earth, faintly murmuring; and, as the severed tail of a mangled snake is wont to writhe, it twitches convulsively, and with its last dying movement it seeks its mistress's feet" (557–60). When Procne eventually learns this awful truth, she vows to her sister that

Figure 4. Nancy Spero, *Codex Artaud, I,* detail, 1971.
Courtesy of the artist, New York City

she will murder Tereus in revenge, never hesitating about this end, only
about the means, whether death by conflagration or mutilation: "to cut out
his tongue and his eyes, to cut off the parts which brought shame to you,
and drive his guilty soul out through a thousand wounds" (616–18). Procne's
revenge on Tereus is child-murder. She wavers only briefly, and then "with
no change of face" (642), with the deliberate rationality of Medea's slaughter of her children to revenge Jason's erotic infidelity, she kills their son Itys
and serves him as banquet fare to the unwitting king.[5] In spite of the fact
that the human meat is cooked, the taint of cannibalism remains. In addition,
Philomela flings the child's severed head in the face of Tereus. The king draws
his sword against the sisters. In the *Metamorphoses,* the gods release the humans
from the cycle of violence by transforming them into birds.[6]

For contemporary feminism, the emblematic status of this legend lies not it its violence (awful though it is) but in Philomela's breaking of the silence imposed on her, as celebrated by the artist Nancy Spero in her focus on the tongue as the instrument of female vindication (fig. 4). Even though she is mutilated and mute, Philomela weaves her story in a tapestry and thus communicates the outrage to her sister. Patricia Joplin's important article on this tale, "The Voice of the Shuttle Is Ours," after a phrase from Sophocles' lost play *Tereus* (recorded in Aristotle's *Poetics* [16.4]), revises Geoffrey Hartman's gloss of this same phrase in his *Beyond Formalism: Literary Essays 1958–1970*. She writes that "he celebrates Language and not the violated woman's emergence from silence. He celebrates Literature and the male poet's trope, not the woman's elevation of her safe, feminine, domestic craft—weaving—into art as a new means of resistance" (26).

In her version of the ancient myth, *The Love of the Nightingale* (first performed in 1988), the contemporary playwright Timberlake Wertenbaker rewrites the tale so that the expression of truth is accomplished through theater. In the midst of the bacchanal festivities, Philomele *[sic]* represents the rape and mutilation with huge dolls (scene 18). At the moment when the third doll, a queen, is made to weep and embrace the other female doll, the real Procne, who has been watching with the crowd, approaches her sister. Theater is a sign of the difference between civilized Greece and barbarian Thrace ("Do you have good theatre in Thrace?" asks King Pandion of Athens; "We prefer sport," responds King Tereus of Thrace [scene 5, p. 9]). Its function is not recreation but illumination: "I find plays help me think. You catch a phrase, recognize a character. Perhaps this play will help us come to a decision," suggests King Pandion (scene 5, p. 9). Whether the art form is the specifically feminine one of tapestry weaving or that of theatrical mime, its function is to express what the dominant culture represses. It becomes the voice, the tongue, of the silenced victim. The visual is thus a powerful speech act, not so much a voice as a scream, an urgent cry not to contemplation but to action. In both cases, what is important is that the artist who creates the reenactment is the female victim. In the play by

Guillén de Castro the true representation, Philomela's woven tapestry, is superimposed on Procne's own artistic re-creation of her sister's alleged accidental death: "Here will I set the cliff, and here upon it / the stumbling horse, / and here my sister, beautiful though bloodied, / falling, and if I can find a way / I'll paint my grief throughout" (2.146b). The purpose of Procne's artistic elaboration is introspective. She wishes to commit the scene to memory as part of her mourning; she refuses to let go of her grief: "Here will I draw / the wretched reason of my forlorn woe, / so that with greater assiduousness / I may lament the original upon seeing the copy" (2.146b). When the true version is delivered to her in the form of Philomela's tapestry, its effect is not remembrance but revenge—she calls for a sword and decapitates her son ("Because he is the image of that man / who drives me to this vengeance, / to bring his soul torment / will I take this one's life" [2.148a], adding that "solely for being a man / would I take many lives from you" [2.148b]).

The myth exemplifies—literalizes—the concept of woman's tongue as her weapon. Accordingly, "[to] reduce woman to silence is to reduce her to powerlessness; that is how the masculine will to castrate operates. . . . Thus—perhaps because of this—women's will to revolt necessarily passes through the use of language, the tongue *[la langue]*. Language, the tongue, is woman's weapon" (Debax 33, qtd. Brooke-Rose 310). The threat of her tongue is, in popular culture, postcoital: the shrew, the nag, are wives, not virginal maidens (a headline in a June 28, 1994, issue of the sensationalist newspaper *Weekly World News* exclaims that in Vienna "FED-UP HUSBAND RIPS TONGUE OUT OF NAGGING WIFE'S MOUTH!" He used a pair of pliers [6].) The symbolic equivalence between tongue and sword is made explicit in Tereus's angry condemnation of Philomela's lethal weapon that can be used against him after the rape in Guillén de Castro's play:

> Oh cursed instrument,
> tongue and woman's tongue!
> False, frivolous, and indiscrete

towards itself and towards others,

with sharper edge and venom worse

than lance, sword, or arrow. (2.142a)

As in the source story, succinctly stated by Apollodorus (*The Library* 2:98), the marriage is posited as a gift rewarding political allegiance: "But war having broken out with Labdacus on a question of boundaries, he [Pandion] called in the help of Tereus, son of Ares, from Thrace, and having with his help brought the war to a successful close, he gave Tereus his own daughter Procne in marriage" (qtd. Joplin 39, n. 27). The alteration in the Spanish versions involves a confusion of merchandise, which is accomplished (anachronistically) by introducing the custom of portrait exchange in the business of royal marriage brokerage (Davies 302): King Pandion gives Tereus the option of choosing one of the sisters and, accordingly, sends portraits of both. But the names identifying the portraits have mistakenly been inverted. Although he requests Procne, Tereus had meant, from the beginning, to have Philomela as his wife. Although his brother tries to convince him of the superior worth of Procne on the basis of a supposedly quantifiable measure—beauty ("To forget your anger, / consider that your wife Procne, / fairer is than Philomela" [Guillén de Castro 1.126a]), Tereus's desire has focused on the image of Philomela; it is she he wishes to possess ("I filled my eyes with her, / she entered in my soul" [Guillén de Castro 1.126a]). She has acquired a surplus value, which is further intensified by the fact that she is also desired by the brother, whom Tereus then suspects of intentional fraud in regard to the portrait error.

The addition of another male in competition for the same object has the effect of displacing the locus of attention to rivalry between men (Tereus and his brother Teosindo/Hippolytus). The tension that subtends this economy of desire is one of sibling rivalry, as evinced in the allusion to Cain and Abel when Tereus berates the younger Teosindo: "Why have you slain me? / For what wrongs and to what end / have you sought to be Cain / to one always your Abel?" (Guillén de Castro 1.126a). Only after intercepting a note between the lovers planning their escape to Greece is the enraged King Tereus spurred to commit violence. He dismisses any claims his brother may have and asserts his proprietary rights to ownership:

> Yes, but is it not excess of daring,
> nay, treason could it not be called,
> that he should take as wife
> the woman I chose for my own?
> Married those two are not,
> and I want Philomela. (Rojas Zorrilla 2.481–86)

In Guillén de Castro's play, Philomela's pleading for mercy because of her pregnancy (a unique plot alteration) only provokes Tereus's rage against his brother ("Ah traitor! So he has enjoyed you?" [2.141b]), and he vows revenge on the fetus:

> I will rip it out by pieces
> if your will will not yield to
> mine, for I yield myself
> to my jealousy. (2.141b)

He does not commit this savage act, but before readying his dagger to cut out Philomela's tongue and rape her ("I plan to cut out your tongue / and afterwards enjoy you" [2.142a]), he reiterates his motivating passion— not lust but jealousy: "I am dying of jealousy" (2.142a). In this sense the woman Philomela is but a pretext; the primary bond subtending the narrative is between men, locked in a passionate power struggle.[7]

The erotic conflict erupts openly into political upheaval in Guillén de Castro's play, when Tereus is banished from the kingdom after the murder of their son and the macabre banquet. More than seventeen years of civil strife ensue between Tereus and his queen, who is supported by her father, King Pandion, as well as by Tereus's brother. If the play begins with war between countries, at the end the most dreaded of all hostilities—internecine warfare—threatens the destruction of Thrace. The crisis is averted by means of a resolution of peace making among the warring parties that avoids death for the legitimate king, and the play ends in a frenzy of coupling—Procne and Tereus are reunited; Philomela and Teosindo are to be wed; the respective children of these couples (Procne's daughter Arminda and Philomela's son Driante) are to be united.

Ideological and aesthetic reasons have been suggested for Castro's ending: Jean Schneider Escribano views the play as a mythic plot rewritten *a lo divino* (allegorized), and, in keeping with Counter-Reformation tenets, "the pagan myth with all its passion, lust and hate, functions in the theater of Guillén de Castro to teach a moral lesson on repentance, forgiveness and redemption" (50–51); according to Edward Friedman, the fact that "Castro, in effect, writes a tragedy in Acts I and II of *Progne y Filomena,* then 'rewrites' the prescribed ending in Act III, a *comedia* of youthful love and averted catastrophe, in which the end justifies the means" (216), marks a time of aesthetic transition in Spanish dramatic practice between the older classical models and the new, highly successful Lope formula for the *comedia nueva.* I would add that, as bizarre and improbable as this ending may seem, its symbolic dimension reveals an underlying structural coherence.

Implicit in the resolution is the mechanism of the substitute sacrificial victim. According to René Girard, "ritual victims tend to be drawn from categories that are neither outside nor inside the community, but marginal to it: slaves, children, livestock" (*Violence and the Sacred* 271). It is Itys's death that accomplishes the beneficial healing required for the community to continue intact. In the myth the cycle of violence is not broken by the murder and ingestion of the child Itys: Tereus's intended revenge is stopped only by the miraculous metamorphosis, which finds him wielding his sword against the sisters, and even in his avian transformation he looks warlike (6.674). In Guillén de Castro's play, on the other hand, the innocent and powerless child Itys, whose physical resemblance to his father makes him a particularly appropriate substitute ("Because he is the image of that man / who drives me to this vengeance" [2.148a]), is signaled as sufficient atonement for Tereus's violence against Philomela to break the cycle of reciprocal reprisals. When Procne reminds her sister that "and it costs us both a son" (3.163b), Philomela accedes:

> You are right, and had I
> known it before, I would not have been silent
> so many years, nor would I have sought
> worse vengeance for my wrong. (3.163b)

Itys becomes imbued with a sacred aura.

In addition, though, there is another crucial factor in Guillén de Castro's version that enables the restoration of political order: Tereus did not rape Philomela. Thus her chastity (though not her virginity, in this instance) has been maintained:

> Tereus on that
> miserable day,
> attempted his evil urge,
> but did not succeed. (3.162a)

Tereus later adds, addressing his wife:

> I did not wrong your sister
> though I tried to possess her;
> I admit that cutting out
> her tongue was a great sin. (3.162a)

His offense, therefore, is limited to intent ("he has offended you with his intent," says Procne to her sister [3.163b]).

In her fundamental work *Purity and Danger,* Mary Douglas posits the human body as the symbolic basis of social structure. She adds: "The body is a model which can stand for any bounded system. Its boundaries can represent any boundaries which are threatened or precarious." Furthermore, "all margins are dangerous. . . . The mistake is to treat bodily margins in isolation from all other margins" (121). The metaphoric equivalence between the (specifically) female body and the body politic provides the essential underpinning for Castro's happy ending. What is at stake throughout the play in the political arena is a country's safe maintenance of external boundaries (Greece, then Thrace). Unlike the myth, where the distinction and potential rivalry between two nations and two kings fade from the scene of action, the play accentuates the tensions, and in the final act the aged King Pandion is at war against Thrace on behalf of his daughter Procne. Peace, as the maintenance of national boundaries and avoidance of invasion by an outside force, is made possible by Philomela's intact chastity, which in turn obviates the need for revenge and enables a marriage to take place. Tereus has not unlawfully transgressed the boundaries of her body; there has been no sexual pollution. Philomela's body and the body politic mirror one another. Though both are threatened, both remain intact and whole at the end.

In contrast to Guillén de Castro, Rojas is praised by Raymond MacCurdy for having "had the dramatic insight to perceive the inevitability of a tragic situation" in the case of his version of *Progne y Filomena,* adjudged, with other works in his opus, as "the most skillful tragedies of revenge composed in Spain's Golden Age" (31). In the myth, and in Guillén's play, the boy-child Itys served as substitute victim for Tereus. Children are absent from Rojas's version, and the sisters together wreak revenge on their antagonist, before father (King Pandion of Greece) and husband (Hippolytus) arrive on the scene, intent on accomplishing the same goal. Unlike the myth, and unlike Castro's version, there is no substitute victim. Tereus indeed does rape Philomela in Rojas's play, and the incestuous implications of Tereus's sexual transgression are doubled, because he is her brother-in-law twice over: husband to her sister and brother to her husband. Her love relationship with Hippolytus has been consummated, as is delicately intimated in a garden scene of floral eroticism:

the lullaby of your voice,
put to sleep my honor
as though it were a young child,
and kept my hope awake.
Not even the flowers bore witness,
because the maiden rose
hid in her green cocoon,
through caution or chastity;
Shrunk down inside its bud
the bashful lily hid,
and to vie with our entwinement
the green ivy revealed itself. (1.181–92)

Thus when Philomela escapes Tereus's first illicit approach and turns to her sister for support, she states that "you are a betrayed wife / and my husband is his brother" (2.123–24) and proceeds to itemize the king's offenses:

Four offenses has he incurred
with his tyrannical intent:
he has offended through me his brother,
and the law with his triumph,
me with all his desire
and you with total disregard. (2.125–30)

The seemingly extraneous plot accretion of the Spaniards—the subtext of sibling rivalry—acquires narrative logic in Rojas's play, for the younger brother becomes the rightful heir to the kingdom on the death of his brother Tereus. Both father-in-law and new king manifest their satisfaction at the end of the play: "Happy am I," says Pandion (Pandrón in the text); "I hold a scepter," announces Hippolytus (3.1190, 1191). Philomela's honor is restored; war is averted; national boundaries are maintained. Unlike the myth, then,

where "[t]he sacrifice of the innocent victim, Itys, continues, without alter-
ing it, the motion of reciprocal violence" (Joplin, "The Voice of the Shuttle
Is Ours" 45), the endless cycle of revenge is, in fact, broken in Rojas's play.
It, too, can be said to have a comic resolution.

This is a novel ending within the *comedia* honor code, which assigns the
role of revenge to the male, and a demonstration of Rojas's uniqueness,
observes Américo Castro in his edition of *Cada qual lo que le toca,* which he
compares to *Progne y Filomena* in terms of the prominent role of the women:
"But the author's idea is clearly that wives can execute vengeance for their
dishonor as legitimately as can their husbands" (192). In addition, Raymond
MacCurdy notes, Rojas refutes the double standard of marital fidelity by
empowering the aggrieved wife to punish her adulterous husband (x). After
all, Procne asks her sister, who answers affirmatively: "Tell me, when a
woman commits adultery / does she not deserve / death?" (3.1107–9).

Is it, in fact, Rojas's "unwonted feminism" (MacCurdy x) that determines this unfolding of the plot? Are we to imagine the audience of the
public theater applauding Procne and Philomela, as they knife Tereus to
death in sororal splendor? It is possible, of course. A theme based on classical myth is distanced in time and space; its unconventional outcome
would prove less threatening than a similar ending in a play of contemporary manners, such as *Cada qual lo que le toca.* I would like to suggest,
however, that, if we read more closely the details of the play *Progne y Filomena,*
another, more obscured interpretation emerges, more powerful because
it is repressed. Américo Castro makes the point in his comparison of the
two plays that "[t]he same device of a dagger is used to prevent, rhetorically speaking, the wife's arrogating to herself the husband's basic authority" (192). It is clear in both plays that the instruments used belong to the
respective husbands. Philomela explains:

> This sword belongs to my husband,
> and it is the sword that once
> was author of my offense;

and given that I hold it,

I will use my arm's own strength,

since he supplies the instrument. (3.1128–33)

She recalls the moment when, after her rape and mutilation, *"bathed in blood, hair loosened, and barefoot"* (2.stage directions after 1070), she encountered the horrified Hippolytus and, unable to speak, borrowed his dagger to write her tale of horror in the sand.

Rojas has negated key elements of the myth. He has erased the weaving of the tapestry, a crucial aspect for the interpretation of this tale in terms of a "feminist poetics": "As an instrument that binds and connects, the loom, or its part, the shuttle, re-members or mends what violence tears apart: the bond between the sisters, the woman's power to speak, a form of community and communication" (Joplin, "The Voice of the Shuttle Is Ours" 51). Furthermore, Hippolytus is interposed between the sisters in the line of communication; it is to him, her "husband," rather than to Procne, that Philomela initially expresses her grief and outrage. Joplin remarks that the myth is structured in such a way that "the end of the story overtakes all that preceded it; the women are remembered as *more* violent than the man" (45), quoting as an example Achilles Tatius's allusion in *Leukippe and Kleitophon* to the sisters' "'exorbitant revenge'" and his conclusion that: "'Only passionate women making a man pay for a sexual affront, even if they must endure as much harm as they impose, count the pain of their affliction a small price for the pleasure of the infliction'" (45–46, n. 36). The dagger-wielding sisters, determined to obtain reprisal, constitute the final scene of Rojas's stage spectacle. The spectators witness the successful murder in a discovery scene, in which *"Tereus is revealed dead in bed"* (3.stage directions after 1179). Father and husband applaud the deed with terms of praise usually reserved for the heroic male: "Great courage!"; "Noble wrath!" (3.1180, 1181).

In this final scene the men watch the women; the audience, in turn, watches the men watching the women. If father and husband react with awe, a similar response of "fear mixed with dread, veneration, reverence, or wonder" (*Webster's Third New International Dictionary*) can be posited for the other viewers. If, as Joplin contends, a female perpetuation of violence is the final impression left by the classical text, then this is all the more true of Rojas's version. The Ovidian tale may, as Joplin suggests, suppress the significance and radical possibilities of Philomela's artistry, but Rojas erases it altogether. He denies the specifically female formulation of resistance to violence through "the voice of the shuttle," transposing the sexual imagery from the female warp and woof of the loom to the male dagger point, inevitably taken from the male (Philomela uses Hippolytus's weapon and Procne, Tereus's) because the female does not have one.[8] His Philomela is not an artist but a mere scribbler in the sand. And what she, the victim, has written—the story of Tereus's crime—will vanish with the next gust of wind or lap of water. What will remain for future generations is the story of the sisters' crime against their victim, Tereus. This, according to Procne, will bring her renown: "that Procne's name be writ / in bronze eternal" (3.1100–1101). And the ambivalence regarding victimization is heightened by the playwright's characterization of the Thracian king as a man whose suffering and guilty conscience (toward both his wife and Philomela) are portrayed and analyzed. "Indeed," concludes MacCurdy in an interpretation with which it is difficult not to concur, "Tereo's abiding passion for Filomena is a 'rebellion of the blood'—one that raises him above the commonplace rapists and invests him with a true tragic weakness. Having acquired new insights into his own being, Tereo realizes better than anyone else that only death will quiet his rebellious blood" (52–53).

One may well wonder who the victim is and who the aggressor in Rojas's reworking. For in her first appearance after the rape Philomela emerges as a *mujer salvaje* (wild woman), "*dressed in animal skins with a bared dagger*" (3.stage directions after 298), and anything in heaven and earth that by analogy can be considered "king" of its respective kingdom is subject to her savage wrath, even the pine on the mountain ("botanical king of that mountain" [3.308]) or the lily of the field ("since it is king among the

flowers" [3.312]). In a distorted reminiscence of Segismundo's first mono-
logue in *La vida es sueño (Life Is a Dream)*, when he bemoans his lack of
freedom compared with other creatures in nature, Philomela expresses
her own frustration that, "The air, the seasons, and the murmuring crys-
tal waters / all find revenge, and I can find it not" (3.347–48).

In the Ovidian tale, Philomela begins the patient labor of weaving
during her imprisonment in order to communicate with her sister; in
Progne y Filomena, Rojas presents on stage a Philomela who has been transformed into a savage creature, dangerous and bloodthirsty. She has
lived the two years since her rape alone in the wilderness, with the
knife edge sharpened and ready for use. Read symptomatically, the
departure from the narrative source points to the emergence of the
image of the phallic female. Rojas projects on stage a powerful visual
image, which both reflects and affects a fantasy that is as much a part
of the cultural imaginary as it is the product of an individual psyche.
In her reformulation of Freud's theories in *The Taboo of Virginity*, Mary Jacobus
uses the same Judith-and-Holofernes example as Freud (Hebbel's play
Judith, in which the still-virginal widow beheads the rapist Holofernes),
and writes: "In order not to be a paralyzing threat, Judith must have phallic attributes, like the phallic woman fantasized by the boy as a defense
against castration anxiety. Instead of being mutilated by a cut, woman
has a sword in her hand; the mark of castration is replaced by the castrating instrument" (119). Functioning with the alacrity and mobility
of fetishistic displacement (Bersani and Dutoit), it is a substitutive
mechanism that offers oblique reassurance. In Freud's essay on Medusa
he speaks of the "consolation to the spectator" (212) offered by her
head full of (penile) snakes, as the effects of terror and erotic excitement coincide.

Yet another mechanism of reassurance emerges. In an idiosyncratic
departure from the source tale, Philomela's tongue heals in both Spanish
plays (although in Castro's version Philomela feigns muteness, for "I swore
I would not speak / with any till I had / avenged such outrage" [3.151b]).

The wound, therefore, is not permanent. The manifest purpose of the mutilation—silencing the victim—would seem to have been invalidated. Only the logic of the unconscious renders such restitution meaningful. If the cutting of the tongue, like decapitation, can be considered an upward displacement of castration according to the rhetorical dislocation of dream language, then such healing constitutes a magical undoing of the (imaginary) wound of castration.

The myth of Procne and Philomela: we imagine a stable story, unchanging in its significance in spite of time and space. But this is not so—as we have seen in the versions of Guillén de Castro and Rojas Zorrilla. The etymology of "version" is apt here, for its root verb is *vertere*, meaning "to turn," and the twists and turns in the storytelling are the most revealing of the subjective and culturally specific symptoms. Mieke Bal proposes the following definition:

> Thus conceived, myth cannot be defined but as an empty screen, a structure that appeals to the individual subject because of its pseudostability, a stability that helps overcome the feeling of contingency. And the screen can be seen as an empty canvas or etching plate, as well as a finished work which the reader or viewer approaches as if it were empty—ready to be filled. (*Reading Rembrandt* 98)

The process is akin to that of psychoanalytic transference, whereby source texts become the bearers of subjective projection, "providing the subject's projection with a means of getting rid of its subjectivity and thereby granting subjective projections universal status" (99).

Onto the empty screen of myth, seventeenth-century Spanish dramaturgy has projected a phallic female, whose contradictory effect on the (male) viewers is both to terrify and to reassure. Viewers of such a representation, then, would experience a mitigation of their own anxiety. The result, according to Jacobus, is that "[o]ne might expect, therefore, to find powerful representations of the phallic woman arising in the context of feminization" (127). Fear becomes the motivating impulse behind the fantasy projection—fear of castration, fear of impotence. In this and other plays, a link is established between rape and castration, in a context of political turmoil, between nations either at war or potentially at war, or between classes, whose interests and values conflict. The voice of the texts speaks of violent, uncontrollable passion; the whisper of the subtexts betrays the secret of insecurity. The wrongful appropriation and wounding of the female is a speech act, Bal has argued, where language has failed: "The meaning of the speech act of rape is hatred of the male competitor, of the woman who may not be possessible; it is a hatred spoken through metonymy. The hatred comes from fear and is acted out—spoken—through the actual body of the object of fear" (*Reading Rembrandt* 85).[9] In a fascinating gesture of exposure, Guillén de Castro and Rojas lay bare this latent structure of competition in their versions by positing sibling rivalry as a motivating factor of conflict.[10] Because Rojas eschews the romance of Guillén de Castro's ending and allows the power struggle to run its course, the result is that the younger brother wins the woman and the throne. What in the first act appeared hallucinatory—Tereus's brother perceived as his enemy—becomes true by the final act.

Another peculiar dramatic manifestation in this and other plays of Rojas Zorrilla deserves mention: the intrusive comic grotesque of the *gracioso* subplot, which in *Progne y Filomena* consists of Juanete "the glutton" and Chilindrón "the greedy" staging practical jokes designed with each one's particular vice in mind. Juanete, having succumbed to the lure of a jar of preserves that his counterpart has filled with purgatives, writhes in pain in a scene of "farcical diarrhea" (MacCurdy 73), which has, in turn, created discomfort among literary critics: "No aspect of Rojas' dramaturgy has been subject to more unanimous censure than his introduction into the plot of extraneous elements which allegedly detract from the proper atmosphere of tragedy" (MacCurdy

72).[11] Considered a facet of the aesthetic grotesque (Leavitt 77), the mixing of comic and tragic elements was standard practice according to Lope's formula for the *comedia nueva* and was a characteristic of Spanish dramaturgy that even the neoclassical Alberto Lista accepted. Why then, asks MacCurdy (79), did Lista single out Rojas for negative criticism of the "comic scenes, with which Rojas takes pleasure in weakening the effect of the tragic scenes" (*Ensayos literarios y críticos* 2.137)? MacCurdy conjectures that perhaps the reason is Rojas's exaggerated use of these effects ("Certainly Rojas exceeded his contemporaries more in the cult of the comic than in the cult of the violent" [79–80]) and grants that the effect "sometimes borders on the freakish": "The results can be disturbing—even to an admirer of the Baroque" (80). He further notes that, in the case of *Progne y Filomena*, there occurs a virtual juxtaposition at the end of act 2 of the *gracioso*'s impending diarrhea and Tereus's rape of Philomela (73) and categorizes "Tereo's desire for Filomena coupled scenically with Juanete's desire to relieve his stomach cramps" as another example of Rojas's "deliberate cult of the grotesque" (76).

Though not identified as such, *Progne y Filomena* and the other two plays discussed by MacCurdy (*El Caín de Cataluña* [The Cain of Cataluña] and *El más impropio verdugo* [The Most Ill-Suited Executioner]) as being the most subject to criticism for the intrusiveness of their comedy share a feature: scatological humor.[12] This is interesting for several reasons. At the level of sociohistoric practice, within the controlled and decorous aristocratic milieu of nobility and court, the lower-class lackeys become the signifiers of the carnivalesque grotesque body (Bakhtin, *Rabelais and His World*). They become the bearers of what the general culture is increasingly repudiating as part of conscious civilized discourse—in particular, the lower body functions of urination, defecation, and fornication, as well as the digestive functions of an excessive intake of food and drink. In their study of the transformations and displacements of carnival practices, Peter Stallybrass and Allon

White chart the marginalization in terms of class and "gradual reconstruction of the idea of carnival as the culture of the Other" (178), a process that Golden Age dramatic practice articulates. Inherent in the noble/plebeian dichotomy of the *comedia* is the systematic binary classificatory pattern of high /low, refined /vulgar, civilized /uncivilized, and so on, basic to the defining of the self as against the other. The "disturbing" effects of Rojas's *gracioso* activity that MacCurdy recognizes, of an atmosphere "too frequently and too ruthlessly penetrated by foreign elements" (80), may be due to the manifest irruption of the abject in his comic humor, to the bodily waste and filth alluded to in the scenes of purgatives *(Progne y Filomena)*, enemas *(El Caín de Cataluña)*, and chamber pots *(El más impropio verdugo)*. Urine and excrement are, in fact, considered filth and, as such, elements foreign to the clean and proper body.

If we return to the context of *Progne y Filomena* and to the scenic contiguity of Juanete's stomach cramps and Tereus's erotic ache, a metaphoric relationship asserts itself in the thematic linkage of desire posited by MacCurdy: the *gracioso* seeks anal relief; the king genital relief. As Marcela Trambaioli has suggested (294, n. 40), the quince confectionery (containing the laxative) emblematically conjoins sexual and appetitive pleasures. In Alciatus's *Emblems* the delicious fruit of the quince tree *(membrillo)* is a suitable gift for one's wife ("it leaves a pleasant odour in the mouth").[13]

What is at stake in both scenes is pollution—a culturally defined danger: "Each culture has its own special risks and problems. To which particular bodily margins its beliefs attribute power depends on what situation the body is mirroring" (Douglas 121). In the context of seventeenth-century Spain, excreta are funny and are a prevalent source of literary humor (Sancho Panza's loss of bowel control is but one example [1.20]). But excreta are also associated with violence, as occurs in *El Buscón* (The Swindler) (Martínez Vidal 88). The low social status and generally infantile characterization of the *gracioso* figure, whose concerns are alimentary, minimize the potentially subversive quality of his transgression of a social prohibition.[14] Sexual pollution, on the other hand, is supremely dangerous. Tereus's unlawful penetration of the body of the younger daughter of the king of Greece incites war and results in death.

The scenic association of defecation and rape has the effect of thoroughly stigmatizing the sexual act. Sexual activity is already besmirched by its localization in the lower body stratum; it is already subjected to the degrading implications of the increasingly stringent Christian body /spirit separation and differential evaluation, whereby "[e]ventually, all of the body's products, except tears, become simply unmentionable in decent society" (Greenblatt 10). In *Progne y Filomena* Tereus's lust, divorced from the sacralization of marriage and procreative intent, is nothing but shit. The results of the two scenes stand in stark contrast because of the different social classes and different pollution taboos, but in and of themselves they become assimilated by metaphoric similitude as well as by metonymic contiguity. Instead of being a gratuitous and distracting element, the scatological humor results in a strong statement on the part of the playwright. Both the medical and dramatic senses of *katharsis* are put into effect in this conjoining of psychology and physiology (Martínez Vidal 89–90).

Rojas's *Progne y Filomena* was staged before the king and court on January 10, 1636 (MacCurdy 66). Might Philip IV have echoed King Pandion's self-reflexive words in Wertenbaker's *The Love of the Nightingale*— "I find plays help me think. You catch a phrase, recognize a character. Perhaps this play will help us come to a decision" (scene 5, p. 9)? And if it did cause him to think, could King Philip have understood that silencing by force irrupts into ever more grievous violence? Or did King Philip so safely distance himself and his world from the barbarian King Tereus as to preclude thinking at all? In all probability he took home a sadly familiar lesson: the victim is blamed for unleashing the tragic sequence of events. In the prologue to his *Tragicomedia llamada*

"Filomena" (Tragicomedy Called "Philomela," 1564), Juan de Timoneda addresses the audience thus:

> Therefore I do advise you,
> make a correction
> and set a rein and bridle
> on unmarried girls,
> who left to go unfettered
> lose their greatest jewel:
> this that I say,
> let all men understand,
> trust your daughters
> with neither friend nor kinsman,
> but keep them always guarded
> beneath your protection and cover. (212–13)

The Transformation of Tamar

This Old Testament story is short, simple, violent. The main dramatis personae are all children of King David: The mother of Amnon, his firstborn, is Ahinoam; the mother of Absalom, his thirdborn, is Maacah (2 Sam. 3:2–5). Not named in the first list is Absalom's beautiful sister (2 Sam. 13:1), Maacah's daughter Tamar. Amnon rapes his half-sister; Absalom kills him in revenge and is himself subsequently killed after a failed attempt to usurp the crown, making way for the eventual legitimate accession of Solomon to the throne. Many years transpire in the biblical narrative: between the rape and the revenge, two years; Absalom flees for three years and after his father's dispensation returns to his own home, but remains away from the court for two years; then, after four years of seditious activity, Absalom starts the revolt. The time is condensed in the plays to one continuous action in an insistent cause-and-effect sequence. The sense of implacability is overwhelming.

The story of Tamar is embedded in the Great Succession narrative of the house of David, immediately relevant to Christians because both Matthew and Luke trace the genealogy of Jesus Christ through fourteen generations, from Abraham, through David, to Saint Joseph (Matt. 1:1–17). It is understandable, therefore, that both of the major Golden Age authors who deal with this episode (Tirso and Calderón, who adopted Tirso's final act as his own second act)[15] are concerned with the character of King David as revealed in his response to his family catastrophes and that literary critics have also looked to David for the significance of the plays, with particular attention to the quality of mercy he displays, variously adjudged as saintly or indulgent.[16]

This Davidic focus is inherent in the text. In addition, however, in the plays certain modifications of source materials serve to further deflect attention from Tamar's violation. In particular, the characterization of Absalom is altered in terms of his motivation for killing Amnon. The biblical narrator explains that "Absalom hated Amnon, because he had forced his sister Tamar" (2 Sam. 13:22). There is no mention whatsoever of any aspirations to the throne.[17] In the plays, on the other hand, Absalom's political ambitions emerge as a salient factor in his decision to kill, especially in Calderón's rendition. As Francisco Ruiz Ramón states: "Thus, before Amnon violates Tamar, Absalom is already planning to rebel against his father and usurp the throne of Israel. . . . In Calderón's Absalom, unlike Tirso's, the theme of vengeance appears as a contributory motive, not a central one, in the service of a fiercer passion: the ambition to reign" (163). This is all to the good, adds the critic: "By this means Calderón imbues with a new depth and meaning the act he borrows from Tirso, at the same time rendering it more coherent in relation to the rest of the action" (163).[18] Such political coherence, needless to add, diminishes the impact and import of Tamar.[19]

In the Samuel narrative Tamar vanishes after her rape, sent to live in the seclusion of Absalom's country estate, leaving the subsequent

plotting of the revenge to her full brother. Her disappearance from the theater of action ensures the preservation of her characterization as innocent victim. Although her continued stage presence in the plays could,
in principle, confirm such a representation, it does just the opposite. She
exults on seeing Amnon's dead body (*La venganza de Tamar* 3.966–76; *Los cabellos de Absalón* 2.17.1848–58),[20] and she aggressively supports Absalom's ambitious designs against their father's throne.[21] There is a hint of this facet of
her character in Tirso (when Absalom admits that "You know I intend
to take the throne," she replies, "Then may sweet heaven grant your wish"
[3.977–78]), and Calderón develops it as a intrinsic quality, predating the
rape. Amnon's illness excites Absalom's desire to inherit the crown, and
Tamar admits that "Although I would grieve his death, / I would joy to
see you on the throne; / for in fact you and I are siblings / of the same
father and mother born" (1.2.219–22). By the final act she is praising his
"splendid ambition" (3.11.2414) and literally champions his cause, wielding the sword and planning to lead the revolt in Geshur (the kingdom
of their maternal grandfather). When verbal appeals fail to ward off the
aroused and dangerous Amnon, she expresses her resolve ("great strength
have I, and courage" [1.15.980]) and snatches Amnon's sword from its
sheath, wounding him slightly. The impact of the transformation from
pitiful and wronged maiden to potent and avenging Amazon is not celebratory but negative. In this play about mercy, Tamar is portrayed as
merciless, which has led some literary critics to judge her harshly, as witnessed in such statements as the following: "Tamar, before burying herself *in deserved obscurity,* admits that her brother's death was a just, albeit
lamentable, punishment" (Dixon, "El santo rey David y *Los cabellos de
Absalón*" 97, emphasis added).

   These are not only dramatic texts; they are also theatrical spectacles,
and the visual rhetoric of stage performance must be looked at as a key element in determining audience understanding and response. After all, the
public would know the story (from preachers, from *romances*);[22] the nov-
elty for them would be in its representation. In both plays the *apariencias,*

or discovery scenes (usually indicated by stage directions to draw open a curtain) punctuate key moments of particular intensity in the dramatic composition.[23] Thus, for example, the scenography accentuates Absalom's ambition with the visual impact of an almost dreamlike *apariencia* scene, in which he comes upon the king's golden crown, tries it on, finds that it fits, and threatens to kill any and all who present an obstacle in his path to kingship, including his brother and father. In addition to being a literal discovery space on stage, the scene acquires figurative meaning as psychological discovery, for King David, finding his son crowned, is forced to recognize the threatening implications (*La venganza de Tamar* 3.415–43; *Los cabellos de Absalón* 2.10).[24]

Tirso's *La venganza de Tamar* includes two violent acts, which Calderón replicates with slight modifications: Amnon's rape of his half-sister Tamar and her full brother Absalom's subsequent killing of Amnon, whose crime King David had forgiven. The events leading up to the rape and those immediately following it are enacted: the rape scene itself is completely elided. The aftermath of the homicide, on the other hand, is rather elaborately staged. In the *apariencia* scene, a set banquet table in a state of disorder is disclosed; on it lies the dead Amnon, a goblet in one hand and a knife in the other, with a dagger through his throat (3.211). In *Los cabellos de Absalón,* Amnon lies across the table, bathed in blood. Reference is made to the blood of revenge—still warm—that Tamar may drink as the sign of her restored honor (2.17.1840–44). White tablecloth and red blood present a stunning visual contrast. The histrionic excess of the scene is memorable, to say the least, and justified by the public character of the crime.[25] Nevertheless, the effect is one of displacement. The sexual crime against Tamar, private and intimate, is effaced. The only visible signs of her bodily damage are symbolic—she is dressed in mourning and has covered her head with ashes. Her body bears no marks of the hurt; she is neither disheveled nor bruised nor bloodied. In her long and ultimately futile plea to King David to take revenge, the mention of hymenal blood remains taboo. Institutional arguments concerning family blood line and the blood code of honor prevail (*La venganza de Tamar* 3.176–281). Tamar, as a victim, is aestheticized. Her body is kept distant from the audience.

In salient dramatic and performative aspects, the plays of Tirso and Calderón seek to repress violence against the woman Tamar. I should like to unearth this discrete incident of sexual violence from the encompassing layers of its destructive domestic repercussions on the house of David and on the land of Israel. Because Calderón concludes his *Los cabellos de Absalón* with the next portion of the succession story—Absalom's attempted usurpation of the throne and subsequent death—Tamar moves farther into the background as the epic dimensions are foregrounded. Yet Tamar—whose very powerlessness as a young female has served to conceal the centrality of her narrative role—is pivotal to the plot development. It is she who defines the relationship of the males to each other, which in turn determines the future of the kingdom; it is she who serves as a catalyst provoking the emergence to the light of obscured passions and pathologies. It is she, finally, who provokes the disintegration of the usually polarized gender representations and expectations, which results in a feminization of the males as they play out the tragedy. The obscuring of Tamar reflects underlying ideological assumptions concerning the importance of men and their deeds—a bias shared, to be sure, with the Bible.

But there is a further discomfort with the female and her sexuality in this tale. Amnon is sick with longing for Tamar but cannot act on his desire: "for she was a virgin, and it seemed impossible to Amnon to do anything to her" (2 Sam. 13:2). But he does do something to her, and she is accordingly defiled. Then there is the matter of familial relationship. Though the biblical narrator states first, "And Amnon was so tormented that he made himself ill because of his sister Tamar" (2 Sam. 13:2), two verses later Amnon confesses to his friend that "I love Tamar, my brother Absalom's sister." The change in designation is subtle but significant: "For the first time, fraternal language enters to indicate friction between the royal sons. The designation 'sister of Absalom,' supports this tension while deflecting Tamar's kinship to Amnon. . . . According to Amnon, Absalom, not virginity, stands between the object and his desire. If this male can be removed, the female becomes accessible" (Trible 40). Later, when Tamar pleads with Amnon to act sensibly, she says, "Now therefore, I pray you, speak to the king; for he will not withhold me from you" (2 Sam. 13:13). This is not simply a delaying tactic or evasion on Tamar's part; marriage between half-brother and half-sister would not have been prohibited in the Jerusalem of King David's time,[26] and Calderón's Tamar reasons accordingly: "Under our law is permitted / the marriage of kin with kin. / Ask my father's permission" (1.15.963–65). Amnon's crime is thus, technically speaking, rape, not incest. This technicality is conspicuous by its absence in Tirso's text, where Amnón recognizes his desire as unnatural, freakish, and clearly forbidden:

> Of Nature's freaks my love's the worst.
> My only hope is desperation.
> They talk of the singer and the dolphin,
> the plane tree and the Persian King.
> They talk of one who loved a statue,
> the horse and the Assyrian queen.
> My torture's a sterile madness,
> more cruel than any other.
> I lost my heart to a woman's voice,
> and became my sister's lover. (1.707–18)[27]

Even where the possibility of legitimization through marriage suggests itself, the discomfort caused by the closeness of familial ties is felt: in the Bible there is an insistent and redundant occurrence of the sibling terms "brother" and "sister" in the brief account (Ridout 75–78); in *Los cabellos de Absalón* Tamar's identification as Amnon's sister or half-sister well exceeds the demands of character identification. And in all versions Amnon repudiates Tamar—immediately and ruthlessly—after the rape. A swift and stunning reversal occurs: the biblical narrator writes, "Then

Amnon hated her with very great hatred; so that the hatred with which he hated her was greater than the love with which he had loved her" (2 Sam. 13:15); the Amnon of Tirso and Calderón rids himself of Tamar saying, "I dread your eyes upon me! Go! / My hatred's stronger than my love / ever was. Servants, throw her out!" (*La venganza de Tamar* 3.18–20). This is the first, and primary, reversal charted (A and A'). The biblical account, in fact, traces a flawless, chiastic arrangement, at the center of which occurs the rape, albeit "only briefly noted" by the narrator of Samuel:

> The inversion of emotions reported here highlights the series of contrasts upon which the entire chiastic structure has been built. The beautiful Tamar comes innocently to her brother (B), but leaves with her life ruined (B'). Amnon pushes his servants out that he might be alone with Tamar (C), but then calls one back to dispose of her (C'). Amnon's coaxing his sister into a private room with him (D) contrasts diametrically with the curt manner in which he dispatches her after satisfying his lust (D'). (Ridout 83)

Mutatis mutandis, the same pattern prevails in the plays. This chiasmic trope dominates the dramatic movement, and the deceptions and homicides that follow as its direct consequences are linear, tracing a straightforward, albeit deadly, pattern of cause and effect. It has been suggested that the purpose of such a rhetorical strategy in the biblical narration is "to stabilize the material enclosed, to enable a story to better resist change in the course of transmission, and to provide a pattern which makes more likely the recall of elements of the whole" (Ridout 80, n. 10). Trapped at the pivotal center of this formal perfection of the doubling and inversion lies the body of Tamar.

The enormity of the repudiation cannot be overemphasized. And King David's silence on the matter is deafening: "When King David heard of all these things, he was very angry" (15.21). The Greek Bible (which became the Christian Old Testament) is more explicit: "When King David heard of all these events, he became very angry. But he did not trouble his son Amnon because he was his first-born and he loved him" (Ridout 77). The playwrights, following Christian commentators (Dixon, "El santo rey David y *Los cabellos de Absalón*"), provide a motive for the king's long-suffering mercy by having him recall God's forgiveness of his own sins of adultery with Bathsheba and the murder of her husband, Uriah (*La venganza de Tamar* 3.368–81; *Los cabellos de Absalón* 2.7). It has been pointed out, however, that these acts are not equivalent:

> In the Bath-Sheba story we are explicitly told that Bath-Sheba was ritually clean when she cohabited with David and also that Uriah did not afterwards have sexual connection with his wife. David's offence is against the property rights of Uriah, it is not a "sin" which entails ritual contamination. In sharp contrast, the real gravity of Amnon's offence is not that, as a royal prince, he cohabited with his royal sister, which borders on the legitimate, but that having cohabited, he then discards her, destroying her virginity without giving her the status of wife. The offence is one of ritual contamination. Absolom [sic] must avenge her not because his property rights have been infringed but because she has been dishonoured. Appropriately David's offence, which is a crime rather than a sin, ultimately results in the triumph of Solomon. Amnon's offence, which is a sin rather than a crime. . . . ultimately results in the total destruction of all concerned. David's offence amounts to giving greater weight to the moral principle of endogamy than to the civil law concerning a husband's property rights over his wife. Amnon's offence is that he carried the moral principle of endogamy to excess, to a point at which "correct" behaviour becomes sinful. (Leach 71–72)

Love—or rather desire, as Trible justifiably prefers to translate the word for Amnon's yearning (58, n. 6)—turns into hate. In the plays the *gracioso* Jonadab tries to mitigate the peculiarity of Amnon's response by uttering a generalization about objects used and then discarded: "Tamar came just like a letter. / He's read her, now he tears her up" (*La venganza de Tamar* 3.84–85), but even he in an aside expresses surprise: "It's most strange. After so much love, / who'd think that hate could go so far?" (*La venganza de Tamar* 3.92–93). In *Los cabellos de Absalón,* although Jonadab had brushed aside Amnon's momentary hesitation about forcing his half-sister, saying "I tell you I'd do the same, / were she my full sister / if I were angry enough" (1.5.582–84), he is also bewildered by his master's reaction.

Trying to detain Amnon, Tamar implores him not to rape her, "for such a thing is not done in Israel" (2 Sam. 13:12) and would make of him "as one of the wanton fools in Israel" (2 Sam. 13:13), a translation of the term *nebalah,* "reserved for extreme acts of disorder or unruliness which themselves result in a dangerous breakdown in order, and the end of an existing relationship" (Phillips 238). Tamar's appeal is not to divine law but to the custom of the land. The rule that is breached "is the ancient prohibition on casual sexual relations outside marriage with women whom one could expect to find living under the same family roof" (Phillips 239), which would apply even though in King David's time princes were housed separately. Marriage would have been permitted, but by forcing her Amnon breaks an ancient taboo.

The narrator of Samuel and Calderón's play abruptly confronts us with a lusting Amnon. Tirso's text is unique in its creation of a prehistory for Amnon's yearning. The elaboration of desire as a process rather than as a given invokes the dynamics of the incest dread, which explains why *La venganza de Tamar* is so erotically charged, to be rivaled only in the twentieth century by García Lorca's poem of forbidden love, "Thamar and Amnón," in the *Romancero gitano* (*The Gypsy Ballads*). Amnon willfully and knowingly trespasses on the boundaries protecting against dangerous incursions of desire: bored and curious, he scales the garden wall of his father's palace, at great risk to himself if discovered, for the punishment for this infraction is death ("If he finds out, you know quite well, / any man caught within these walls / would not survive to tell the tale, / however high his birth might be" [1.255–60]). In the darkness, in the oppressive heat of a still night, amid the garden fragrances, he hears the dulcet tones of an unknown female voice singing a song of passionate longing near a fountain. It has been pointed out that the images are all of sensual pleasure (Hesse, "Imágenes"; *Tirso's Art*), and Amnon's fall from the wall as he moves closer (460) indicates psychologically the movement into the realm of irrationality and morally the impending collapse into sin (Hesse, "Imágenes" 165–66).

The equation of reason with law and unreason with sin and its expression in a dualistic pattern of images is, of course, a familiar structure in Golden Age drama. We need only recall Rosaura's fall from her horse that initiates the action of *La vida es sueño.* But in this private, secluded, and protected place, the transgression is more profound and archaic, and its meaning moves us into a pre-Oedipal maternal matrix of rhythm, sound, smell, and warmth of instinctive attraction previous to the intrusion of knowledge of the law in a secluded and private place. Amnon's subsequent realization that his object of desire is his sister ("Is that not / my sister in the scarlet gown? / Great Heavens! Is that not Tamar?" [1.674–76]) is dreadful, literally filling him with the dread of Oedipus.[28] Harking back to the erotic pull of a world of affect ("I lost my heart to a woman's voice" [1.717]), the primary world of undifferentiated desire of the child for the mother, this scene is particularly radical in its incestuous implications precisely because it lacks the scopic dimension that typically characterizes (adult/heterosexual) male desire. The attraction of an infantile, presymbolic space is again suggested in an analogy offered by Amnon himself as he convinces his sister to "play pretend" and assume the role of the dead Ammonite princess in a fictional tragedy of his own creation:

> A baby cries and asks its nurse
> for milk, yet may suck contented
> at some other's dried up breast,
> believing fondly that it feeds. (2.673–76)

Tamar is to be the wet nurse, the maternal substitute whose breasts can satisfy his demand.

During his feigned illness he requests, and is granted, the king's permission to have Tamar prepare his food and feed him. Dutifully following instructions, she prepares and kneads the dough and bakes the cakes,[29] but this is not sufficient, for then she is asked to bring them into his chamber and feed him by hand (2 Sam. 13:7–10): "My lord the king commanded me / to bring food to Your Royal Highness, / that you may eat from my own hand" (2.1069–72). It is at this point of marked psychosexual regression that the rape occurs, when Amnón demands, "Come, lie with me, my sister" (2 Sam. 13:11). The sequence is followed by both playwrights. This is all, of course, a ruse to maneuver Tamar into his inner sanctum where he may be alone with her; nevertheless, the explicitness of the details of the feeding procedure is odd, and the plot sequence charges the scene with anticipatory sexual excitement.

The request is apparently unusual, for it requires parental approval. One assumes that a princess is not usually asked to perform the duties reserved for servants. But the detail specifying that Tamar touch the food that will enter his mouth ("merely by placing hand or eye / on any sustenance or drink, / or even on the humblest broth, she [Tamar] would halt this fatal journey / that my life has undertaken" [2.1038–42]) points to a deeper level of disturbance than that of hierarchical social norms. Restrictions in the handling and partaking of food figure among the examples Freud offers in *Totem and Taboo* of avoidance customs or laws that serve to protect against the risk of incestuous relationships (814–15). If at the beginning Amnon's unlawful behavior caused him to succumb unintentionally to incestuous longing, here he intentionally and with permission circumvents normal restrictions, which then enables him knowingly to satisfy the forbidden desire.

The sexual tension that pervades Tirso's elaboration of the prelude to the rape can be attributed to a rich pattern of erotic imagery (gustatory, visual, and aural). The formal surface pattern is energized by an underlying psychosexual current of a boy child's incestuous longing, which Tirso has captured and expressed with particular vividness here (and in several of his comedies, as studied by Sullivan). I attribute this to his having insinuated into the given plot of sibling yearning the other forbidden object of primal desire—the mother, assimilating one into the other and blurring the distinctions between the two. The inclusionary gesture is inherent in the biblical narration, where the image of the nurturing mother feeding the sick child originates, but Tirso has extended and elaborated the suggestion, more fully developing its potential. In a manifestation of narcissistic entitlement (Giacoman, *Los cabellos* 52), Amnon offers a self-serving justification to the effect that sibling alikeness—or lack of difference—argues for a natural law in favor of their union: "If love consists in like attracting like / and between a brother and a sister / no distinction can be made, being in blood, / appearance and in merit equally / deserving of each other's devotion, / what law can prevent what love has decreed?" (2.1009–13). This negation of boundaries (here conscious, with malicious intent) resonates to the earliest infantile identification with the maternal body. Henry Sullivan has demonstrated the applicability of Lacanian terminology to Tirsian drama: at this radical moment of willful denial of limitations, Amnon rejects the intrusion of the law of the Name-of-the-Father, the imposition of culture on nature. The consequences are tragic.

After the physical violation Tamar is overwhelmed by Amnon's hatred ("Then Amnon hated her with very great hatred; so that the hatred with which he hated her was greater than the love with which he had loved her" [2 Sam. 13:15]). She experiences this psychological violence as even more cruel: "for this wrong in sending me away is greater than the other which you did to me" (2 Sam. 13:16). She who

was addressed intimately as "my sister" before the rape is now shorn
of either proper name or familial relationship. She is reduced to a
generic identification, to "this woman" ("Put this woman out of my
presence, and bolt the door after her" [2 Sam. 13:17], which Tirso renders as "Remove this woman / and lock the door behind her!" [3.82–83]).[30]
His command that the door be bolted—the same door through which
Tamar entered—dramatically enacts the reinstatement of the very
boundary lines he denounced, slamming the door, as it were, on his
own unconscious to prevent the return of the forbidden desire and a
repetition of the act.

Is this reaction, whether expressed in terms of the taboo and its pro-
tective dynamics of "almost sacred loathing" (Freud, *Totem and Taboo* 817)
or in terms of a Christian code of ethics, an indication of a guilty conscience and the consequent fear of punishment, of self-loathing projected onto the victim?[31] The problem with this as the sole interpretation
is that there is no rhetoric of repentance, no renunciation, no penance.
In his portrayal of Amnon in the final act, Tirso is decidedly explicit on
this point. Touched by his father's mercy, Amnon vows that "and that
great love I shall repay / and sin no more against him" (3.392–93). The
vow is short-lived. On the occasion of the sheepshearing festival at Ball-
hazor, he makes amorous overtures to an attractive shepherdess, and when
she denies him he threatens force. Incest, or at least quasi-incest, uncan-
nily threatens to repeat itself: the veiled figure is none other than Tamar
in disguise, who pointedly exclaims, "You are a man who likes his way"
(3.873). Rape, not repentance, defines the behavior of King David's first-
born son. This is the characterization followed word for word by Calderón
in his second act.

Why does Amnon hate Tamar? The biblical Amnon is not a psychological subject; his suffering is manifested to others as already repressed,
already transformed into a somatic symptom. He has become sick.
Consumption of intercourse cures his hysterical symptom—his illness—
but it also transforms love (desire) into hatred. The before and after are

clearly demarcated in time and space by the rape. The intercourse also marks Tamar for life. Her alteration is described not as emotional but as physical: as Amnon's love has become hate, so her virginity has turned into nonvirginity, and it is a loss she bewails. The condition of Tamar's hymen and Amnon's emotions are intimately related and have been so from the beginning of the story: her virginity, the narrator explains, presented a seemingly insurmountable obstacle to the fulfillment of Amnon's lust ("for she was a virgin, and it seemed impossible to Amnon to do anything to her" [2 Sam. 13:2]).

Pollution beliefs offer an explanatory solution (Douglas): more specifically, the defiling effect of sexual intercourse, which is due to the association with death of the loss of blood and semen, both life liquids (Wenham). But neither time nor cleansing can restore Tamar's purity. More, much more, is at stake here for Tamar, who has lost all value in the economy of exchange. She herself insists on this difference in *La venganza de Tamar*: in her disguise as a shepherdess, she hesitates to look at her reflection in the waters of the river, referring enigmatically to a stain that, contrary to her companions' experience, cannot be washed away with water, only with blood ("If water could wipe out this stain, / my tears would be enough. But this / can only be removed by blood, / the blood of a traitor and a rat" [3.642–45]). Her rhetoric of pollution in her plea to the king (3.176–281), which includes references to pestilence ("a plague that ravaged honour" [202]), contagion ("and I have been infected" [203]), and poison ("I wish I'd given him poison" [207]), evokes her status as unclean, untouchable. Her reference to herself as "garbage" immediately after the rape ("A woman who's been used is dross" [3.29]), is, in fact, quite apt, and she is condemned to a life of desolation, sent away from court to Absalom's house, according to 2 Sam. 13:20]).[32]

The textual gap left by Tamar's disappearance from the biblical narrative after her immediate response to the trauma allowed (or provoked) Tirso to fill in what was missing, to represent on stage an image of a postvirginal Tamar, of a Tamar who has now known a man. Because there is no source for Tirso either to follow or to discard or distort, this sequel acquires the status of a fantasy projection, imagined by Tirso, which then formed the basis of Calderón's version.

The image of Tamar becomes negativized and disturbing, as though Tirso had set himself the task of solving the conundrum of Amnon's violent reaction of hatred. She is portrayed as aggressive, in fact guilty of aggression according to critical commentary. Alan Paterson offers the most detailed commentary on Tamar's characterization, which, although lengthy, merits quotation in full:

> In Act III, this moment [when she is released from a passive role] comes. Tamar is transformed; from playing the victim, she moves to the centre of the stage bent on exacting to the uttermost the due of revenge. Honour acquires the imagery of fire and appetite once applied to love; retribution is her only law. In a dextrous appeal to David, she fashions the image of fiery love into one of bloody revenge (III, 192–9). . . . An inner bleakness dominates these arguments, as repellant as Amón's [sic] tortured love. This is driven home in the pastoral scenes later in the Act. The shepherds inhabit a world of natural generosity; for them, the mirror which exalts Tamar's perfection is the river as it reflects her beauty, not the mirror of honour; if she suffers from some blemish, it can be removed simply by washing in the water. Tamar picks up their simple notion and submits it to a different conclusion: only spilt blood can treat the blemish that she hides. By this simple device of contrast, the law of revenge acquires a terrible inhumanity, complete when we see Tamar rejoicing coldly over Amón's corpse. Her final revenge is bought at the cost of life and charity. Throughout the play, there is a well-defined symmetry between Amón and Tamar. For part of the action

Amón is the aggressor and Tamar the victim; then, in the third act, they each assume the other's role, calling forth a drastic change in our reactions. Each, too, exacts claims upon the other: Amón submits his sister to his rule of passion and she in turn imposes on him a crude code of revenge. ("Introduction," *La venganza de Tamar* 18–19)

Searching for psychological coherence, Paterson looks to earlier scenes for negative signs and finds them—in the passion of her love song in the garden, in "the spirit of the coquette" she displays at the intrusion of the disguised Amnón; in her "ruthless and immediate" response to Amnon's affront during the wedding celebration (18). Much in this analysis (especially the reading for proleptic allusions in act 1 to developments in act 3) reveals an aspect of the ideology of rape, according to which the victim is held responsible—at least in part—for the violation. But the cognizance of Tamar's "transformation" from passivity to activity is not only valid but well stated, for the choice of the verb "transform," meaning "to change completely or essentially," is apt.

Another way of characterizing the difference in her behavior is that the rape signals Tamar's entrance into subjecthood. This is the case also in the Samuel narrative, where she speaks for the first time when threatened by Amnon and utters words of wisdom, perhaps the only words that can be thus described in the whole tale (Hagan 310; Trible 45–46). She had been silently dutiful to her father and brother, voiceless in her obedience. In the plays, anxious about Amnon's declining health, she complies with his request to playact the part of his beloved in a script he has written and directs to suit his needs, and then accedes to her father's command that she feed the patient, specifying to her half-brother that she comes not of her own volition: "My Lord the King commanded me" (2.1069). In *Los cabellos de Absalón,* forewarned by his scripted scene, she does not disguise her hostility: "Amnon, do not thank me / for this visit; for I come today / because my father / commands me to serve you" (1.14.899–902).

In the normal course of events, Tamar would have passed from being her father's property into the hands of her husband. Her passive, object status would have remained undisturbed.

Yet it is the aggressor who casts out his victim, who accuses her of being deceitful, of harboring death and destruction: "Get out of here! Out I said! Out! / You poison in a golden cup! / So beautiful on the outside, / yet putrid as the grave within! / You vile and loathsome animal, / you harpy with an angel's face!" (3.1–5). Above all, it is her gaze that he cannot abide, for he fears it: "Don't look at me, you basilisk! / There's venom in your eyes and death. / Their evil gaze has maimed my life" (3.6–10). In the later scene, when Tamar, disguised as a shepherdess, reveals her countenance to him, Amnon reacts with horror: "I'd rather have torn out my eyes / than let them light on you again! / You defile the name of woman! / I'll quit the sight of you, because / your very sight is death to me!" (3.899–903). The fact that these two moments provoke a similar reaction establishes a metaphoric connection between the veil covering her face and her hymen.

Defilement is mutual: her blood and his semen have been discharged in the encounter. But, unlike Tamar's complaint, the image cluster of his tirade does not refer exclusively or primarily to pollution. What emerges is his fear of her look. Tamar, who has existed as the object of Amnon's desirous and appropriating gaze, suddenly assumes the subject position of looking, and he cannot bear it. The biblical narrator alerts us to the taboo of virginity; Tirso's metaphoric sequence discloses the element of fear inherent in Amnon's reaction of hatred; Calderón literalizes the implicit metaphoric connection between defloration and castration by having Tamar (in attempted self-defense) brandish Amnon's own sword at him and draw blood. Later, girded with a sword (3.11.2416), she commits herself to a leadership role in Absalom's insurrection against their father.

Danger emerges as one of the salient themes in Freud's essay on "The Taboo of Virginity" (TV). Although danger is present in all of men's dealings with women (TV 75), he ascribes the particular danger of virginity to the dreadful risk of invoking the female's anger; he has known cases of women "who after the first act of intercourse . . . openly express their enmity against the man by reviling him, threatening to strike him or even actually striking him" (TV 79). After suggesting, then discarding, several explanations, Freud proceeds to locate the cause of the threatening anger in female penis envy, the etiology of which can be traced to the moment described in "Some Psychological Consequences of the Anatomical Distinction between the Sexes" (PC) when the little girl "has seen it and knows that she is without it and wants to have it" (PC 188). As a result of this "wound to her narcissism, she develops, like a scar, a sense of inferiority" (PC 188). What emerges most clearly in the essay, according to Mieke Bal, is "the object of Freud's dread, whom I will designate the post-virginal woman" (*Death & Dissymmetry* 52). His "entangled" argument is constructed in such a way that

> From lasting bondage, defloration leads to lasting hostility; from a value, virginity becomes a danger. From a danger to the woman who is subjected to it, it becomes a danger to the man, subjected to the subjection of the woman who, from an innocent and ignorant virgin, becomes overnight a deadly, phallic woman. By the time we reach the second half of the essay, the prototype of the virgin has been named Judith. (55)

The reference is to Friedrich Hebbel's tragedy, *Judith* (1840), an adaptation of the book of the Old Testament Apocrypha that recounts the story of the heroic Jewish widow who saves her people from an attack by Nebuchadnezzar's general, Holofernes. As Mary Jacobus pointed out, Hebbel's version includes significant changes from the source: according to the Book of Judith, the pious widow remains untouched by the enemy general and beheads Holofernes while he is in a drunken stupor; according to Hebbel, the widow in the story, whose husband "was paralysed on the wedding-night by an inexplicable fear and never again dared to touch her" (TV 84), is raped by Holofernes and kills him in revenge.

Freud, recalling the dream of a new bride that "betrayed unmistakably the wish to castrate the young husband and keep his penis for herself" (TV 83), concludes: "Decapitation is to us a well-known symbolic substitute for castration; so Judith is a woman who castrates the man by whom she was deflowered, just as the newly married woman wished to do in the dream I mentioned" (TV 84–85).

Jacobus's revisionary reading of "The Taboo of Virginity" discloses the essay's basic confusion between penis envy of the female and castration anxiety of the male. Freud notes that primitive man, failing to distinguish between actual physical danger and imaginary psychic danger, "has the habit of projecting his own inner feelings of hostility on to the outside world, that is, of ascribing them to whatever objects he dislikes or even is merely unfamiliar with. Now woman is also looked upon as a source of such dangers and the first act with a woman stands out as a specially perilous one" (TV 78). Jacobus's comment is that, "For Freud himself, it seems, the projected danger is as real as for primitive man" (116). What is at stake here is not females' "narcissistic wound" (TV 80) but rather males' "narcissistic interest in their own genitals" (PC 185). Viewing the female genitalia as lack, he reacts with "horror of the mutilated creature or triumphant contempt for her" (PC 187). As analyzed by Jacobus, the fantasy of the phallic woman corresponds to the same substitutive mechanism as occurs in fetishism to avert the fear of castration. If "the fetish is a substitute for the woman's (mother's) phallus which the little boy once believed in and does not wish to forego" (Freud, "Fetishism" 215), then the image of castration (the sword-bearing female) also serves as an image of reassurance against the fear it incites (119).

At work in the Samuel narrative of Amnon's lust are the dynamics of a perverse desire, defined as an "erotic form of hatred" (Stoller, *Observing the Erotic Imagination* 8). Although hostility may be an element in all erotic excitement, Amnon's actions betray a pointedly aggressive hurtfulness: he deliberately humiliates and hurts Tamar by raping her, instead of gaining possession of her lawfully, as she begs of him; then he further degrades and insults her by repudiating her, which she experiences as even more painful and insulting than the violation. What enables such a sudden reversal of affect is the dehumanization of the object of desire—in other words, the fetishization of Tamar, broadly conceived: "The word 'dehumanization' does not signify that the human attributes are completely removed, but just that they are reduced, letting the fetish still remind its owner of the original human connection, now repressed," and one of the mechanisms of dehumanization is to rid a person of individuality by considering him /her as an abstraction, a representative of a group (Stoller, *Sexual Excitement* 7). Tamar, accordingly, is obliterated; Amnon dismisses her as "this woman" (2 Sam. 13:17). The same linguistic disavowal of intimacy is registered in Tirso's scene, as the gentle playfulness of word play with her name (in Spanish, "Tamar, amar" [2.1101]) is reduced irritably to the generic designation of "woman" ("No te quieres ir, mujer?" [3.41]).

And yet, Tirso's feat of dramatic appropriation of the rhetoric of victimization by Amnon converts the aggressor into the aggrieved; Calderón's feat of theatricalization whereby Tamar wields Amnon's own sword and wounds him makes visible to the audience her potentially lethal aggression. What she mirrors—Amnon's instrument of rape that leaves her bloodied—remains invisible.

By comparing critical commentaries, we can see the effects of Tirso's and Calderón's versions of Tamar. Based on his reading of the Great Succession narrative, the biblical scholar Harry Hagan reaches the following conclusion about Uriah (Bathsheba's husband, whom King David had killed) and Tamar:

> Both of these stories are preparations for the rebellions which follow, for they deal with the destructive desire within a man for the possession of what is not his by right. Uriah and Tamar (who is one dead among the living) represent the innocent victims of this force. . . . The author uses the deception in each case to underline the evil. Uriah and Tamar are sheep led to slaughter, and their deception shows how cold-blooded and unfeeling both David and Amnon have become in the heat of passion with its abandonment of fidelity. (323)

In his interpretation of Tirso's play, Paterson writes:

> We have already mentioned the purpose in the pastoral
> scenes in Act III; they establish a contrast between goodness
> and Tamar's obsession for revenge. . . . As Amón [*sic*] crosses
> the pastoral scene, he is associated strongly with the appeal
> of innocence, for it is on his behalf that the shepherds are
> arguing. The more we feel the inhumanity of Tamar's argu-
> ment, the more our sympathies gather round the unsus-
> pecting, trusting victim. But there is another purpose behind
> the rustic scene; it suggests a concealed metaphor. . . . What
> Tirso has done is to plant an analogy in the mind of his spec-
> tators; and it is an analogy which has a particular signifi-
> cance in the light of our play's central conflict. By seeing a
> relationship between the "innocent" Amón about to pay
> the sacrifice of honour and the sheep awaiting the shep-
> herds' shears, we are within a step of the major Christian
> image of the slain lamb, that is, Christ. If this step is taken
> and the analogy completed, we arrive at a stable symbol of
> divine justice and mercy. (23–24)

Susana Hernández-Araico's close textual reading (which focuses on the
different role of the *gracioso* in Calderón's play) discloses a Tamar who is hypocritical, "secretly passionate" (103), herself responsible for the scandalous
union. Her half-brother's wrath, therefore, is well deserved: "Amnon's
loathing is due, nonetheless, to his resentment at having been undone by
trickery. . . . Amnon discloses through these images that Tamar enjoys him
sexually, and he rejects her as a hypocrite" (109–10).

The playwrights' deviant readings and renditions of the source, as
expressed in their works, anachronistically appear to be complicitous
with Freud's fabrication in "The Taboo of Virginity." Both bear the hallmarks of a fantasy, an imagined creation that is distorted. Texts are always

responses to other texts; we cannot know if the authors intentionally or polemically deviated from the source or did so unwittingly and unconsciously. But we can question the significance and function of the projection on stage of a Tamar who is revengeful, implacable, dangerous—whose look, it is feared, can kill.

Answers, however speculative, may be found in a consideration of theater as an institution both defined by and defining the prevailing cultural and ideological traditions. Among other issues of hierarchy—be they rank, age, race, or religion—the structure of gender relations is one of the most passionate areas of dramatic conflict. A thematics of gendered violence emerges insistently from consecrated sources—biblical, mythological, historical—to be presented again. The transmission from poetic or narrative source to dramatic text for the consumption of the public playhouse audience, by all indications noisy, diverse, and demanding, entails adjustments for the purposes of audience reception. What this may entail in terms of spectator identification and recognition becomes important. The theatrical experience was, after all, a social event, with pleasure as one of its primary goals.

Any consideration of the main female character in the plays necessitates a scrutiny of the male roles and their sex/gender identity in the context of the culturally defined norms and expectations. What is disclosed is a pattern of male feminization, present in the biblical narrative and increasingly evident in the dramas, in which, in contrast to the stark and skeletal Samuel account, the authors explore motivations and elaborate on the perceptions of other characters. From the opening scene, Amnon occupies an interior space—the home, traditional domain of the female—and is relieved to have left the scene of war: "Remove these spurs / take off the boots" (1.1–2). His lust turns him into a bedridden melancholic, and he uses ploys usually associated with women, such as deception, feigned illness, and playacting, to achieve his desire.[33] In the Tirso drama, he is described as uninterested in women prior to this encounter with Tamar: the comment is made to him that "Splendid soldier though you may be, / you never were a great lover" (1.82–83), to which Amnon later replies, "You'll never see me fall in love;

my nature is far too nasty" (1.143–44). He states his aversion to marriage and admits to the truth of the observation that "You're not your father's son in that" (1.162–63)—a difference both agonizing and humiliating for this son of the heroic King David, argues Raymond Conlon, and the source of his sexual pathology. Cast in the role of a reluctant bride, Amnon does not remain unpunished for his recalcitrance to love. The obstacles in his choice of sexual object cannot, however, have a comic resolution.

Absalom, on the other hand, considers any woman except his mother fair game: "I only spare my natural mother" (1.187). He is vain, boasting of the physical beauty that makes him irresistible to women ("since fate gave me so much beauty / I share it with all womankind" [1.89–90]) and as proud as a maiden of the heavy, golden locks that will be his undoing when they catch in the tree branches, leaving him at the mercy of his father's forces. Adonijah describes his half-brother as the one with the "softest skin and prettiest face" (3.113) and predicts that his would be an effete and effeminate rule:

> Your council would be a clutch of women,
> your crown a ring of plaited hair and your
> illustrious father's throne a boudoir.
> For armour, you'd wear linen and brocade.
> For a shield, you would grasp your looking glass
> and fall in love with your own reflection
> and, whereas I prefer to use a sword,
> you would no doubt repel me with your fan! (3.120–27)

Angry at the insult to his masculinity, Absalom invokes his sword: "My blade is bright with uncircumcised blood" (3.148).

King David is all-forgiving: of the legal options available to him upon learning of the rape—marrying the pair or invoking the death penalty—he chooses neither; furthermore, once Absalom has killed Amnon, David becomes responsible for taking revenge. Instead, an eventual reconciliation takes place between Absalom and his father (Hagan 311). David, in fact, can be considered "the most important figure of weakness. . . . His weakness is no longer size or youth; it is the weakness of a man with all his foibles and misplaced love and trust" (Hagan 325). Subjected to deceits and buffeted by misfortunes, he will triumph in the end in his dynastic succession. The presentation by the narrator of Samuel is, nevertheless, "sympathetic, but not uncritical" (Conroy 112). Closely following the Samuel narrative, in *Los cabellos de Absalón* David's commander Joab decides to take matters in his own hands and kill Absalom—against David's express orders to treat his rebel son gently:

> Of less moment is one life,
> even that of an heir apparent,
> than the general unease
> of the rest of the realm.
> Just reason of state
> cannot be reduced to precepts
> of love: I must slay him.
> Fainting youth,
> die, though the King did command
> me not to touch you. (3.28.3141–50).

The most flagrant sign of King David's loss of political power is the rupture of his daughter's hymen—by one of his sons and within the home, the very locus of patriarchal power. By logical extension, as his home has been violated, so will his kingdom be threatened—by yet another of his sons. His failure to protect his daughter by indulging Amnon is equivalent to his failure to protect his kingdom by indulging Absalom.

It is in the context of this feminization of the males that the "logic" of Tamar's transformation emerges: her phallic attributes serve to allay male fears concerning their own masculinity (Jacobus 127). Situated as the male characters are within the feminine domain of hearth and family and their attendant pleasures, with war and heroic action a memory, their masculine identification is already at risk. Returning to Freud's "The Taboo of Virginity," we read:

> Perhaps this fear is founded on the difference of woman from man, on her eternally inexplicable, mysterious and strange nature, which thus seems hostile. Man fears that his strength will be taken from him by woman, dreads becoming infected with her femininity and then proving himself a weakling. (76)

It is Amnon who has succumbed to passion and irrationality; it is he who has behaved hysterically, betraying repressed feelings in somatic symptoms. Paradoxically (but not inexplicably), after raping Tamar, an act of cruel mastery, he manifests fear of her femaleness as a threat to his male power and control: "and realization of the influence gained by the woman over a man as a result of sexual relations, and the favours she extorts by this means, may all conduce to justify the growth of these fears" (TV 76). Tamar's empowerment begins at the moment of the rape. In the Samuel narrative, at the moment her virginity is threatened Tamar emerges from silence and gains her voice, and a voice of wisdom, at that (Hagan 310). In the plays, Tamar, no longer the dutiful and devoted daughter and sister, makes demands and is satisfied only when she sees her assailant with a dagger through his throat. As Jacobus has pointed out about the Judith and Holofernes story, there is a deadly complementarity at work in the tale of rape and revenge: "Freud's famous equation in 'Medusa's Head' (1922), 'To decapitate = to castrate' (*SE* 18:273) is reformulated by the play to read: 'To rape = to be castrated' and 'To castrate = to be raped'" (120). Amnon is not decapitated, but his death is certainly its functional equivalent.

What is at stake here is power, which in the system of representation bears a phallic signifier. The dread of being like a woman, of becoming a woman, is mitigated by projecting onto her the phallic symbol, which thus ensures the continued rule of the masculine. Thus, with implacable if perverse logic, in *Los cabellos de Absalón* it is only after order is restored to the kingdom that Tamar is reinscribed in her codified feminine role of passive victim. Following Absalom's murder, her life-in-death will be one of utter solitude: "I shall entomb myself alive, / in the very darkest place, / where no one may know whether I live, / or whether I die" (3.31.3191–94). Tamar, it seems, has assumed the guilt of the rapist and the rebel; her self-imposed exile is here equivalent to suicide.

The throne, the home, the bed—all sites of kingly and patriarchal authority—are threatened in this tale of rape, fratricide, and attempted usurpation of a father's throne. It is at this time of chaos, when the lines of a clearly delineated male hero falter, that the rigid gender demarcations become blurred, even interchanged. Hinted at in the Samuel narrative when Tamar's tongue is unleashed, the fantasized phallic woman emerges with unmistakable contours in *Los cabellos de Absalón* when Tamar takes Amnon's sword and wounds him. When throne and home are reinstated as loci of power, the distinctions between masculine and feminine roles revert to the status quo of polarization.

One can read the playwrights' transformation of Tamar as evidence of a conscious, intentional deformation of the source, in order to: what? Mitigate the blameworthiness of Amnon, the rapist, by impugning the victim and, once Tamar's character is assailed, render less objectionable her father's failure to protect her and subsequent failure to enforce reparations?[34] The ideological commitment, after all, is to King David and his succession. We cannot know the authors' intentions. We can assume, however, that such a negativized representation would be familiar and recognizable to a Golden Age audience, for it accords with a long, interpretive tradition of biblical "lethal ladies" (Bal, *Death & Dissymmetry* 24), who, starting with Eve, caused trouble in the orderly world of men.[35] The acrobatics of interpretation could render even innocuous females guilty. For example, according to the rabbis, it was Bathsheba who seduced King David, not vice versa: after all, she was bathing nude on the roof.[36]

But such programmatic, propagandistic intentionality on the part of the Tirso and Calderón is untenable. We must look, rather, to the unconscious of the text, to representation as a fictional construct that is itself the result of a dynamic process of reading and responding to previous texts. The ancient biblical narrative has mythic status, giving it the illusion of objectivity and stability. Yet, as we have seen in our analysis of the plays, there are extensive displacements and distortions. Bal's concept of the "emptiness of myth," of a blank screen ready to receive the projections of the reader or viewer (*Reading Rembrandt* 98), is particularly relevant to the terse narrative stance in 2 Samuel: the gaps and ambiguities left for the reader to fill in are central, rather than marginal, to the plot development in terms of motives and emotions (Sternberg 186–229). The story of King David and his children thus provides a mythical screen that invites subjective projections—of personal concerns, certainly, but more significantly for our purposes, of collective preoccupations. The plot tells the story of a crisis of masculinity and a concomitant destabilization in the body politic. The fantasized phallic female, terrifying but at the same time reassuring in her fetishized projection, provides a mechanism for mastering, or at least assuaging, the anxiety produced by the threatening evidence of woman's difference. In their subject matter, the plays thus correspond to the contemporary preoccupation with power—or rather its loss, and it was commonly perceived that one the first somatic signs of a state's weakening was the blurring of gender distinctions. Both María de Zayas and Gracián, for example, point to effeminacy in the current male population as an index of the decadence that afflicts the state.[37]

I began by stating that the story of Tamar is embedded in the Great Succession narrative. It is evidently a preamble to the story of Absalom's revolt: Tamar's rape provides justification both for a sibling rivalry that leads to fratricide and for a son's rebellion against his father. Her sacrifice (psychological death) literally enables the plot to unfold. In the Samuel narrative, the erotic is displaced very quickly by the political, and Tamar's effacement from the plot after the rape eliminates the disturbing effects of her body. The Samuel narrative thus facilitates "reading for the plot."

The playwrights' transformation of Tamar has the paradoxical effect of unmasking the subplot that underlies this tale of power politics, disclosing a radical anxiety about gender. In the dramas, we are confronted not with Tamar's effacement but, rather, with her radical incorporation. What is disclosed is the extent to which a woman's body poses a sexual and political threat. The source plot tells us of a violence done to the woman; the dramatists' distortion of the plot provokes a shift in victimization, "twisting" (in accordance with the Latin root, *torquere*) the meaning of the violence. *Torquere* is the etymological root of "torture" also. Blaming the victim is a familiar trope in the ideology of rape and is, therefore, useful to the maintenance of patriarchy. But the particular twist of the Spanish playwrights—the projection onto the "empty screen" of myth of a phallic female—unmasks the fear and hostility latent in the Samuel narrative. Her wielding of the sword and killing look disturb the plot space assigned to her, although at the end she is restored to the customary symbolic space of the female: passive and therefore good. As phallic female, Tamar is a reminder to the reader and the viewer of the violence inherent in the construction of femininity as mutilation, as lack. In the system of representation, she comes to represent not only difference but also potential loss. Imbuing her with a phallic indicator is a mechanism for mastering anxiety, assuaging the crisis of masculinity.

In Calderón's play, King David prefaces his reconciliation with Absalom by saying: "Concerning Tamar I ask you nothing, / lest it should arouse / on this occasion any ill will" (3.7.2213–15). The conscious decision to repress reference to her—his daughter, after all—may provoke outrage in us. But the unconscious speaks through this, for the power of difference cannot be repressed.

FIVE

A Contemporary Rape Narrative

Julia: The Prison House of Silence

O Rose, thou art sick!
The invisible worm,
That flies in the night,
In the howling storm,

Has found out thy bed
Of crimson joy,
And his dark secret love
Does thy life destroy.

—William Blake, "The Sick Rose," *Songs of Experience*

"Wound," according to *Webster's Third New International Dictionary,* is "an injury to the body consisting of a laceration or breaking of the skin or mucous membrane usually by a hard or sharp instrument forcefully driven or applied"; it is also "a mental or emotional hurt or blow to the pride, sensitivity or reputation"; in addition, it means "a similar hurt or blow affecting a political body or a social group and usually giving rise to resentments or animosities." The wound inflicted by rape is deep. "It as an assault on one's most private being," writes a survivor, which violates the core of female identity, an identity that is "enhanced by the cultural and symbolic values that the woman's body represents. It is this essence that is also violated: what she is and what she means" (Metzger 407). The rapist "Has found out thy bed / Of crimson joy."

In the seventeenth-century (and earlier) texts I have discussed, two of these meanings are explored: rape as the literal infliction of bodily hurt, and rape as the metaphorical wounding of the social body. Socially constructed codes of honor and personal revenge dictate the scripts of these rape narratives. Not until the twentieth century, with Ana María Moix's *Julia,* does the remaining metaphorical meaning receive expression, as the devastating psychological effects on the victim are brought to the fore. This intimate violation—unspoken, untold—constitutes a particularly incapacitating kind of violence, for it is turned inward, against the protagonist's self.

Although the narrative voice recounts her memories in the third person, the story is her own. The insomniac Julia at twenty years of age reviews the trajectory of her life, economically privileged yet emotionally deprived, in seemingly chronological sequencing. The years pass by, marked by memories of school and then university (during a time of student protests). The years include an extended stay in the country home of her paternal grandfather, parental fights, separations, and lackluster reunions (for the sake of public appearance), and deaths—of a grandmother, of her beloved grandfather, and of the younger of her brothers, who suffered a brain tumor at age nineteen after a prolonged illness. In its re-creation of the politically and socially repressive Spain of the Franco era, the novel presents a cultural context familiar to the reader, well within our realm of expectations. An intimate, psychological novel removed from the realm of political commitment, the portrait of Julia's bourgeois family does, in fact, verge on being a caricature (Nichols 123). The connection between the

personal and the political is nevertheless clear: the weight of the past sti-
fles a younger generation's access to a future of its own making (Christopher
Soufas); the seeds of the collective illness are sown within the bosom of
a dysfunctional family such as this one (Thomas 111).

But the actions, characters, and plotline act as a screen, blocking rather
than facilitating our access to signification. For there is another frame, a
still one frozen in time and space, occupied by the subject of narration as
a young child, sitting alone. The nodal point that controls Julia's life and
attempted death by suicide is her rape at six years of age by a family friend.
The story *Julia* as recounted by Julia with herself as protagonist is, properly speaking, a rape survivor's narrative.

It is a repressed memory, one that Julia in a reflective moment recognizes as such: she acknowledges that, in the trajectory of her mental journey backward in time, "the outcome of that trip she, Julia, had erased,
hidden away outside of herself" (54). This site of self-censorship is never
named in Julia's utterance but expressed in the pictorial language of
dreams. As many commentators have noted (in particular Bush, Schumm,
and Jones), the impact of the trauma is expressed by means of the twin
tropes of metaphor and metonymy, mechanisms of dream language as
well as of poetry. The associative chain emanating from the rape and its
particular setting (on a hot summer day, on a beach by the sea, with a sea
urchin as the only means of defense) imprisons Julia thereafter in a private world of distorted semantics. The usual positive connotations of
water become negativized into a signal of distress: in a school washroom
scene with her classmate (and tormentor) Lidia, Julia's panic reaction to
sexual tension is conveyed by the sound of dripping water, associated with
the seaside location of the rape: "The sink faucet was dripping and the
sound of the water falling on the porcelain echoed in her head like the
pealing of bells" (174).[1] The literal weight of the rapist's body on her small
frame, repressed as a memory, is expressed metaphorically, converted
into a somatic symptom—a feeling of asphyxiation when frightened
(which happens very frequently). Or, as Andrew Bush states more

precisely, the stifling of speech that follows the rape "is then converted into the symptom, or trope, of stifled breathing" (143). In the same washroom scene, when Lidia lays a hand on her shoulder, Julia tries to free herself: "She couldn't get loose. For some moments it seemed to her that air couldn't reach her lungs and that she was going to suffocate" (173). Here triggered by a specific external event perceived as threatening, the sensation is pervasive in Julia's life: "Julia had on occasion felt the exhaustion of anguish, an invisible weight on her body, an unrest that stopped her from breathing, a pain in her chest and in her throat that somehow she had to resist" (64). The threat of suffocation can be seen to have a causal role even in her aesthetic response to architecture and decor. The clutter of her maternal grandmother's bedroom makes it akin to "a torture chamber" (151) in Julia's eyes; her home, with its "oppressive drapes" and bibelots, is unbearable: "The whole house was like that. Julia gnawed her fists when she walked through it, not knowing what to do" (39). The spaciousness and sparsely decorated white walls of her beloved Eva's apartment (183), in contrast, are experienced as pleasing and comfortable.

The train of association, seemingly ineluctable in its poetic logic, determines that, for Julia, meaning is always elsewhere, not in the present but in the past. Her reactions and perceptions are determined by a secret causality over which she has no control. At key moments the temporal frames of the narration are conflated. The storyteller does not (is unable to) consciously mark the different times between the present "telling" (as an adult) and the past traumatic experience (as a child). The pictorial frame of the assault thrusts itself into the narrator's consciousness as a vision of heat, sand, sea urchin, and blinding light, not subject to Julia's reflection or analysis. As a result of these uncontrollable and terrifying memories, she can never feel safe or secure. Julia's flashbacks, which "may be characterized as waking nightmares in that they are vivid experiences accompanied by similar physiological reactions and intense feelings of anxiety" (Calhoun and Atkeson 73), are triggered by physical contact with a male, to which Julia responds with repulsion. Carlos's attempt to kiss her make her nauseous, provoking in her a need to scream and kick (208). Her nightmare that same evening includes images of asphyxiation ("the feeling of being locked up in a wardrobe or in a coffin" [208]), of herself, nude, as the object of Carlos's sexual activity, to which she reacts with "deep revulsion" (209) though unable to move. Upon waking her mind is flooded with "the image of a beach, rocks, a sea urchin, the paddle boat floating on the sea" (209). She showers, needing to cleanse herself from the residue of the nightmare.

Julia's dislike of sex is such that she cannot even bear to hear others talk about it. A young maid's unsolicited confessions about her relationship with her boyfriend provoke Julia to irritation and silent anger; then she is left with "the same anxiety, the same anguish" (51).

The impact on sexual functioning is but one of the effects described in the novel that coincides with clinical findings of a "rape trauma syndrome" (Burgess and Holsmstrom) or, more broadly, a post- traumatic stress disorder (outlined in Dahl 25–26).[2] The youth of the victim, the secrecy she maintains (succumbing as well to the verbal threat of her assailant, "You'll say nothing, you idiot" [61]), the lack of mediating factors such as family support (her mother, in fact, screams at her and hits her in punishment for the anxiety produced by her absence [62]), all exacerbate the traumatic effect. Julia's young life is marked by behavioral as well as psychological disturbances. She is plagued by nightmares, sleeplessness, fears of intruders ("The ghostly visions were what most terrified Julia. She knew they were the product of her own imagination. She had to conquer the fear" [45]). Compulsive patterns dominate her actions—attempts to exercise some sense of control (Quina and Carlson 73): "Any innovation, however small and insignificant, frightened her. She always left things in the same place. . . . Every day she would organize the identical little disorder and before going to bed she felt compelled to check lest anything had been left in the wrong spot. The same with articles of clothing and some of the rag dolls that watched her from the shelves. It irritated her to see herself dominated by that obsession" (145).

She reacts with guilt ("She, Julia, was bad" [15]), shame, self-loathing, and depression—when anger would have been a more appropriate (as well as beneficial) reaction. Harassed by the malicious Lidia and her friends, she describes her state of mind: "She was full of resentment but not towards her companions. She told herself she was weak and cowardly; they would always defeat her. She felt ashamed of herself" (177). The expression of anger is difficult, in literature as well as life: "Expressing rage is especially difficult for most women, who are socialized from childhood not to express any negative emotions. When feelings of anger do emerge, they tend to be either diffuse, directed at the wrong targets, or self directed" (Quina and Carlson 148): thus Julia's suicidal ideation and final attempt on her life. Julia's rage is released in fantasies of hurting fellow students (with a shower of stones or a douse of petroleum [30]), of killing her father by shoving him into a well (72). Her intense jealousy of her brother causes Julia to feel responsible for his death (16); the excessive fear of her mother's death may be interpreted as guilty atonement for her own murderous rage against her (Schumm 154). The cycle of shame, rage, and guilt propel the child into a constant state of misery. Feeling happy at the thought of her mother's return, she corrects herself:

> Suddenly she felt an urgent need to punish herself for that happiness. She didn't deserve it. That morning she had committed a grave fault. She was guilty. Pappa appeared in her mind, and then the well, dark, deep, swallowing him up. Julia remembered that that afternoon, in the doorway of the house, in summer, in Sitges, under the sweltering sun, she experienced for the first time the need to think of something that would fill her with pain, with fear, with anguish. She imagined Mamma dead, in that train that would arrive

any minute now, and she, Julita, would never see her again, never, never. (76)

A dissociative state has been identified as one of the coping techniques of avoidance adopted by victims of violent assault, "who may literally watch the world 'go flat' during periods of stress: other people acquire a distant, two-dimensional quality like actors on a television screen" (Quina and Carlson 154). Watching her brother in the emergency ward, "it seemed to her that they were advancing slowly, as if it were a movie sequence shot in slow motion" (141).

But Julia's dysfunction is more acute, for in the coexistence of Julia and Julita, it involves a splitting syndrome (but one of the facets of doubling in the novel [Bellver]). She is at an emotional remove not only from others but also from herself: "Raphael's memory linked her to a time in the past that she felt was hers, lived by her. Everything else was like a movie seen in dreams, the leading character of which was named Julia and had her very face, but who wasn't really her" (147). The peculiarity of a third-person voice to express a first-person narratological stance has been stressed by Sandra J. Schumm: "The use of this type of third-person narrative helps to convey the pathological division of self that results from Julia's traumatic childhood rape and the ambivalent attitude of her mother" (150). In effect, Schumm concludes, "The use of a third-person narration with a first-person perspective suggests that the Julia thinking of her life does not see that life as her own. She narrates as if she were talking about another person by not using the pronoun 'I'" (166).[3]

Julita in the diminutive—in her identity as a child—ceased to exist on a sunny afternoon at the beach. After the rape she was disowned, for Julia wanted to, had to, forget her in her shame and helplessness.[4] For abandoning her at the scene of the crime, Julita cannot forgive Julia. In the confrontation between the two personalities at the end of the novel, Julita "would lead her through small, sun-baked streets towards the corner of a lonely beach. She would make her feel once again all the summer sun sliding down her flesh and an old pain lodged inside her body. She blamed her for having abandoned her there; for the ignorant arrogance of thinking she could go on living without her" (217). The self turned against the self, fractured, and never reintegrated. Julita is gone—temporarily—but hardly forgotten:

> The scene of violation is seared into the victim's imagina-
> tion. That scene may hover at the periphery of awareness
> or instead repetitively replay itself in consciousness, fantasy,
> or night terrors. The scene also may be banished from aware-
> ness, fully disowned, resulting in the self becoming frozen,
> statuelike. (Kaufman 121)[5]

Without any positive counterbalancing forces to effect reintegration, the ruthlessly disowned self buried within acquires independent being and emerges, vengeful and angry.

Within the narrative structure of *Julia,* the negative poetics of the trauma (the concatenation of images triggered by sensations or sights that recall the event) is countered by a powerful and positive image of a party, which Julia associates with early memories of her mother: "She created a festive atmosphere, a childish carnival of unrestrained gaiety" (37). At the end it is written that:

> Julita spoke to her about a strange and unforgettable party
> that lasted only five years of her life and about which Julia
> could only recall the end. A party for other people, which
> took place in an immense garden, as big as the world, adorned
> with little lanterns, where people teased one another with
> games, words, laughter, and dreams. A party that promised
> to last a lifetime and from which Julita had been excluded
> without knowing why. A splendid party, an endless party
> in which everyone, except Julia, took part. (217)

There is loss—of childhood—and mourning for that loss. If the male world is experienced by Julia as violent (in word, the command to silence; in deed, her rape and her father's hitting both her mother [66] and her brother Ernesto [150]), the maternal plenitude recalled by Julia is a hallucination, a memory trace marked by absence. But the intense longing for the nurturing and gentleness of maternal love is obsessively reiterated by Julia in her relationships with older females (her aunt, the director of the school, the university professor, Eva). Eva's perceived abandonment, which repeats her maternal abandonment, proves literally unbearable. Her longing is thwarted once again. When Julia recognizes that "there was something abnormal about her, something that made her different, but she didn't stop to think about it" (180), the reader in turn recognizes another strategy of evasion. The word "rape" remains unspoken; so, too, does the word "lesbian." She does not dare speak of her love, any more than she dares speak of her hurt. She is locked in a prison house of silence.

Julia never recovers. She reappears in Moix's next novel, *Walter, ¿por qué te fuiste?* (Walter, Why Did You Leave?) (1973). I quote Catherine Bellver's succinct and poignant synopsis of Julia's trajectory:

> We discover in *Walter* that after her suicide attempt, Julia's estrangement grew to include a withdrawal from the basic physical activities of living—speaking, eating, moving— until non-action coincided with death. In the end, Julita, her pursuing inner half, alienates her from society, from the present, and from her self, first killing her spirit and finally her body. (32)

Although *Julia* is the story of the rape of a child, this in no way limits the painful accuracy with which it depicts the emotional aftereffects of rape. The dreadful choreography between power and powerlessness, innocence and victimization is starkly naked, free of the ideological presuppositions of victim culpability or complicity. Accordingly, her narrative voice is trustworthy. Yet with *Julia* we have moved far from the perorations concerning honor, from swords drawn and ready for revenge. The stage of rape was formerly populated by family members and authority figures, all men, acting out socially scripted roles prescribed by tradition and law. The stage is now emptied out, the cast of characters is reduced to two: victim and assailant. No longer a shame culture, no longer a community event, the stigma of rape is nevertheless retained. But it has been internalized, even by a child, and the hurt is, if possible, even deeper, because of the isolation of the victim. A survivor writes:

> Rape is loss. Like death, it is best treated with a period of
> mourning and grief. We should develop social ceremonies
> for rape, rituals, that, like funerals and wakes, would allow
> the mourners to recover the spirits that the rapist, like death,
> steals. The social community is the appropriate center for the
> restoration of spirit, but the rape victim is usually shamed
> into silence or self-imposed isolation. (Metzger 406)

Novels such as Moix's, by memorializing the event, critique rape as a social practice and expose the ideological underpinnings that permit, and thus perpetuate, this violence done unto another.

AFTERWORD

Laws distinguish between legitimate and illegitimate sexuality. For thousands of years rape has been illegal; this, therefore, is not the question. But there are serious obstacles to reportage (guilt, fear of retribution on the part of the victim, reluctance to incur the shame that may follow public exposure, as Leocadia's father argued in "La fuerza de la sangre"). Then there is the issue of nonexistent or differential enforcement based on social and economic qualifiers, which continues to haunt the courts today, just as it did centuries ago.

In his analysis of rape cases in Renaissance Venice, Guido Ruggiero shows that victims from a lower class were the least likely to merit any attention (99), whereas the rape of a noble by a non-noble was considered a most serious offense (92); in medieval England the crime of a nonnoble against a noble was "a supreme taboo" (J. M. Carter 66). The acquittal of William Kennedy Smith for his alleged rape in March 1991, in Palm Beach, Florida, raised similar issues of power and powerlessness, for the celebrity and wealth of the Kennedy family were pitted against the obscurity of a woman of mediocre means. On April 19, 1989, when a privileged, white investment banker was raped and brutally beaten while jogging by a group of black project youths in New York City's Central Park, the media coverage was inflammatory. Male-on-female violence became a tangential issue to the central manifestation of violence in contemporary America: race.

Traditionally the rape of a married woman has been considered the more egregious fault. The sexual laws in Deuteronomy stipulate the death penalty for rape of a betrothed woman in the field, where cries for help would be of no avail (22:25–27). The thirteenth-century *fuero* of Ubeda specified death by burning for the rapist of a married woman, whereas if the victim were unmarried the penalty was a fine (Segura Graiño 89–90). Even when only fines were exacted, the highest amount pertained to the rape of a married woman (according to the amounts stated in Alfonso X's *Fuero Real,* 300 sueldos for a married woman, 200 for a widow, 100 for a single woman [Asenjo González 56, n. 4]). The legislation devolves from the concept of a woman as male property, whose value diminishes considerably when violated: "From their inception, rape laws have been established not to protect women, but to protect women's property value for men" (Herman 22).

The possibility of marriage—and thus of an "honorable" solution— has served as a mitigating factor in the severity of punishment meted out for raping an unmarried woman. This assumption, as reflected in legal discourse, is still in force. On March 12, 1997, the *New York Times* recounted the rape of a seventeen-year-old in Lima, Peru, by a group of drunken men. After the assailants were identified and one of them offered to marry the young woman, pressure was put on her to accept: "In Peru the penal code exonerates a rapist if he offers to marry the victim and she accepts. The law, which was written in 1924, was modified in 1991 to absolve defendants in a rape case if one of them marries the victim" (A1). Similar laws pertain in other Latin American countries. A few weeks later, activists in the Peruvian Congress managed to legislate the repeal of this law; but one wonders whether many citizens do not still agree with the opinion of a taxicab driver quoted in the article: "Marriage is the right and proper thing to do after a rape. . . . A raped woman is a used item. No one wants her. At least with this law the woman will get a husband" (A8). The late-eleventh-century Latin *Fuero de Jaca* provides an early Spanish example of this solution, in a clause "compelling a man who raped an unwed woman either to marry her or to find her a husband, provided that the victim asked for justice within three days and could prove the rape by means of witnesses. Where there was consent on the woman's part the man bears no responsibility" (Orcastegui Gros 118).

What is now referred to as the "corroboration rule" (Herman 30–31) in presenting rape evidence before a jury is already in effect in this medieval document and demonstrates the excruciating problem of a rape victim's credibility. For a rape victim is contending with a cultural stereotype that consistently undermines her authority and plausibility. After all, as Dianne Herman points out, a lack of witnesses is also typical of an assault, where the possibility of falsified charges also exists, yet no such evidenciary rules pertain (31). The compensatory offer of marriage seems to make a victim even more vulnerable to disbelief: an accusation of rape could be used as a means of obtaining a dowry (Ruggiero 9), or, as the medieval Soria *fuero* would have it, it could be deviously employed to circumvent parental decisions about a suitable marriage in order to marry the partner of choice or to circumvent the payment exacted for a broken betrothal agreement (Asenjo González 53–54). In addition, the suspicion that the accuser might contrive to "marry up" eviscerates her credibility. This was suggested in the Kennedy trial, where the Palm Beach woman was viewed as "some sort of *arriviste*," according to Martha Howell of the Institute for Research on Women and Gender at Columbia University: "it's possible to imagine she's using her sexuality for social advancement" (*Newsweek,* April 29, 1991, 31). Dorotea's convoluted and contradictory reconstruction of her sexual encounter with don Fernando (*Don Quixote* 1.28) manifests a keen awareness of the cultural stereotype against which she will be judged. Though wealthy and an old Christian, her bid to marry the aristocratic don Fernando is a transgression of class boundaries ("'I shall not be the first,' I said to myself, 'who has risen through marriage from a lowly to a lofty station, nor will Don Fernando be the first led by beauty or, as is more likely, a blind attachment, to marry below his rank'" [1.28.215]). Prescriptive codes concerning signs of forcible resistance are the implicit intertext of her narration, and thus she attempts to justify her failure to scream for help when Fernando enters her chamber secretly at night ("'The apparition so astounded me that it deprived my eyes of sight and my tongue of speech. I was unable to utter a cry nor, I think, did he give me time to utter one, as he immediately approached me and took me in his arms. Overwhelmed as I was, I was powerless to defend myself'" [1.28.214]). For the censors of the time there was apparently too much consent in evidence, and in 1624 the Portuguese Inquisition excised her account from the text of the *Quixote* (1.351, n. 14, Murillo ed.).

This most intimate of crimes can also be the most invisible in terms of the harm inflicted. There may not even be lesions or bruises on the surface of the body to signify the physical hurt. The first stanza of Marge Piercy's "Rape Poem" (in *Living in the Open* [1976])—"There is no difference between being raped / and being pushed down a flight of cement steps / except that the wounds also bleed inside" (164)—recognizes the differences between physical and psychological wounds, between the exterior and the interior. Yet invisible wounds challenge a listener's /reader's /viewer's ability to believe a rape narrative. An alleged victim's credibility is conditioned by factors such as social standing and reputation, by her ability to create a plausible narrative. It is also—and very forcefully—conditioned by the cultural ideology pertaining to rape, and the stereotypes about gender and sexuality are tenacious. The bias is against the victim. Concerning the "corroboration rule," a 1970 comment in the *University of Pennsylvania Law Review* (118:3) states that:

> Women often falsely accuse men of sexual attacks to extort money, to force marriage, to satisfy a childish desire for notoriety, or to attain personal revenge. Their motives include hatred, a sense of shame after consenting to illicit intercourse, especially when pregnancy results, and delusion. (460, qtd. Herman 32)

The stereotypical scenario of conniving female and innocent male is replayed and corroborated during Sancho Panza's governorship of Barataria in the case of an alleged rape by a herdsman (2.45). The woman's accusation is proven false by means of a clever strategy. A purse of silver coins is awarded to her; the herdsman is then ordered to follow her and steal the purse, which he is quite unable to do. This proves to Sancho that the plaintiff has lied, and he admonishes her sternly: "'Sister, if you had shown as much, or only half as much, spirit and vigor in defending your body as you have shown in defending that purse, the strength of Hercules could not have forced you" (2.43.674). In a note in the *Psychopathology of Everyday Life,* Freud points out that Sancho's equation of sexual and other violent assaults is erroneous, for the role of the unconscious in a sexual attack contours the body's reactions differently, rendering his judgment " psychologically unjust" (125, n. 1). A seeming paralysis of bodily defense reactions is typical in cases of sexual assault. The sense of powerlessness described by Dorotea in the *Quixote* episode is even more acute in the case of Leocadia, abducted by Rodolfo and his companions in "La fuerza de la sangre." The narrator specifies that, even before fainting, the maiden "did not have the strength to resist and the shock left her speechless and unable to protest" (132). But then, as now, these responses can be interpreted—in fact, are interpreted—as complicity with the assailant.

Although sexual activity seemingly corresponds to the most private of bodily functions, its intersection with the power relations of domination and submission extends its significance to the public, political realm. As a torturer inflicts pain on the victim from a position of control, so is the rapist's act instrumental as an insignia of power. The abuse of military authority, which in Calderón's *El alcalde de Zalamea* is associated with the billeting of troops and the class arrogance of the young captain, is being reiterated in contemporary America in U.S. Army training bases, where, according to the disciplinary rules, "[d]rill sergeants are entrusted with absolute authority over young recruits, who must obey their every order, no matter how unreasonable it may seem." "A Base Out of Control" is the headline accompanying the report of the situation in an Aberdeen, Maryland, base, rife with allegations of sexual harassment and multiple rapes, which led to an investigation of bases worldwide (*New York Times,* April 15, 1997, A8). The accused drill sergeant was convicted by a military jury of raping six trainees (*New York Times,* May 7, 1997, A17).

It has long been acknowledged that rape is one of the by-products of war: lands are plundered and women are raped. The gang rape by German soldiers of Jewish women, the enforced sexual slavery of Asian women, mainly Koreans, by Japanese soldiers, and the rape of German women by invading Russian soldiers during World War II were all reported and investigated. A documentary film, *Rape: A Crime of War* (National Film Board of Canada, 1996), stresses the historic nature of the Hague Tribunal's charges in the Bosnia-Herzegovina War. It is the first time that rape has been acknowledged as a weapon of war and prosecuted as such, leading to the conviction on December 10, 1998, of a Bosnian Croat paramilitary chief for failure to stop the rape of a woman by a subordinate (*New York Times,* December 11, 1998, A10). Serbian soldiers interrogated in 1992 admitted to raping Muslim women under orders: their youngest victim was twelve years old. According to a military court in 1993, at least forty women held in a prison were gang raped, then killed. Male prisoners were also sexually assaulted and tortured (in one instance, prisoners were commanded to bite off the testicles of fellow prisoners). The comment was made that the humiliation involved reduced the men "to the level of women."

If greed was the motive and cruelty its means of realization, no less an instrument in the Spanish Conquest of the Americas was humiliation by and through women's bodies. One of the many examples offered by Bartolomé de las Casas describes the soldiers' treatment of one of the kings of Hispaniola: "The recompense they gave this great and good Indian ruler was to dishonor him through his wife, who was raped by a Christian officer" (46–47). "Through his wife": here the woman's body is explicitly recognized not as an end but as a means to the end of communicating a message between men. One of the witnesses in the trial of the Aberdeen drill sergeant noted that it was common knowledge that the men in charge were vying competitively with one another: "That's what everyone talked about when you got here, that him [Sergeant Delmar G. Simpson] and Drill Sergeant Cross had a thing going to see who could get more women" (*New York Times,* April 15, 1997, A8).

The *Toronto Star* (July 22, 1997, A1) quoted the executive director of the United Nations Children's Fund as saying that, "In today's world, to be born female is to be born high-risk. . . . Every girl grows up under the threat of violence" (A1). One in five, or one in seven, women will be the victim of rape; as many as 50 percent will suffer abuse at the hands of the their "intimate partner," according to the same article (A1). In fiction, as in fact, lust (or the sudden, blinding, uncontrollable desire suggested by many of the texts here considered) is not the motivation behind rape. In an article entitled "The Mind of the Rapist" (*Newsweek,* July 23, 1990), anger, power, and sadism are the three broad motivational typologies suggested by psychologist Nicholas Roth (48). Rage, a need for mastery to overcome insecurities, a need to humiliate one's victim—these are the dominant emotions. Even sadism, defined as "eroticized aggression," is marked most clearly by anger (49). Lust and its familiar cluster of images act as a rhetorical smoke screen, obscuring the dynamics of power and powerlessness at work in the personal and social circumstances of rape: "to possess and punish in one act" (Piercy 165).

By reading the cultural scripts that underpin these narratives, by understanding the ideological structures that subtend the plots, we can hope to disarticulate the armature that enables the violence, which is so naturalized that it is barely noticeable. In her reflection on the rape of Persephone by Pluto (Hades), god of the underworld, the American poet Jorie Graham recalls "[t]he other one the mother the one whose grief is the visible world / a wound she must keep open by beginning and beginning" ("Self-Portrait as Demeter and Persephone" st. 1, p. 59). Like Demeter, we, too, can keep the wound open through the act of remembering. By reading the violence back into texts that in various and sundry ways erase it, we can detect Persephone's girdle; we can reconstruct her silenced story.

Notes

Introduction

1. Diane Wolfthal ("The 'Heroic' Rape") discusses certain traits as characteristic of representations of the heroic rape in Athenian classical art, which include the victim's absence of resistance, an absence of any threatening weapons or explicit genitalia or even nudity, the physical beauty of all involved, and concentration on the pursuit rather than the assault. One of the examples cited is a terra cotta sculpture of Zeus's abduction of Ganymede (ca. 470 B.C.).

2. For dates I have referred to Harold E. Wethey.

3. These paintings were a gift to Charles V from Federigo Gonzaga of Bologna. According to Cecil Gould (131), the exact date of the *Io* is uncertain but can be assigned safely to the last four years of the painter's life (1489–1534).

4. In his discussion of *Fortunas de Andrómeda y Perseo* (The Fortunes of Andromeda and Perseus), Thomas O'Conner cautions against the stringency of allegorical appropriations that negates the experiential dimension of the events:

> Rape, as traditionally viewed in allegorical terms, was an ambivalent act. It could, as in Neptuno's rape of Medusa, destroy the *concordia discors* by dividing the soul from wisdom, or, as in Jupiter's rape of Danaë, produce the ideal balance in the human soul symbolized by Perseus. Instead of negating divine justice, rape actually presages it. While these allegorical interpretations indeed form part of the intellectual background to plays such as *Fortunas,* Calderón's depiction of the rape of Danaë fundamentally challenges such an allegorical scheme. Perhaps the realization of the horror of rape prevents, or forecloses on, the textual harmony that such allegorical interpretations set as their goal. There could be no heroic dimension to rape, and for this reason the allegorized approaches to the play fail to come to grips with the inner dynamics of *Fortunas.* (*Myth and Mythology* 91)

5. Froma Zeitlin describes the Greek vase paintings of the early fifth century B.C. as follows:

> Suddenly, for the first time, we find representations of amorous assaults by gods and mortals, a motif that will establish its characteristic conventions and persist with remarkable popularity to the end of the period. The god either

> pursues the girl with outstretched arm, his instrument of power in the
> other, or he has caught her and grasps her arm, shoulder or back. She, in
> turn, usually registers terror and shock (in the convention of the upraised
> arms) and resistance, thrusting forth one hand, sometimes in a gesture that
> may seem to supplicate or ward off her pursuer, and the movement of her
> feet and body often represent her attempt to flee. If female age-mates accom-
> pany her, they are often depicted as more agitated than she is, even rushing
> off to the girl's father seated upon his throne who seems to be uncompre-
> hending or else helpless to intervene. ("Configurations of Rape" 128)

Examples from the *Metamorphoses* include Daphne's anguished and fearful flight from Apollo, until she begs for release, preferring death through metamorphosis to capture (1.452ff.); Peleus manages to overcome the sea-goddess Thetis's efforts to evade him only after he receives assistance from the sea-god Proteus (11.221ff.).

6. The issue of violence takes an unexpected turn in these plays. In her relationship with Narcissus, Liriope corresponds to the "terrible-mother image" who seeks to devour her son (Hesse); she also, in an act of symbolic castration, mutilates the nymph Echo by depriving her of her voice. Thetis retaliates against Peleus—"Him I killed, and the island / I burned" (2.220c), a fascinating and original addition to the myth on the part of Calderón. She, too, becomes a "devouring" mother in her efforts to protect her child. The emergence of a deadly female following rape implies a fear of women and of their retaliatory powers (as posited in Freud's essay, "The Taboo of Virginity").

7. In her study of Rubens's *Rape of the Daughters of Leucippus* (1615–1618), Margaret D. Carroll considers the cultural context of its production, namely "a tradition that emerged among princely patrons at the time, of incorporating large-scale mythological rape scenes into their palace decorations" (5), in keeping with the absolutist political theory in the sixteenth century. The painting is taken as a reference to the double marriage contract (the future Philip IV of Spain was betrothed to Louis XIII's sister, Elisabeth, and the French king was betrothed to Anne, sister of Philip). Such manifest glorification or "mystification" of violence among later-sixteenth-century French political theorists (Jean Bodin's *Republic* [1576] is cited [26–27, n. 53]) is not to be expected in Spain, with the anti-Machiavellian bias of its theorists—in principle, at least, if not in actuality (see Maravall, "Maquiavelo y Maquiavelismo"). Friedrich Meinecke (who does not include Spanish political theorists) makes the following point about "Machiavellism": "There were those who fought it wholeheartedly as an evil enemy. And there were others who made a great show of fighting it, but at the same time borrowed from it freely" (50).

8. Carroll notes that in a later painting commemorating these nuptials, the *Exchange of Princesses* (ca. 1622–1625), Rubens cites traditional Visitation scenes between Mary, mother of Jesus, and Elisabeth, mother of John the Baptist: "By implicitly identifying the royal brides with these holy mothers, Rubens turns our attention away from the violence of the brides' induction into sexuality and toward their future maternity and the birth of divinely favored heirs for the French and Spanish thrones" (17–18). A similar shift of attention is achieved by Calderón in *Fortunas de Andrómeda y Perseo.*

The emphasis on sacralizing offspring characterizes the allegorical interpretations, which are predicated on the identification of Jupiter and God. As C. A. Merrick explains:

León Hebreo explains Jupiter's rapes—so shocking in a deity—as the seemingly evil but essentially good emanation of divine being required to produce blessed offspring like Perseo, image of the human mind. They represent the strife-ridden but fruitful marriage of matter and form which generates the only created being capable of balancing heaven and earth, angel and beast, in his own nature. Discord, then, is necessary to creation; evil is an apparent absolute—the danger which Danaë fears— concealing a providential good. And the rape, which seems to negate divine justice, is really a presage of that justice because Perseo, the offspring of their union, is destined to achieve the ideal *concordia discors,* the balance of all the faculties in the glorious soul of man. (322–23)

Merrick cites Hebreo's *Philosophy of Love,* translated by F. Friedeberg-Seeley and Jean H. Barnes (London, 1937), 145–47, and signals similar interpretations of the Danaë rape (322, n. 3) in P. Sánchez de Viana, *Las Transformaciones de Ovidio* (Valladolid, 1589), 96–97, as well as in Giovanni Pietro Valeriano Bolzani, *Hierglyphiques,* translated by J. de Montlyart (Lyon, 1615), 791.

9. Thomas A. O'Conner ("The Politics of Rape and *Fineza* in Calderonian Myth Plays") stresses the importance of the rape motif in Calderonian drama in general, in both the secular and the myth plays, and emphasizes the theme of redemption through love— selfless as opposed to selfish love. O'Conner thus distinguishes the tragic ending of *Eco y Narciso* (Echo and Narcissus) from the comedic, "happy" resolution of *Fortunas. Eco y Narciso* qualifies as a tragic myth in which the characters remain subjected to the rule of Fate—"linked to cyclical time in that, in this instance at least, the children of violent and erring parents somehow come under the influence of a 'tragic inheritance'" (181). In *Fortunas,* on the other hand, the salvific action of Christian providence "allows Perseo

to escape his inheritance of violence and rape so that he is able to realize to the full his human potential" (179). See also O'Conner's "Violación, amor y entereza en *Fortunas de Andrómeda y Perseo* de Calderón de la Barca" and "On Love and the Human Condition: A Prolegomenon to Calderón's Mythological Plays."

10. I wish to thank Patricia E. Grieve of Columbia University for bringing this text to my attention.

11. I thank Theodore Kassier for pointing out this version to me. In *Flor nueva de romances viejos,* the editor Menéndez Pidal (67, n. 1) notes that this is a seventeenth-century version of a traditional ballad.

12. This point is made by Colbert Nepaulsingh (209–11), who cites H. B. Workman's appendix to his *Persecution in the Early Church* (London, 1923), entitled "The Punishments of Women" (371). The punishment of being subject to men's lust or delivered over to it is a prominent aspect in the tales of female saints: the stalwart virgin Agnes is threatened with a house of prostitution (Prudentius 2:339); St. Juliana and St. Petronila prefer death to the contamination of marriage; St. Justina of Antioch is steadfast against the designs of Cyprian, whom she eventually converts—and so on, according to Voragine's compilation, *The Golden Legend.* Miraculous deliverance from harm is a feature of the legends that is absent in the epic poem.

Kathryn Gravdal stresses the gender-specific nature of hagiographies of the Middle Ages: "There is a sexual plot peculiar to the female saint's legend. Rape, prostitution, seduction, and forced marriage are the signal variations in this gendered plot. The construction of sexual assault runs through hagiography like a shining thread in a tapestry, highly valued and useful" (22). She identifies four basic plot types: the threat of rape, forced prostitution, seduction, forced marriage (22–23). (Gravdal's notes 10–13, pp. 152–53, offer more specific information.)

13. Colin Smith ("On the Distinctiveness of the *Poema de Mio Cid*") makes the interesting suggestion that the marriage between the Cid's daughters and their husbands was not consummated until the night before the assault, thus allowing for a two-year lapse of time between the ceremonies in Valencia and the lion episode, in deference, he conjectures, to the daughters' young age at the time of the betrothal. His textual evidence includes the fact that the Infantes have to request paternal permission to take their wives away from Valencia and that the dowry is handed over only at this time (168).

14. The analogy to St. Agnes's beheading, which Nepaulsingh cites as "the most famous of all the erotic martyrdoms" (210), is relevant. Agnes praises the virility of her executioner, pleased that he is not "listless, soft, womanish" (Prudentius II: 343).

15. The setting corresponds with scenes of sacrifice in the Old Testament. Mieke Bal *(Death & Dissymmetry)* compares Abraham's "proper" sacrifice of Isaac (Gen. 22:2) with Jepthah's "improper" sacrifice of his daughter (Judg. 11) and comments that "Both Isaac and Bath go to the mountains, to the wilderness of transition" (110). In the case of Isaac, he is accompanied a (loving) father and survives the test; the daughter goes alone to the hills, unaccompanied by her (unloving) father—and for her there is no future. In addition, a similar setting is the most likely for martyrological traditions of early Christianity (Nepaulsingh 207–8). In their response to Roger M. Walker (who argues for the thirteenth-century French *Florence de Rome* as a possible source), Alan Deyermond and David Hook point to more likely similarities to the Tereus/Philomela tale of the *Metamorphoses,* including the setting for the scene of violence.

Deyermond and Hook's inquiry into source possibilities ends with a cautionary statement: "The background to the *afrenta de Corpes* is much more complex than any attempt to indicate a single source would allow since there are also the folkloric and martyrological parallels to take into account" (26).

16. The authors add "that early mediaeval laws were mainly concerned with actions and their effects, and very little with intentions, good or bad. . . . It is clear that nothing about *mens rea* or intention to murder figured in the laws of Castile at the time of the poet, about 1200 (still less in the Cid's day, if the poet were looking back to practices of that time)" (104).

17. Here Deyermond differs with Menéndez Pidal *(La España del Cid),* who looks for glimmers of historicity (22–23).

18. Date according to S. Griswold Morley and Courtney Bruerton, p. 550. It was published in the Parte XXIII (1638) of the *Comedias de Lope de Vega.*

19. A tribal prerequisite to marriage, unrelated to matters of faith (*Interpreter's One-Volume Commentary* 25a).

20. Edmund Leach stresses the important role of endogamy and protection of monotheism as salient factors in Old Testament history.

21. As quoted in Castro's edition (pp. 176–77) from *Teatro de los teatros,* Bibl. Nac., ms. 17459, fol. 78r. M. Serrano y Sanz published the work in the *Revista de Archivos,* 1901 and 1902. This particular quotation is found in vol. 6 (1902): 76 (177, n. 1).

22. All citations (act followed by verse numbers) refer to the edition of Américo Castro.

23. Castro points out that Calderón's *El médico de su honra (The Surgeon of His Honour),* translated by Roy Campbell (Madison: University of Wisconsin Press, 1960) contains analogous materials, although "Isabel, however, went beyond Mencía in her intimacies" (194).

24. All citations (act followed by verse numbers) refer to the edition of the *Obras completas* edited by Agustín Millares Carlo.

25. The greater constraints imposed on a playwright are particularly pertinent when the author is female, as pointed out by Elizabeth Ordóñez (9), by Lola Luna in her introduction to the edition of Ana Caro's *Valor, Agravio y Mujer* (Valor, Offense, and Woman) (31), and by Teresa Soufas (*Dramas of Distinction* 35).

26. In a note, Elizabeth Patton specifies that Harvey espoused the Ramistic view, which argued for a separation of rhetoric from logic and philosophy (8, n. 12).

27. First published in Antwerp in 1524, it was then revised for a second printing in Basel in 1537. In her chapter on Vives (157–96), Patton stresses the fact that the 1529 English translation by William Hyrde *(The Instruction of a Christen Woman)* remained the basis for English readers, who accordingly were unaware of the revisions. The first Spanish translation by Justiniano appeared in 1528. Not until the 1947 translation by Lorenzo Riber were the changes incorporated into the Spanish-language text. Patton's thesis is that "the revisions were primarily motivated by a concern to clarify and strengthen his views in support of the education of women. . . . [T]he revised and expanded version leaves no room for doubt as to the author's positive stance on the subject" (178–79).

28. All page citations (book, chapter, section, page) refer to the English translation from Latin of the first book by C. Fantazzi in vols. 6 (first book) and 7 (second and third books) of the *Selected Works of J. L. Vives.*

29. The reference to Thucydides is to a funeral oration delivered by Pericles (fifth century B.C.) concerning the widows of fallen soldiers: "and the highest praise you can win is to be spoken of by men as little as possible, whether for good or ill" (Patton, qtd. 85, n. 31 from *History of the Peloponnesian War* Loeb Classical Library, 2:45).

30. For the history and impact of these statutes, see Albert Sicroff.

31. On the subject of the valorization of the old Christian peasant as idealized in the theater of the period, see Noël Salomon's fundamental study.

32. I am indebted to Patton's note (169, n. 8) for awareness of this issue as a problem in Vives studies. In the introduction to his edition of *In pseudodialecticos,* Charles Fantazzi conjectures that Vives's Jewish origins were the probable cause of his critical neglect (5). In his 1903 study, Adolfo Bonilla y San Martín's mention of the issue is buried in a note (31, 573–74). Here he writes that José Amador de los Ríos, in his *Historia social, política y religiosa de los judíos de España y Portugal* (Madrid: Fortanet, 1875) indicates Vives's *converso* origins (14n) and later specifies Abraham Aben-Vives (listed among the Jews in the *Repartimiento de Valencia*) as the ancestral head of the family (404–5n.). Bonilla y San Martín responds that "We do not know on what grounds Mr. Amador de los Ríos formulated such astonishing assertions, which we judge fantastical" (574). He goes on, however, to allude to a document from the Valencian Inquisition in which reference is made to a "Luis Vives, Merchant" (who lived around 1476) whose possessions were confiscated because of heretical practices. Bonilla y San Martín then asks, "Could this be the father of our Vives?" (574). Resistance seems to give way to doubt in the note.

A more recent translator and editor, Lorenzo Riber, rejects the notion that Vives could have an "ancestral stain" because he was himself such a fervent suppressor of Muslims and Jews (1:15). But a different kind of logic reveals Vives's position as perfectly coherent. It is a psychological commonplace that one repudiates and disavows what one hates in oneself. In 1964 Miguel de la Pinta Llorente and José María de Palacio y de Palacio published the inquisitional proceedings against Vives's mother, Blanquina March, and refer to a second volume on the proceedings against Miguel Vives, the humanist's father.

33. The punishments meted out include that of Hippomenes, prince of Athens, who shuts his sullied daughter in a stable with a stallion, without food, until the maddened horse devours her. Both classical and contemporary accounts are relayed, including a childhood memory of his own, of three girls who suffocate a companion whom they surprise "in an obscene act," and of brothers from the province of Tarragona who, on discovering that their sister is pregnant, wait until she gives birth and then stab her to death in the stomach (1.6.§42.61).

34. Examples from Greek and Roman history are given of women who chose death over dishonor, and Vives adds Christian saints: "What number can be devised for those women who readily and willingly allowed themselves to have their throats cut, be slain, dismembered, suffocated, drowned, cut to pieces, burned alive, as long as they could preserve their chastity?" (1.10.§91.123). A listing of pagan women who preferred death to dishonor, beginning with Lucretia, is found in the second book (2.2.§13.17) as well as an enumeration of wives who preferred death to surviving a deceased husband (2.3.§19.25), and includes such examples as Marcus Brutus's wife, Portia, who stuffed live coals in her mouth, and the Lydian queen Artemisa, who drank her dead husband's diluted ashes until she too died (2.3.§20.25–26).

Mutilation of self is praised in the cause of not betraying a secret. Reference is made to a "disciple of Pythagoras who bit off her own tongue and spat it in the face of the tyrant, who was torturing her, so that she could not be forced to speak," and to a certain Epicharis, who refused to betray her knowledge of a conspiracy. In such a weakened condition after an initial torture session, she had to be carried on a saddle to be tortured again the next day. It was then that "she took a band that was tied around her breasts, fastened it in the form of a loop to the pommel of the saddle, then tied it around her neck and let her body fall under its own weight and breathed forth the little life she had left in her" (1.11.§108.145).

35. As William Pietz writes in "Fetish II":

> Despite the use of this terminology in a variety of disciplines that claim
> no common theoretical ground—ethnography and the history of reli-
> gion, Marxism and positivist sociology, psychoanalysis and the clinical
> psychiatry of sexual deviance, modernist aesthetics and Continental phi-
> losophy—there is a common configuration of themes among the vari-
> ous discourses about fetishism. (23)

36. I am indebted to my conversations with Mary S. Gossy for the application of the Freudian fetish model to the economy of purity of blood.

Chapter One: Rape and the Resolution of Class Conflict

1. Friedman, by focusing on the irreconcilable incongruities between ending and plot, between the literal and figurative levels, convincingly demonstrates the latent

irony inherent in such a destabilization of the generic conventions of romance. Readers' unease upon completion of the tale is thus both inevitable and intentional, controlled by a discourse that is "self-consciously ambiguous" (154). Previous critics have noted genre tension—without fully confronting their own insights: Forcione admits to "anti-generic tendencies in this miracle" (362) but largely relegates to the footnotes his many meticulous observations concerning the literal level of the narration; Slaniceanu alludes to Cervantes's exploitation of the inherent element of parody in romance (102, 109, n. 3). Friedman makes manifest, so to speak, what has remained at the latent level of interpretive strategy.

2. All citations from "La fuerza de la sangre" are to Lesley Lipson's translation of the *Exemplary Stories.*

3. According to María Elisa Ciavarelli, the first actual blood recognition (as opposed to recognition by a sign) occurs between mother and daughter in Heliodorus's *Ethiopic History,* a text favored by Cervantes as a model for the epic in prose (62).

4. Luce Irigaray distinguishes between male eroticism, characterized by "the predominance of the visual" (25), and female eroticism, which privileges touch, not sight (26). According to Irigaray, the dominance of the male "scopic economy" (26) has relegated woman to the passive status of an object of desire. Rodolfo is no exception.

5. El Saffar points out that this type of female figure is rare in Cervantes until his later fiction (*Beyond Fiction* 45). In her role as maternal mediator, doña Estefanía also recalls Demeter, with the obvious difference that she strives to join her "daughter" Leocadia/Persephone with her rapist-husband instead of negotiating a separation for a portion of the year.

6. For the concept of art as resistance in the myth of Philomela, see Joplin, "The Voice of the Shuttle Is Ours," 43–53.

7. Diana Wilson (*Allegories of Love,* chap. 6) has observed that this episode is comparable to the paternal passivity of Mauricio Fitzmaurice in the *Persiles,* whose resignation in the face of his daughter Transila's potential victimization as a candidate of legislated rape is tantamount to an endorsement of the barbaric custom of *ius primae noctis.*

8. Here, too, the female characters are comparable to Transila Fitzmaurice in the *Persiles,* who seizes both word and deed from her father in a radical stance of self-preservation. (See Wilson, *Allegories of Love,* chap. 6.)

9. Nina M. Scott stresses the unusual role of the parents in "La fuerza de la sangre" who protect their daughter instead of banishing her to a convent or condemning her to death (127). In her comparison of male and female friendship patterns in the interpolated tales of *Don Quixote,* Debra D. Andrist shows that, because their goals are not in competition, women avoid the dynamics of sacrifice typical of the male relationships: "As a consequence, the threat of violence inherent in the male rivalries appears to be non-existent in the female friendships, at least between the women themselves" (158). This holds true for the friendship between Leocadia and doña Estefanía, who work together toward a common good. In myth, Philomela and her sister, Procne, were not able to break out of the vicious cycle of repeated violence.

Chapter Two: Rape and Revolution

1. According to Raymond R. MacCurdy in his critical edition of the play (referred to as *L y T*), the *terminus a quo* is 1635, the date of publication of Rojas's principal source, Francisco Bolle Pintaflor's Spanish translation of the marquis Virgilio Malvezzi's *Tarquino Superbo,* and no authentic play of Rojas's is known after 1640 (4). There is no record of its performance (MacCurdy 47). Juan Pastor's *Farsa o Tragedia de la castidad de Lucrecia* (1528) was probably not known to Rojas (*L y T* 37). Agustín Moreto's burlesque *Baile de Lucrecia y Tarquino* (Dance of Lucretia and Tarquin) (included as an appendix to *L y T* 143–48), though it dates most probably from several years after Rojas's tragedy, is not considered a parody of this play in particular, but rather of the theme in general (*L y T* 142).

2. All citations from the play (act and verse numbers) refer to the critical edition of Raymond R. MacCurdy. In his introduction (10–12) MacCurdy includes the full text of the *romance* (from the *Romancero general en que se contienen todos los romances que andan impresos en las nueve partes de romanceros* [Madrid, 1600–1614], rpt. *Biblioteca de Autores Españoles,* ed. Agustín Durán, vol. 16: 564.

3. For a general overview of the subject see Ian Donaldson's excellent book. The story appears in Dionysius of Halicarnassus, *The Roman Antiquities* (vol. 2, bk. 4), which forms the basis of Juan Pastor's early play on the subject. The main source is Titus Livy, *The Early History of Rome* (1.57–60); it is mentioned in Dio Cassius, *Roman History* vol. 1, "Rome under the Kings," bk. 2), and also appears in Ovid's *Fasti* (bk. 2, vv. 721–852). Livy's history (the *Décadas*) was accessible to Rojas in several Spanish translations, but his main

source was the Spanish translation of Virgilio Malvezzi's *Tarquino Superbo* by Francisco Bolle Pintaflor (Madrid, 1635). (For more information on the possible identity of Pintaflor see MacCurdy's introduction to the play [12–13, n. 8].

4. In his introduction to the Penguin edition of Livy's *The Early History of Rome,* R. M. Ogilvie mentions 510 B.C. as the date traditionally given, but suggests 507 B.C. as a more probable date. According to Ogilvie, both the date and the cause of the overthrow of the monarchy remain uncertain. He writes that "The story in Livy is a melodrama (I. 57–60) of a charming Hellenistic kind" (23).

5. Joseph E. Gillet points out that the first Spanish translation of the *City of God* (by Antonio de Roys) appeared only in 1614. Although Augustine's "censure" of Lucretia would only have been known secondhand to the masses, it nevertheless took hold early (129–30).

6. In his analysis of Richardson's *Clarissa,* Eagleton suggests that Clarissa, as fetishized object, becomes the phallic, "transcendental signifier" (56–63):

> What finally thrusts him [Lovelace] into despair and temporary psychosis is the unspeakable truth that Clarissa is not to be possessed. She is absolutely impenetrable, least of all by rape. Forced into this sole shocking encounter with the "real," Lovelace's precarious self, fantasmal to the core, enters upon its steady dissolution.
>
> In raping Clarissa he unmasks not the "nothing" of her "castration," but a rather more subversive absence: the reality of the woman's body, a body which resists all representation and remains stubbornly recalcitrant to his fictions. (60–61)

Ferguson stresses Clarissa's nonconsent as crucial to the making and meaning of the psychological novel, which delves into the lack of coherence between "states of consciousness" and "forms of action" (105):

> Rape, that is, dramatizes a problematic about the relationship between the body and the mind; although a rake like Lovelace may imagine that carnal "knowing" includes knowing someone else's mind, a character like Clarissa—virtuous even in her violation—suggests that one knows about mental experience as much in despite of the body as through it. (99)

In other words: "What I have been arguing, however, is that Richardson's achievement in *Clarissa* is to insist on a fundamental mistake in the idea of equating epistemology and psychology" (108).

7. Mary Douglas makes the point that pollution beliefs can be brought into play when other sanctions are not available, and thus help uphold the moral code (132–34). In the case of an uprising against the monarchs, otherwise prohibited action by the populace can be justified on the basis of pollution beliefs.

In a patrilineal system a double moral standard prevails, and a wife's sexual offence is much more serious, for "[t]hrough the adultery of a wife impure blood is introduced to the lineage" (Douglas 126). Thus Lucretia refers to her polluted self as a broken mirror and a mud-stained ermine (3.2078–83).

8. In their explanation of Freud's construct, Laplanche and Pontalis write that:

> The origin of fantasy would lie in the hallucinatory satisfaction of desire; in the absence of a real object, the infant reproduces the *experience* of the original satisfaction in a hallucinated form. In this view the most fundamental fantasies would be those which tend to recover the hallucinated objects linked with the very earliest experiences of the rise and resolution of desire. (24)

Described as a "myth of origin," it is

> a mythical moment of disjunction between the pacification of need *(Befriedigung)* and the fulfilment of desire *(Wunscherfüllung)*, between the two stages represented by real experience and its hallucinatory revival, between the object that satisfies and the sign which describes both the object and its absence: a mythical moment at which hunger and sexuality meet in a common origin. (24–25)

9. Juan Goytisolo's important contribution to the study of Zayas signaled the erotic difference that marks her *novelas*. The gothic overtones of many of the stories are mentioned in my article on her work.

10. In addition, we can read this scene of male bonding through boasting as implicitly homosexual in nature. In his discussion of Shakespeare's poem, in which he concentrates on the rhetorical strategies at work, Joel Fineman endorses (though he does not pursue) the viability of a psychoanalytic approach to this scene, according to which Tarquin's desire for Collatine subtends his need to possess Lucretia. Thus Tarquin's rape of Collatine's wife is "of the kind of jealously paranoic defense against homosexuality" (34).

In a more general way, Luce Irigaray ("Women on the Market") considers homosexuality the basis of the symbolic order in which the exchange of commodities—including women—takes place.

11. Karl Marx in vol. 1 of *Capital,* "The Fetishism of the Commodity and Its Secret" (bk. 1, chap. 1, 163–77). The word "fantasy" appears in his description of the falsification that occurs:

> As against this, the commodity-form, and the value-relation of the products of labour within which it appears, have absolutely no connection with the physical nature of the commodity and the material (*dinglich*) relations arising out of this. It is nothing but the definite social relations between men themselves which assumes here, for them, the fantastic form of a relation between things. (165)

In his 1927 essay on "Fetishism," Freud locates fetishism in men in a child's disavowal of the absence of a penis in women (which he attributes to castration), and consequent redirecting of sexual interest to certain objects or parts of the body that "take the place" of the missing organ. As Bersani and Dutoit point out:

> The crucial point—which makes the fetishistic object different from the phallic symbol—is that the success of the fetish depends on its being seen as authentically different from the missing penis. With a phallic symbol, we may not be consciously aware of what it stands for, but it attracts us because, consciously or unconsciously, we perceive it *as* the phallus. (68)

The result for the fetishist is that he "can see the woman as she is, without a penis, because he loves her with a penis somewhere else" (68).

12. Kaplan insists throughout her study that neither of these gendered tendencies is innate to being male or female; both are social constructs: "As everyone knows, female masochism is the result of women's socialization in a patriarchal society" (518).

13. In all parenthetical references to this play, the page numbers refer to the edition of the *Obras de Lope de Vega* of the Real Academia Española. Citations from the text are preceded by act number. The more recent edition of the play in the *Obras escogidas* includes only a very condensed version of the introductory comments by Menéndez y Pelayo. In her edition of the play, María Soledad de Ciria Matilla corrects some of the historical and source details offered by Menéndez y Pelayo's earlier version. For instance, the king is not Sancho II but rather Sancho IV of Navarre, and she deems such sources as Esteban Garibay's *Compendio historial* (1571), as well as others, relevant to Lope's fictional reworking (22–27).

Chapter Three: The Gendering of Violence

1. Dian Fox (85–91) argues, based on textual evidence, that the main protagonists in this play (Elvira, her father, and Sancho) "are not idealized peasants but idealized *hidalgos: hijos de algo,* descendants of bluebloods, a condition that is unobtrusively reiterated throughout *The Greatest Alcalde.* Lope's creations, hailing from a social class rarely commended in Golden Age fiction, are therefore all the more extraordinary: if the 'poor *hidalgo*' is a tautological expression, the productive *hidalgo* amounts to a dramatic oxymoron; it is almost unheard of in fiction for a member of that class actually to make himself useful" (88).

2. For the dating of Lope's plays, see Morley and Courtney; for Calderón's dates, see Shergold and Varey. Citations to *Peribáñez, Fuenteovejuna,* and *El alcalde de Zalamea* refer to the English translations; otherwise, translations are ours.

3. Gayle Rubin points to Mauss's *Essay on the Gift* as the first theoretical statement on the importance of gift exchange in primitive societies: "Mauss proposed that gifts were the threads of social discourse, the means by which such societies were held together in the absence of specialized governmental institutions" (172).

4. The quotation from Emile Beneviste is from *Vocabulaire des institutions indo-européennes* (Paris, 1969), 1:241. The absence of any reference to the religious imprimatur is curious in *Fuenteovejuna:* the marriage is portrayed exclusively as a popular ritual. As might be expected, the formal petition of marriage, consent, and dowry transaction in the play are a domestic arrangement (2.1365–1440). In *El mejor alcalde, el Rey,* on the other hand, the feudal lord, don Tello, as a delaying tactic prohibits the priest from entering to consecrate the marriage (1.12.461) and thus manages to postpone the nuptials. Because the historical settings of both plays precede the Council of Trent, the more casual attitude in *Fuenteovejuna* toward religious benediction cannot be accounted for simply by the fact that its action occurs before the council's rulings for more ecclesiastical supervision of marriage ceremonies. Whatever the reason for the gap in *Fuenteovejuna,* it serves to emphasize the popular community spirit (in matters of both law and religion) that infuses all aspects of this play.

5. Claude Anibal points to the account by Alonso Fernández de Palencia (1423–1492), a historian of "well-established independence, integrity, veracity, and authenticity" (695), who portrays him as loyal to the Catholic kings but inimical to the interests of the Order of Calatrava, members of which fomented the peasants' rebellion. Palencia adds that the peasants, "[i]n order to excuse in some way their crimes . . . accused the deceased of sexual assault and corrupt behavior" (695; qtd. from *Crónica de Enrique IV, escrita en Latín por Alonso de Palencia, Traducción Castellana por A. Paz y Melia,* Colección de Escritores Castellanos, 138 [Madrid, 1903], 4:199–203). Rafael Ramírez de Arrellano's account, "Rebelión de Fuente Obejuna contra el Comendador Mayor de Calatrava Fernánd Gómez de Guzmán," is alluded to in Carter, "*Fuenteovejuna* and Tyranny" (335, n. 50), and in MacKay and McKendrick.

6. The hallmarks of ritualistic violence that MacKay and McKendrick discuss are based on a study by Natalie Zemon Davis. As her subtitle indicates, she focuses very specifically on religious rioting by Catholics and Protestants. Although there may indeed be analogies between religious and political rioting in terms of crowd behavior, goals, and justification, some cognizance of the differing motivations must be taken into account. Either crowd behavior must be held to be similar, regardless of the motivation for riot (religious, political, economic) or, as in the case of Fuenteovejuna, an argument made as to the quasi-religious overtones given to the conflict. The authors investigate the aspersion of "bad Christians" cast on the comendador and his men, whose excommunication for fiscal disagreements with the Córdoba cathedral had adversely affected the residents of Fuentevejuna and Bélmez. This is, however, not posited as a principal cause of the people's disaffection (132).

7. In their excellent article on mob violence in *Fuenteovejuna,* MacKay and McKendrick argue for the legitimacy of the murder of the comendador, citing Davis's study. They fail to distinguish, however, between legitimacy as a concept of law and the strategies of legitimization, or how at the psychological and narrative levels the actions are justified to the self/reader/spectator. As in any recounting or representation, distortion is the handmaiden of ideology.

8. Salomon notes that this detail is not mentioned by Rades y Andrade (857, n. 30) but appears in the Ramírez Arellano document as an action accomplished by an emissary from Córdoba—in which case Cordoban arms would have replaced those of the

comendador. He considers Lope's scene to be based not on a specific historical source but on the customary behavior of villagers in the sixteenth and seventeenth centuries as they symbolically marked the passage from seigneurial ownership to a *realenga*.

9. Whether or not Laurencia remained, in fact, a virgin after her abduction is a subject of critical debate. See Dixon, "'Su Majestad habla.'"

10. The subject of women's hair merits more critical attention literary studies. In *The Bacchae*, a change of coiffure (so to speak) is represented by the messenger to Pentheus as the first indication of the women's entry into a Dionysiac celebratory mode: "First they let their hair fall loose, down / over their shoulders" (695–96). In Ovid's *Metamorphoses*, Apollo's pursuit of the fleeing Daphne is interspersed with references to her locks of hair, which are in disarray (1.477) and which the god imagines combed (1.498). Lavinia Lorch interprets this first metamorphosis as emblematic of the poetic process itself:

> Daphne's hair is in this episode the illustration of the movement, of the flux, and therefore underlines by its own nature the difficulty of imposing an order on, of capturing, the fleeing vision. Hair in this context is much more than an elegiac topos. At first it was *sine lege*, with a *levis aura* blowing through it. . . . Through his breath, the god will impose a law on her hair. By his in-spiration, it will become the *frondem* ("the leafage") (550), eternal symbol of poetic success. (270)

Her analysis includes a discussion of Laura's hair in Petrarch's poetry as emblematic of his poetics (273 n. 19). And so on, I suspect. Woman's hair appears iconographically related to the binarism of order/disorder, whatever significance the dichotomy may, and does, assume.

11. In *Violence and the Sacred*, Girard makes a similar suggestion concerning the Dionysian cult. According to his argument, a sacrificial crisis requires the participation of a whole community. He is suspicious, therefore, about the exclusively female role in the homicide: "We may therefore wonder whether the preponderance of women does not constitute a secondary mythological displacement, an effort to exonerate from the accusation of violence, not mankind as a whole, but adult males, who have the greatest need to forget their role in the crisis because, in fact, they must have been largely responsible for it. They alone risk plunging the community into the chaos of reciprocal violence" (139).

Freud speculates about yet another gendered displacement in *Group Psychology and the Analysis of the Ego* (1921), in which the group is likened to Darwin's primal horde. Discussing the advance in mental development from group to individual psychology, he summarizes his conjectures concerning the primal horde's killing of the father and the formation of a totemistic community of brothers (the subject of *Totem and Taboo* [1912–1913]). He continues: "It was then, perhaps, that some individual, in the exigency of his longing, may have been moved to free himself from the group and take over the father's part. He who did this was the first epic poet; and the advance was achieved in his imagination. This poet disguised the truth with lies in accordance with his longing. He invented the heroic myth. The hero was a man who by himself had slain the father. . . . In the lying poetic fancies of prehistoric times the woman, who had been the prize of battle and the allurement to murder, was probably turned into the seducer and instigator to the crime" (203).

12. In her classic analysis of "The Taboo of Virginity," Mary Jacobus reveals the gender confusion in Freud's essay between the penis envy attributed to the female and the male's castration anxiety. As in Hebbel's play *Judith* (1840), in which sword and woman are closely identified so that "the mark of castration is replaced by the castrating instrument" (119), so, too, do *Fuenteovejuna*'s sword-bearing women function to repress sexual difference by assigning the female phallic attributes.

13. "What is interesting from the point of view that concerns us is precisely to see how the basic antifeudalism that nourishes Lope's play . . . is dissipated, emasculated in Tirso's, because Tirso does not make the conflict between lord and vassal his central theme. . . . On the contrary, Tirso, freed from the patterns of established tradition, does here and there treat the same theme, but much less forcefully, and he proves much more compliant with the dominant feudal ideology" (865).

14. Freud wrote: "The sight of Medusa's head makes the spectator stiff with terror, turns him to stone. Observe that we have here once again the same origin from the castration complex and the same transformation of affect! For becoming stiff means an erection. Thus in the original situation it offers consolation to the spectator: he is still in possession of a penis, and the stiffening reassures him of the fact" ("Medusa's Head" 212).

15. Bal, *Lethal Love* chap. 5.

16. Salomon notes that the servant Gallardo, handed over to the peasants for punishment, is exempt from the seigneurial code that protects his master don Guillén and that Lillo, the comendador's lackey in *La Santa Juana III,* suffers a similar affliction. He

cites this as further proof of Tirso's conservative aristocratism (881–82). There is nothing unusual about the scatological humor associated with the comic /grotesque body of the *gracioso* figure. The best-known example of this kind of Rabelaisian humor in Golden Age Spain is, of course, Sancho Panza.

17. Leviticus specifies a period of seven days of impurity through menstruation. The taboo of menstruation is decidedly cross-cultural: menstruating women are not allowed to enter Hindu temples; other examples are cited in Douglas, chap. 9. See also Kristeva, chap. 3, "From Filth to Defilement," and chap. 4, "Semiotics of Biblical Abomination."

18. The bandit theme in *La dama del olivar* has been linked to Vélez de Guevara's *La serrana de la Vera* (1613) (Salomon 876), though the theme is initiated by Lope's play of the same title, which predates Vélez's (written in 1595–1598), as does his second play on the subject, *Las dos bandoleras y fundación de la Santa Hermandad de Toledo* (The Two Bandoleras and the Foundation of the Santa Hermandad of Toledo) (1597–1603; dates according to Morley and Bruerton). McKendrick specifies that the attribution of *Las dos bandoleras* to Lope is not absolutely certain (109, n. 3). It is assumed that both playwrights used a popular *romance* as their source, which depicts "a seductive and homicidal woman," who in one version, "pays with death her bloodthirsty sensuality" (according to Menéndez Pidal and María Goyri in the notes to their edition, p. 136). Lope's *serrana* play is an exception to the general rule of a dishonored female seeking revenge (McKendrick 110). *La dama del olivar* is also recognized as an exception: "In this play although he leans heavily on Lope, Tirso makes one important departure: the heroine is not seduced or deceived but abducted and raped. She is therefore the most seriously wronged of all the *bandoleras*" (McKendrick 127). (Though the abduction is a fact, Laurencia's alleged innocence is compromised by her complicity with her powerful seducer in previous meetings, as we have noted.)

Though not rape narratives, these plays share a facet discussed as an aftermath of rape—the emergence of the castrating, lethal female. In this sense they, too, ratify Freud's speculations in *The Taboo of Virginity*. The case of Vélez de Guevara's ferocious Gila is particularly noteworthy. She dies shot through with arrows, thus resembling a female Saint Sebastian, to whom she is compared (3.3278) in a curious disregard for the conditions of martyrdom. Her final act is to beg her father to approach so that she may whisper in his ear, which she then bites off (3.3248–49). As sources for this episode, the editors cite Boethius, *De disciplina scholarium,* in which a sentenced son asks his father for a kiss and bites his nose. This example then appears in *Castigos e documentos del rey D. Sancho* and *Libro de los exemplos.* In the *Cifar,* the son bites off his mother's nose; in the *Ysopet* (republished many times from 1489 onward) the robber bites his mother's ear. The editors assume that this popular version was known to Vélez. An earlier example in Valerius Maximus is mentioned, with the qualification that the ear is bitten in different circumstances. Other examples are also mentioned (159–60). This particular daughter's biting off of her father's ear has all the earmarks (if a pun may be forgiven) of an upwardly displaced castration.

Although he respects McKendrick's warnings against reading for sexual preference (315–19), Matthew D. Stroud cautiously notes that, "Indeed, in *La serrana de la Vera,* as in none of the other plays, we do have slight indications of Gila's preference for women over men" (122), and mentions in particular her adoration of Queen Isabella. In this instance it is the queen's power she admires and covets rather than her body, but there are other examples of Gila's expressed affection for women in the play.

19. De Lauretis (37) cites Monique Plaza ("Our Costs and Their Benefits," trans. Wendy Harrison, *m/f,* no. 4 [1980]: 28–39) to the effect that even when the rape victim is a male, he too is raped "as a woman" (31).

20. In the *Siete Partidas* (II-13-xvi): "And therefore the people must not be defiant, in such guise that they lose respect for their king, but rather should they be obedient in all that he commands, so that . . . he may establish justice amongst all who have grievances" (Carter, "History and Poetry" 211, n. 6).

21. Carter cites a relevant passage from the *Partidas* (III-18-lii) concerning "On royal orders that should be carried out without legal debate and without trial." Unless the letter or the informants are proven false, the king's demands are nonnegotiable: "Wherefore we state that he to whom the letter is addressed can advance no defense to justify his failure to comply with what was commanded in said letter" ("History and Poetry" 211, n. 6).

22. The comendador's decision to "take possession" of Casilda via her portrait is curiously reminiscent of an anecdote recounted by Vasari in his *Lives of the Artists:* "It is said that Fra Filippo was so lustful that he would give anything to enjoy a woman he wanted if he thought he could have his way; and if he couldn't buy what he wanted, then he

would cool his passion by painting her portrait and reasoning with himself" (1.216). My thanks to Gridley McKim-Smith and David Cast of Bryn Mawr College for bringing this passage to my attention. They note that the situation is more complex in the case of Fra Filippo, involving the act of painting as well as the act of viewing in the erotic dynamics of artist/viewer and subject depicted.

23. The now-classic study of the theme of honor and Pedro Crespo's embodiment of its ideal is Peter Dunn's "Honour and the Christian Background in Calderón" (see also the introduction to his edition of the play [1–28]). Fox's reading (151–70) focuses on Pedro Crespo's efforts to save his son (who had wounded the captain, his captain in fact) from falling in the hands of a military tribunal. Because the captain is denied any proper hearing, Pedro Crespo's execution can be classified as a "murder of a prisoner in his custody" (155). According to Fox, his sacrifice of his daughter's honor (by making public the offense against her) provides the distraction necessary to save his son. Peter W. Evans considers the execution an act of revenge rather than justice (49). The central paradox of the play for this critic is that the oppressed resort to the ideology of repressive violence of their oppressors.

24. I am grateful to Jane Bennett for so generously sharing her work on the sociolinguistics of rape survivors' oral testimony. Her professional and personal dedication to the survivors' cause have been a source of inspiration to me.

25. In a production (March 1994) of *El alcalde de Zalamea* at the Chamizal Siglo de Oro Theater Festival (El Paso, Texas) by the company of Francisco Portes of Madrid, the passage concerning Isabel's going to the convent was deleted. A colleague suggested that the change made the text more modern. I could not agree with him. The appearance of reintegration in the social fabric violates the meaning of rape as psychological death, which, in its own way, Calderón's text expresses in a compelling and moving way.

Chapter Four: Text and Transformations

1. All citations from the play are from the Aris & Phillips edition translated by A. K. G. Paterson. All other translations from the Spanish are ours.

2. Seneca's two Hercules plays, *Hercules furens* and *Hercules Oetaeus,* were translated into Spanish by Francisco López de Zárate as the *Tragedia de Hércules furente y Oeta,* written by 1629,

though not published until 1651 (Morby). The radical departures from the originals (Megara is replaced by Deianeira throughout, for example, and Hercules' killing frenzy is eliminated) warrant its being considered an adaptation rather than a translation.

3. According to Courtney Bruerton's dating of Castro's plays. Chap. 3 (35–46) of William E. Wilson's book on Castro in the Twayne series is dedicated to "Castro's Versification and the Dating of His Plays." The edition referred to of Castro's play is that of the Real Academia Española, vol. 1. Quotations are identified in parentheses by act, page number, and column (a or b) on the page.

4. According to Raymond R. MacCurdy (66). The edition referred to is that of Alfred Rodríguez and Saúl E. Roll-Vélez. Quotations are identified by act and verse numbers. In the *Biblioteca de Autores Españoles*, the play appears in vol. 54.

5. In Ovid's version, the child's murder is associated with Dionysiac rites, in which Procne participates as a ploy to recover her sister in the woods: she "mimics thy madness, O Bacchus" (6.596). Then, having reached Philomela, she "arrays her in the trappings of a Bacchante" (6.598–99). Patricia Joplin points out the allusion to Agave's murder of her son Pentheus in Euripides' *Bacchae,* adding that "[h]e [Ovid] also trades on misogynist lore by making it clear that his Procne only pretends to be a bacchante, suggesting that the rites are or were only a cover for the unleashing of female revenge against men" ("The Voice of the Shuttle Is Ours" 44–45, n. 35). The point here, though, is the revenge-plot, which a fit of madness would disable. It is the sisters' difference from Agave that is signaled—the responsibility for the act is theirs, not Dionysius's.

For a study of the legends informing the poem and plays, see Fontenrose. For discussion of Medea, see Mills; Foley.

6. Tereus is changed into a hoopoe, "with the look of one armed for war" (6.674). The Latin poets reversed the avian transformation of the sisters, making Philomela the nightingale and Procne the swallow. According to earlier tradition, as apparently represented in Sophocles' *Tereus* (only fragments of which are known to us), the grieving mother Procne, as a nightingale, eternally mourns the loss of her child; Philomela, the swallow, chirps against Tereus. The powerful contemporary play by Timberlake Wertenbaker, *The Love of the Nightingale,* follows the later Latin tradition of metamorphosis. It was a privilege to see this play, directed by Elizabeth Swain, in the Minor Latham Playhouse of Barnard College in November 1992. I thank Professor Swain for making this work known to me.

7. Luce Irigaray, in "Women on the Market" (published originally as "Le marché des femmes" [1978]) argues that this is always so in patriarchal societies: "The use of and traffic in women subtend and uphold the reign of masculine hom(m)o-sexuality, even while they maintain that hom(m)o-sexuality in speculations, mirror games, identifications, and more or less rivalrous appropriations, which defer its real practice. Reigning everywhere, although prohibited in practice, hom(o)o-sexuality is played out through the bodies of women, matter, or sign, and heterosexuality has been up to now just an alibi for the smooth workings of man's relations with himself, of relations among men" (172). The primariness of the homosocial bond among men is the subject of Sedgwick, *Between Men.*

8. Marcela Trambaioli uses this example when she takes issue with a feminist interpretation of the revenge scene: "First of all, the sisters' vengeful attitude derives from the ancient myth; secondly, Procne and Philomela use their respective husbands' swords. Both women serve only as agents of a justice executed through weapons that are symbols respectively of the king's power and Hippolytus's honor" (284).

9. The concept of rape as a speech act, a semiotic message between/among men, is developed in Bal's earlier biblical study, *Death & Dissymmetry.* See in particular the analysis of the rape, murder, and dismemberment of the so-called concubine of the Levite (Judg. 19) (119–27).

10. In her contemporary version, Wertenbaker shows the "narcissistic wound" posited by Freud as being the male's fear, not the female's. After the rape, Philomele *[sic]* reacts with contempt and berates Tereus's sexual prowess as nothing but a sham:

> Did you tell her [Procne] that despite my fear, your violence, when I saw you in your nakedness I couldn't help laughing because you were so shrivelled, so ridiculous and it is not the way it is on the statues? Did you tell her you cut me because you yourself had no strength? Did you tell her I pitied her for having in her bed a man who could screech such quick and ugly pleasure, a man of jelly beneath his hard skin, did you tell her that? (35)

In a frenzied act of symbolic displacement, as though trying to retrieve what he has lost—an erect and powerful member—Tereus cuts out Philomela's tongue, making it his own.

11. MacCurdy (72) cites the following criticisms: Alberto Lista opines that inclusions of "novelistic incidents" "distract the attention of the spectator and weaken the

dramatic effect of the best scenes" (*Ensayos literarios y críticos* 2.136); Mesonero Romanos expresses his distaste by means of the rhetorical question, "Who, for example, can tolerate with patience the inanities of the two clowns in *Progne y Filomena*, side by side the torrents of gallant poetry and the bits of true passion that escape from Rojas's pen in this play (to my understanding the best after *García*)? (*Comedias escogidas, Biblioteca de Autores Españoles*, vol. 54, xx); Valbuena Prat signals the "witty but not pertinent interventions of the comic types" as his only quibble with Rojas's otherwise magisterial tragic art (*Historia de la literatura española*, 2d ed. [Barcelona, n.d.], 2.292).

12. Marcela Trambaioli recalls (284–85) that a salient intervention by *graciosos* is also a feature of Juan de Timoneda's earlier version of the legend (*Tragicomedia llamada "Filomena,"* 1564). The *gracioso* humor in Timoneda's play is, however, strictly appetitive, not excremental.

13. The English translation is from the edition of *The Emblems in Translation* by Peter M. Daly (emblem 204). The full text in English is: "There was a decree of Solon that the quince should be presented as a gift to one's wife, since it is a very healthy and delicious fruit, and it leaves a pleasant odour in the mouth."

14. Contemporary artists have actualized the subversive potential of excremental art. In his contribution ("Phobic Art") to the catalog published in conjunction with the Whitney Museum's exhibition of "Abject Art" (June 23–August 29, 1993), Simon Taylor discusses this under the general heading of "Political Scatology." He makes reference to exhibition of the NO! art movement in 1964, which "consisted of several trompe-l'oeil piles of excrement made of papier-mâché, painted brown, with red areas indicating hemorrhoids" (75). In a photograph, one of the artists, Sam Goodman, is posed in the middle of the excremental piles in mock imitation of Rodin's *The Thinker*. The intent of the group was to protest "the complicity of their fellow artists with the moneyed elite" (75). The paintings and coprophiliac sculptures of John Miller (such as *Untitled* of 1988) are said to "represent the unsublimated expression of the instinctual drives, defeating the anal regime of the puritan mentality" (76).

15. In the introduction to his edition of *La venganza de Tamar*, A. K. G. Paterson suggests (27–28) that the play was first written between 1621 and 1624; there is a surviving variant manuscript dated 1632; the printed version appeared in Tirso's *Parte tercera* (1634). Helmy F. Giacoman, in the preface to his edition of *Los cabellos de Absalón*, cites H. W.

Hilborn (15), quoting an approximate date between 1633 and 1636 (*A Chronology of the Plays of don Pedro Calderón de la Barca* [Toronto: University of Toronto Press, 1938], 25).

Nancy K. Mayberry develops the suggestion first made by J. C. J. Metford (150) that Tirso's *La venganza de Tamar* is the second part of a trilogy, the missing third act of which informs the conclusion of Calderón's *Los cabellos de Absalón.* The reasons remain unknown for this apparently unique instance in Calderón's opus of such flagrant copying. Otto Rank characterizes it as "a case of plagiarism unparalleled in world literature" (464) and attributes it to the playwright's profound and troubled discomfort with the problematics of incest and inability to deal with the subject overtly: "In this plagiarism we see a disinclination to deal with complexes that Calderón, writing under the pressure of powerful repressions, was unable to portray himself" (464). In his preliminary note (661–65), Angel Valbuena Briones summarizes other critical suggestions, in particular those of A. L. Constandse (*El barroco español y Calderón de la Barca,* 1951).

It is interesting to note that Calderón does include a salient fact from the Samuel narrative that Tirso deletes: the legitimacy of marriage between half-brother and half-sister in the Jerusalem of King David. Tamar thus reminds Amnon (to no avail) that "Under our law is permitted / the marriage of kin with kin. / Ask my father's permission" (1.15.963–65). Tirso heightens the tension by stressing the incest implications; Calderón, on the other hand, defuses (or at least mitigates) the explosive potential of the theme.

For discussion of subtle differences between Tirso's third act and Calderón's use of it as his second act, see Giacoman, chap. 6 of his edition, as well as his article, "En torno a *Los cabellos de Absalón* de Pedro Calderón de la Barca." Susana Hernández-Araico's close attention to the expanded role of the *gracioso* provides revealing insights (chap. 4, "Risa y ambivalencia en *Los cabellos de Absalón:* Tamar, el gracioso y Teuca," 99–114).

16. Because Tirso's act 3 is used by Calderón as his own act 2, King David's characterization in *Tamar's Revenge* is important. Paterson's introduction to his edition of Tirso's play considers David "a striking parable of mercy. . . . And it is his infinitely vulnerable form of love that survives tragedy; the day is foreseen when another son will make Godly justice a reality (II,359; III,160)" (22) [the reference is to Solomon]. Jane Albrecht interprets Tirso's David as a much more problematic character, as a failed *imitatio Christi:* "In fact, in not fearing God and punishing his sons, David fails God, his family, and his

kingdom. David's duty was to punish Amón and Absalón. His failure to do so ironically underscores both that God is directing events and his prophecy is being enacted and that David's individual desires have controlled him" (222). Gwynne Edwards believes that Calderón's debt to his predecessor in the characterization of David as morally blameless has been exaggerated ("Calderón's *Los cabellos de Absalón*" 220). She proceeds to counter Sloman's contention that *Los cabellos de Absalón* is an atypical play because it lacks Calderonian insistence on individual responsibility for the fate that befalls one (284–86) and analyzes the fallibility of David as well as the other main characters. Victor Dixon insists on the centrality of King David in the drama (as opposed to other opinions that favor Absalom) and stresses the king's piety and patience before the will of God as his essential characteristics ("El santo rey David y *Los cabellos de Absalón*" 85). Francisco Ruiz Ramón harks back to the curse of the prophet Nathan on the house of David in punishment for his sin with Bathsheba (2 Sam. 12:9–12), comparing it to the implacable tragedies that befall the house of Thebes and house of Atreus in Greek drama (158), and insists on the tragic dimensions of the interrelationship between Divine will and human will in this, as in other Calderón plays: "Once again Calderón shows that the divine will fulfills itself not in opposition to human freedom but rather by means of it, the sole tragic nucleus of the Christian tragedy of freedom and fate" (170). Felipe Pedraza Jiménez, who subtitles his discussion of the character of David "David or the Inconveniences of Affection," cites examples of the king's irresoluteness, inappropriate for a ruler, yet also points out his admirable restraint in the midst of an environment of destructive passion: "But reality is multifaceted, and neither the saintly king's admirable moral outlook nor his paternal tenderness are the best rules for government. Calderón, as in many other plays, does not resolve the difficulty; he limits himself to showing us reality's conflicted profile" (1:558).

17. In his discussion of this issue (102–3), Charles Conroy makes the point that "Political consequences should not be confused with political motivation." According to Conroy, some biblical scholars' assumption of a political, as opposed to personal, incentive for the fratricide is speculative and not corroborated by textual data (36, n. 75).

18. The same point is made by Dixon: "And as Calderón also emphasizes, in the dialogues that follow, Absalom's mistaken interpretation [of Teuca's prophecy], so too does he lay bare Absalom's ambition and his hatred towards all rivals, long before the offense is committed against Tamar" ("El santo rey David y *Los cabellos de Absalón*" 93).

19. This is Mieke Bal's thesis in her study of the Book of Judges: "The political coherence, as I call it, thus functions as closure; it allows critics to escape the painful experience of awareness of the deep-seated relationship between social institutions and violence against women that my analysis has brought to the fore" (*Death & Dissymmetry* 237). Her intent is a reading with a "countercoherence":

> A countercoherence relates the "official" reading to what it leaves out;
> it relates the texts to the needs of the reader; it relates everything that
> is denied importance to the motivations for such denials. The counter-
> coherence will start precisely where repression is the most flagrant. Since
> men are said to lead the game, I will start with the women; since con-
> quest is said to be the issue, I will start with loss; since strength is said to
> be the major asset of the characters, I will start with the victims. (17)

20. Text citations from *La venganza de Tamar* (act, verse numbers) are to the translation of John Lyon (based on A. K. G. Paterson's edition of the play). Citations to *Los cabellos de Absalón* are to the edition of Helmy F. Giacoman (act, scene, verse numbers); translations are ours.

21. Dixon contrasts Tamar's support of her brother's rebellion with Solomon's faithfulness to his father: "She allies herself with her brother against her father, just as Solomon on the other hand is increasingly contrasted with Absalom. . . . The solicitous love of the loyal son contrasts with the ungrateful harshness of the rebellious son" (95). In the same vein, Sloman comments that "Even Tamar, with her essential role in the story, is enigmatic, enlisting our sympathy when assaulted by Amón and then forfeiting it by her support for Absalón in his rebellion against David" (115).

22. In his edition of *La venganza de Tamar,* Paterson (13, n. 2) notes the following collections: *Romancero de la Montaña,* ed. J. M. de Cossío and T. M. Solana (Santander, 1933) 1:27–31; Paciencia Ontañón de Lope, "Veintisiete romances del siglo XVI," *Nueva Revista de Filología Hispánica* 15 (1961): 187; *Romancero general,* ed. Agustín Durán, *Biblioteca de Autores Españoles,* vol. 10 (Madrid, 1849): 299; *Romancero sefardí,* ed. Moshe Attias (Jerusalem, 1956), 175. Juan de Avila's sermon "Audi, Filia" (*Obras del padre maestro Juan de Avila, predicador en el Andalucía* [Madrid, 1577]: fol. 295r) is mentioned for its tracing the cause of the tragedy to David's adultery with Bathsheba and killing of Uriah. In addition, Paterson (13) indicates that several preachers used Tamar's fate as an example to admonish women against the perils of intimacy.

23. Anita K. Stoll's careful analysis of *Los cabellos de Absalón* as a stage text that effectively heightens emotional impact by means of discovery scenes and symbolic and metaphoric visual representations leads her to the most interesting conclusion that: "The fact that the third act demonstrates a greater concentration of visual dramatic recourses than the first two, which are closely tied to Tirso's play, attests to the growing importance of spectacular staging in the later period of Golden Age theater, perhaps influenced in part by Calderón's effective practices" (80).

I particularly wish to thank Leslie Nelson for sharing with me her master's thesis (Bryn Mawr College). Her interest is, of course, on the interrelationship between the genre of the still-life (as executed by Velázquez) and scenography of the period. Her research on the widespread and varied use of discovery scenes in Golden Age drama made me more aware of the visual impact of such scenes. I also thank Gridley McKim-Smith (Department of Art History, Bryn Mawr College) for drawing my attention to this study.

24. In his edition, Paterson quotes Louis Ginzberg (*The Legends of the Jews* [Philadelphia, 1913] vol. 4, p. 118) to the effect that, according to a Jewish legend with particular reference to Adonijah, the royal crown fit only the legitimate heir. The sources of Tirso's probable acquaintance with the legend remain unknown (142, 43n. [to v. 414]).

25. David H. Darst includes *La venganza de Tamar* in a group of five biblical plays that stage an "exhibition of the body" (the others being *La mujer que manda en casa* [The Wife Who Rules at Home]; *La mejor espigadora* [The Best Gleaner]; *Tanto es lo de más como lo de menos* [More or Less; It's All the Same]; *La vida y la muerte de Herodes* [The Life and Death of Herod]). Its intent is didactic—an embodiment of the warning that "the wages of sin is death" (Rom. 6:23): "the curtain rises to exhibit the dead person's body to the other characters and to the audience, mainly to frighten them and give them an example of what can happen to them if they follow the same path" (224). (The exception is *La mejor espigadora.*)

26. According to *The Interpreter's One-Volume Commentary on the Bible:* "Marriage between half brother and sister was forbidden in later legislation (Lev. 18:9, 11; Deut. 27:22) but at this time was still acceptable" (2 Sam. 13:1–22). See also Conroy (17–18, n. 3); Fokkelman (1:103–4): "He does not commit incest but rape. . . . In this way, Tamar's argument in v. 13cd becomes quite reasonable; it is a genuine alternative which she proposes to Amnon, not an escape but a plea."

27. When confronted with these examples of impossible love, one cannot help but recall the dominance of this theme in García Lorca's plays, from his earliest staged work, *El maleficio de la mariposa (The Butterfly's Evil Spell)*. Before his death in 1936, the playwright spoke of writing a biblical trilogy, which would include the destruction of Sodom, Lot and his daughters, and Thamar and Amnon. Rafael Martínez Nadal recalls that in his last conversation with the poet, García Lorca said that "The drama of Tamar and Amnon attracts me enormously. Since Tirso nothing serious has been done with this stupendous incest" (13).

28. In a series of articles, Henry W. Sullivan has accomplished a Lacanian reading of the incest motif in Tirsian drama. In broad terms, society's imposition of restraints on desire harks back to the law of the Name-of-the-Father that provokes separation (and hence individuation) from the primary mother-child dyad—a necessary but alienating process, always accompanied by a sense of loss and lack. Amnon's moment of recognition of his object of desire as his sister is a stunning example of the restraining impact of "naming" on natural instinct and its relationship to the law of the Name-of-the-Father.

29. Fokkelman (1:105–6) notes that Amnon's word choice for the food he requests is suggestively ambiguous and can signify "let her knead two *heart*-cakes" (emphasis added), "evoking the association of an aphrodisiac." In addition, the denominative of the word "kneading" can refer also to a charm of love.

30. Phyllis Trible points out that most translations are not accurate here: "he does not say, 'Send away this woman from me.' The Hebrew has only the demonstrative *this*. For Amnon, Tamar is a thing, a 'this' he wants thrown out" (48).

31. In his discussion of the Joseph and Potiphar incident, Meir Sternberg points to Amnon's reaction as "the bible's classic formulation of how guilt breeds hate" (532, n. 8).

32. Everett Hesse makes the following statement in *Tirso's Art:* "Whether she ever marries Joab is left to the reader's imagination" (38). He then immediately adds that "Tamar subverts love by her concern only for herself and her honor," implying that a character flaw, rather than ritual uncleanliness, makes her an unfit wife.

In his study of the textual history of the play (a 1632 manuscript, the 1634 edition, and an eighteenth-century *suelta*) Paterson notes that in the last version, a defective copy of an early manuscript, now lost, the play ends with David's promise to wed Tamar and Joab (388, n. 1). Because this subsidiary love plot is unique to Tirso's development of the Samuel story, Mayberry considers this further evidence of an original Tirso trilogy (123,

125). Without the plays, the matter remains in the realm of speculation. If, as is supposed, Calderón had access to the missing acts, why did he reject this resolution? Although Mayberry states that Tamar's decision to exile herself in *Los cabellos de Absalón* "is not based on scripture" (125), the romance ending of marriage is inconceivable in a tragedy—which this story is, both in the Bible and in the plays. Biblical criticism assumes that Tamar suffers a psychological death after the tragic events.

33. The motif of deception is pervasive in the Samuel narrative and functions within the "larger theme of fidelity and infidelity which in the ancient Near Eastern world defines especially the relationship between the king and his men" (Hagan 303). In trying to ascertain the audience impact of this motif in the seventeenth century, we must take into account the different genre. In terms of a specifically theatrical tradition, deceit is clearly marked as a gendered trait. After reviewing the tragic corpus, Froma Zeitlin lists among her conclusions: "Second, whereas deceit and intrigue are condemned in woman, they are also seen as natural to her sphere of operations and the dictates of her nature. For the male, however, resort to *dolos,* trickery, is what most undermines masculine integrity and puts him under the gravest of suspicions" ("Playing the Other" 76). Zeitlin adds that the negative impact on masculine honor is mitigated only when the object of deceit is an enemy king: the intrafamilial deceit of the Great Succession narrative is painfully distant from such a justification.

Another dramatic topos enters in. Donald Beecher has demonstrated the existence of the melancholy lover as a "theatergram" in both Renaissance English and Spanish theater. The locus classicus is the story of the fourth-century B.C. physician Erasistratus and his diagnosis of Antiochus's illness as lovesickness for his young stepmother Stratonice. It entered medical literature through Galen and had a distinguished literary tradition, including Petrarch and Bandello, probably the best-known sources in Spain and England. Beecher mentions Tirso's play among his examples. It should be added that, although a salacious doctor story is related in *La venganza de Tamar* (2.50–162), it is actually the cunning Jonadab who intuits the problem—"Amnon is mad or he's in love" (2.284)—both in Tirso's play and in Calderón's (1.565–74).

34. James Ackerman, basing himself on Sternberg's *The Poetics of Biblical Narrative* and its positing the "epistemological gap" as central to the narrative style of the Bible, concentrates on the many gaps and ambiguities in the Great Succession narrative. He

enumerates the many questions left unanswered in the text concerning David's behavior in the matter of Tamar and Amnon:

> Note that only here in the entire chapter is David called "*King* David." Is the text ironically suggesting that he is so soft-hearted as a father that he cannot properly function as king by dealing with this crime? Or is it the reverse— is he so busy as king that he never gets around to handling a family matter? What blocks his action? Guilt? A further instance of sangfroid? Or is it that David, knowing that Amnon is the heir to the throne and hoping that time will heal all wounds, does not want to take any action that will exacerbate family unity and jeopardize dynastic continuity? Or, if he deliberately sent Tamar to Amnon in the hope that something was developing between the two, his anger might be more directed at the crown prince's precipitous action—terminating the relationship by expelling her from his house. The narrator forces us to intuit the mixed motivations within David, beneath his anger, that are immobilizing him from taking action. (45–46)

35. Diane Wolfthal shows that in the late fifteenth and early sixteenth centuries the topos of the Power of Women became a popular artistic subject: "Here again, women formerly viewed as virtuous heroines were transformed" ("A 'Hue and a Cry'" 62). In Altdorfer's print of 1513 and Lucan van Leyden's *Power of Women* series of 1516–1519, Jael, formerly deemed a heroine for killing the enemy commander Sisera (Judg. 4), is turned into a male-destroying villain (62–63).

36. Cited by Sternberg (26, n. 10), quoted from *Ginzei Schecter: Midrashim* (New York, 1929) 1:166. The discussion focuses on the gaps in the biblical narrative: "For example, it is impossible to determine Bathsheba's attitude, though one would not imagine that she showed much resistance."

37. At the end of *The Disenchantments of Love,* Lisis berates men for their diatribes against women and connects their lack of respect and protection of females with their lack of virility, which has disastrous consequences on both home and state:

> ". . . Where do you think the lack of courage you all exhibit nowadays comes from? That lets you tolerate the enemy within Spanish borders, and while our king is doing battle you sit in the park and stroll along the river all dolled up in feminine frippery? The few men who do accompany the king long only for the fleshpots of Egypt. It comes from your low regard for women.

"I swear if you did love and cherish women as was the way in former times, you'd volunteer not just to go to war and fight but to die, exposing your throat to the knife to keep them from falling into the hands of the enemy. This is the way it was in earlier days, particularly under King Fernando the Catholic. Then it wasn't necessary to conscript men, forcing them into service almost with their hands tied, the way it is today (causing our Catholic king unhappiness and great misfortune). Men used to offer up their possessions and their lives. . . .

"How can you sit back and see us almost in the power of the enemy? From where the enemy is to where we are, the only defense is your heroic heart and your brave arm! Aren't you ashamed to be here at court donning your gala outfits and curling your hair, strolling through parks and gallivanting in carriages instead of defending us? On top of that, you ruin our good name and our honor by telling tales about your love affairs, which I think are more malicious fiction that fact!" (400–401)

In *El Criticón,* before the spectacle of the great Wheel of Fortune, Critilo is dismayed by the differences between the men of yore and his contemporaries:

Oh, what a sight—said Critilo—the former dressed in coarse cloth and the latter in brocade; the former crushing steel and the latter silk; the former bejewelled in soul and naked in body, the latter draped in finery and bare of deeds, devoid of information and saturated with pleasures! (3.10.969)

As generations succeed one another in a satirical spectacle, the conclusion is that

But that which is past is cause for regret, not amusement, for everything grows ever worse. . . . Men were once made of gold and dressed in woollen cloth; now they are make of filth and flaunt damask silk. And despite there being so many diamonds, there is neither refinement nor resolve. (3.10.973; Translations are mine. Only part 1 of the three-part novel is included in Paul Rycaut's English translation [London, 1681], *The Critick.*)

Gracián also views Ferdinand's reign as paradigmatic, as attested to by his treatise dedicated to the Catholic king.

Chapter Five: A Contemporary Rape Narrative

I am indebted to Natalie Shainess for knowledge of William Blake's "The Sick Rose" and its relevance to the subject of rape. She quotes it at the end of her article on the "Psychological Significance of Rape" (2048).

1. Anny Brooksbank Jones comments on this particular passage, which includes subsequent allusions to obscene scribblings on the wall that acquire a life of their own, imagined as ants crawling over Julia's body. Jones's analysis is marked by witty word-play: "Here we have the sound of water only, and the encounter is less littoral than lit-eral: the 'language of the washroom.' . . . At the same time, the adolescents' crude and (in Franco's Spain) presumably ill-understood graffiti, the swarm of words, conflates prurience with itching and fornication with formication" (81).

2. The clinical literature on rape is extensive and shows a great consistency. For a clear and succinct presentation, see Quina and Carlson, chap. 8, "Emotional Aftereffects" (143–74).

3. Schumm interprets this narrative trait as a linguistic indicator of the protago-nist's schizophrenic division. Nichols characterizes the filmic imagery as "the tone of schizophrenic objectivity" (116).

4. It should be noted that Spiegel considers multiple personality disorder a special instance of post-traumatic stress disorder.

5. Kaufman notes that the terminology employed is imprecise and that the clinical terms *schizophrenic* or *schizoid, borderline* or *narcissistic* overlap (146–57). Calhoun and Atkeson write that "Many, if not most, people diagnosed with multiple personality have histo-ries of severe sexual abuse at an early age. In addition, this disorder has been found to be associated with an increased incidence of forcible rape during adolescence and adult-hood" (Coons and Milstein, 1984). Spiegel (1984) suggested that multiple personality represents a special type of PTSD [Post-Traumatic Stress Disorder]" (19).

BIBLIOGRAPHY

Ackerman, James S. "Knowing Good and Evil: A Literary Analysis of the Court History in 2 Samuel 9–20 and 1 Kings 1–2." *Journal of Biblical Literature* 109, no. 1 (1990): 41–64.

Albrecht, Jane W. "Divine Providence and Human Morality: The Ironic Perspective of *La venganza de Tamar.*" *Bulletin of the Comediantes* 43, no. 2 (1991): 215–24.

Alciatus, Andreas. *The Emblems in Translation,* edited by Peter M. Daly. Toronto: University of Toronto Press, 1985.

Alfonso X. *Primera Crónica General de España, que mandó componer Alfonso el Sabio y se continuaba bajo Sancho IV en 1289,* edited by Ramón Menéndez Pidal, in collaboration with Antonio G. Solalinde, Manuel Muñoz Cortés, and José Gómez Pérez. 2 vols. Madrid: Gredos, 1955.

Allende, Isabel. *The Stories of Eva Luna.* Translated by Margaret S. Peden. New York: Bantam, 1992.

Andrist, Debra D. "Male versus Female Friendship in *Don Quijote.*" *Cervantes* 3 (1983): 149–59.

Anibal, Claude E. "The Historical Elements of Lope de Vega's *Fuenteovejuna.*" *PMLA* 49, no. 3 (1934): 657–718.

Asenjo González, María. "La mujer y su entorno social en el fuero de Soria." In *Las mujeres medievales y su ámbito jurídico.* 45–57. Actas de las Segundas Jornadas de Investigación Interdisciplinaria. Seminario de Estudios de la Mujer. Mardrid: Universidad Autónoma de Madrid, 1983.

Atwood, Margaret. "Letter from Persephone." In *Selected Poems II: Poems Selected and New, 1976–1986,* 134–35. Toronto: Oxford University Press, 1986.

Augustine. *The City of God against the Pagans.* Translated by George E. McCracken. 7 vols. Loeb Classical Library, vol. 1. Cambridge: Harvard University Press; London: Heinemann, 1957–1960.

Babb, Lawrence. *The Elizabethan Malady: A Study of Melancholia in English Literature from 1580 to 1642.* East Lansing: Michigan State University Press, 1951.

Bakhtin, Mikhail. *Problems of Dostoevsky's Poetics.* Translated by R. W. Rotsel. Ann Arbor, Mich.: Ardis, 1973.

———. *Rabelais and His World.* Translated by Hélène Iswolsky. Cambridge, Mass.: MIT Press, 1968.

Bal, Mieke. *Death & Dissymmetry: The Politics of Coherence in the Book of Judges.* Chicago: University of Chicago Press, 1988.

———. *Lethal Love: Feminist Literary Readings of Biblical Love Stories.* Bloomington: Indiana University Press, 1987.

———. *Reading Rembrandt: Beyond the Word-Image Opposition.* Cambridge, U.K.: Cambridge University Press, 1991.

Bandello, Matteo. *Le novelle,* edited by G. Brognoligo. Vol. 3 of *Scrittori d'Italia.* Bari, Italy: Laterza, 1911.

Beecher, Donald A. "Lovesickness, Diagnosis, and Destiny in the Renaissance Theaters of England and Spain: The Parallel Development of a Medico-Literary Motif." In *Parallel Lives: Spanish and English National Drama 1580–1680,* edited by Louise and Peter Fothergill-Payne, 152–66. Lewisburg, Pa.: Bucknell University Press, 1991.

Bellver, Catherine G. "Division, Duplication, and Doubling in the Novels of Ana María Moix." In *Nuevos y novísimos: Algunas perspectivas críticas sobre la narrativa española desde la década de los 60,* edited by Ricardo Landeira and Luis T. González-del-Valle, 29–41. Boulder, Colo.: Society of Spanish and Spanish-American Studies, 1987.

Belmont, Nicole. "The Symbolic Function of the Wedding Procession in the Popular Rituals of Marriage." In *Ritual, Religion, and the Sacred,* edited by Robert Forster and Orest Ranum. Translated by Elborg Forster and Patricia M. Ranum. Selections from the *Annales,* vol. 7. Baltimore, Md.: Johns Hopkins University Press, 1982, 1–7.

Benjamin, Jessica. "Master and Slave: The Fantasy of Erotic Domination." In *Powers of Desire: The Politics of Sexuality,* edited by Ann Snitow, Christine Stanselle, and Sharon Thompson, 280–99. New York: Monthly Review Press, 1983.

Bennett, Jane. "'None So Deaf': A Study of Credibility in Autobiographical Rape Narratives." Ph.D. diss., Teachers College, Columbia University, 1992.

Bergmann, Emilie L. *Art Inscribed: Essays on Ekphrasis in Spanish Golden Age Poetry.* Harvard Studies in Romance Languages, vol. 35. Cambridge, Mass.: Harvard University Press, 1979.

Bersani, Leo, and Ulysse Dutoit. "Fetichisms and Storytelling." In *The Forms of Violence: Narrative in Assyrian Art and Modern Culture,* 66–72. New York: Schocken, 1985.

Blake, William. *Poems*, edited by W. B. Yeats. Cambridge, Mass.: Harvard University Press, 1969 [1905].

Bonilla y San Martín, D. Adolfo. *Luis Vives y la filosofía del Renacimiento.* Madrid: Imprenta del Asilo de Huérfanos del S. C. de Jesús, 1903.

Braun, Theodore E. D. "Cervantes and Hardy: From 'La fuerza de la sangre' to *La force du sang*." *Anales cervantinos* 17 (1978): 167–82.

Brooke-Rose, Christine. "Woman as a Semiotic Object." In *The Female Body in Western Culture,* edited by Susan Rubin Suleiman, 305–16. Cambridge, Mass.: Harvard University Press, 1986.

Brown, Jonathan, and J. H. Elliott. *A Palace for a King.* New Haven, Conn.: Yale University Press, 1980.

Brownmiller, Susan. *Against Our Will: Men, Women, and Rape.* New York: Simon and Schuster, 1975.

Bruerton, Courtney. "The Chronology of the *Comedias* of Guillén de Castro." *Hispanic Review* 12 (1944): 89–151.

Bryson, Norman. "Two Narratives of Rape in the Visual Arts: Lucretia and the Sabine Women." In *Rape,* edited by Sylvana Tomaselli and Roy Porter, 152–73. Oxford: Basil Blackwell, 1986.

Burgess, A. W., and L. L. Holmstrom. "Rape Trauma Syndrome." *American Journal of Psychiatry* 131 (1974): 981–86.

Bush, Andrew. "Ana María Moix's Silent Calling." In *Women Writers of Contemporary Spain: Exiles in the Homeland,* edited by Joan Lipman Brown, 136–58. Newark: University of Delaware Press, 1991.

Calcraft, R. P. "Structure, Symbol and Meaning in Cervantes' 'La fuerza de la sangre.'" *Bulletin of Hispanic Studies* 58 (1981): 197–204.

Calderón de la Barca. *El alcalde de Zalamea*, edited by Peter N. Dunn. Oxford: Pergamon Press, 1966.

———. *Los cabellos de Absalón*, edited by Helmy F. Giacoman. Estudios de Hispanófila, vol. 9 (Department of Romance Languages, University of North Carolina). Valencia, Spain: Artes Gráficas Soler, 1968.

———. *Los cabellos de Absalón.* In *Obras completas*, edited by Angel Valbuena Briones. Madrid: Aguilar, 1959, 1: 666–701.

———. *Life is a Dream.* Translated by Edwin Honig. New York: Hill & Wang, 1970.

———. *The Mayor of Zalamea.* In *Four Plays.* Translated by Edwin Honig. New York: Hill and Wang, 1961, 141–215.

———. *Obras de Calderón de la Barca.* 4 vols. *Biblioteca de Autores Españoles*, edited by Juan Eugenio Hartzenbusch. Madrid: Atlas, 1945. Vol. 2: *Eco y Narciso,* 575–94; *Fortunas de Andrómeda y Perseo,* 631–53. Vol. 4: *El monstruo de los jardines,* 213–34.

———. *The Painter of His Dishonour* (El pintor de su deshonra). Edited and translated by A. K. G. Paterson. Warminster, United Kingdom: Aris & Phillips, 1991.

———. *The Surgeon of His Honour.* Translated by Roy Campbell, with an introduction by Everett W. Hesse. Madison: University of Wisconsin Press, 1960.

Calhoun, Karen S., and Beverly M. Atkeson. *Treatment of Rape Victims: Facilitating Psychosocial Adjustment.* New York: Pergamon Press, 1991.

Caro, Ana. *Valor, agravio y mujer*, edited by Lola Luna. Madrid: Castalia (Instituto de la Mujer), 1993.

Caro Baroja, Julio. *El carnaval.* Madrid: Taurus, 1965.

Carreño, Antonio. "The Poetics of Closure in Calderón's Plays." In *The Calderonian Stage: Body and Soul,* edited by Manuel Delgado Morales, 25–44. Lewisburg, Pa.: Bucknell University Press, 1997.

Carroll, Margaret D. "The Erotics of Absolutism: Rubens and the Mystification of Sexual Violence." *Representations* 25 (Winter 1989): 3–30.

Carter, Jon Marshall. *Rape in Medieval England: An Historical and Sociological Study.* Boston: University Press of America, 1985.

Carter, Robin. "*Fuenteovejuna* and Tyranny: Some Problems of Linking Drama with Political Theory." *Forum for Modern Language Studies* 13, no. 4 (1977): 313–35.

———. "History and Poetry: A Re-Examination of Lope de Vega's *El mejor alcalde, el rey.*" *Forum for Modern Language Studies,* 16, no. 3 (1980): 193–213.

———. "*Peribáñez:* Disorder Restored." In *What's Past Is Prologue: A Collection of Essays in Honour of L. J. Woodward,* edited by Salvador Bacarisse, Bernard Bentley, Mercedes Clarasó, and Douglas Gifford, 17–27. Edinburgh: Scottish Academic Press, 1984.

Casalduero, Joaquín. *Sentido y forma de las "Novelas ejemplares."* Buenos Aires: Instituto de Filología, 1943.

Casas, Bartolomé de las. *The Devastation of the Indies: A Brief Account.* Translated by Herma Briffault. New York: Seabury Press, 1974.

Cascardi, Anthony J. "The Old and the New: The Spanish *Comedia* and the Resistance to Historical Change." *Renaissance Drama,* n.s., 17 (1986): 1–28.

Castro, Américo. "Algunas observaciones acerca del concepto del honor en los siglos XVI y XVII." *Revista de Filología Española,* 3.1 (1916): 1–386.

———. *De la edad conflictiva: El drama de la honra en España y en su literatura.* Madrid: Taurus, 1961.

———. *La realidad histórica de España.* 3d ed. Mexico City: Porrúa, 1966 [1954].

Castro y Bellvis, Guillén de. *Progne y Filomena.* In *Obras,* 1: 121–64. Real Academia Española. Biblioteca selecta de clásicos españoles, 2d ser. Madrid: Rev. de Archivos, Bibliotecas y Museos, 1925–1927.

Cervantes, Miguel de. *Don Quixote.* Translated by John Ormsby. Rev. edited by Joseph R. Jones and Kenneth Douglas. New York: W. W. Norton, 1981.

———. *Exemplary Stories.* Translated by Lesley Lipson. Oxford: Oxford University Press, 1998.

———. *El ingenioso hidalgo Don Quijote de la Mancha,* edited by Luis Andrés Murillo. 2 vols. Madrid: Castalia, 1987.

Ciavarelli, María Elisa. *El tema de la fuerza de la sangre.* Madrid: Porrúa, 1980.

Cohen, Ada. "Portrayals of Abduction in Greek Art: Rape or Metaphor?" In *Sexuality in Ancient Art: Near East, Egypt, Greece, and Italy,* edited by Natalie B. Kampen, 117–35. Cambridge, U.K.: Cambridge University Press, 1996.

Conlon, Raymond. "Amnón: The Psychology of a Rapist." *Bulletin of the Comediantes* 45, no. 1 (1993): 41–52.

Conroy, Charles. *Absalom, Absalom!: Narrative and Language in 2 Sam. 13–20.* Analecta Biblica. Investigationes Scientificae en Res Biblicas, vol. 81. Rome: Biblical Institute Press, 1978.

Covarrubias [Cobarrubias] y Horozco, Sebastián de. *Tesoro de la lengua castellana o española.* Madrid: Ediciones Turner, 1979 [1610].

Curran, Leo C. "Rape and Rape Victims in the *Metamorphoses.*" In *Women in the Ancient World: The "Arethusa" Papers,* edited by John Peradotto and J. P. Sullivan, 263–86. Albany: State University of New York Press, 1984.

Curtius, Ernst Robert. "Calderón's Theory of Art and the *Artes Liberales.*" In *European Literature and the Latin Middle Ages,* translated by Willard R. Trask. New York: Harper, 1963, 559–70.

Dahl, Solveig. *Rape: A Hazard to Health.* Oslo: Scandinavian University Press, 1993.

Darst, David H. "La muerte y el matrimonio en el teatro de Tirso de Molina." In *Tirso de Molina: Immagine e rappresentazione,* edited by Laura Dolfi, 219-31. Segundo Coloquio Internacional, 1989. Naples: Edizioni Scientifiche Italiane, 1991.

Davies, Gareth Alban. "'Pintura': Background and Sketch of a Spanish Seventeenth-Century Court Genre." *Warburg and Courtauld Institutes Journal* 38 (1975): 288–313.

Davis, Natalie Zemon. "The Rites of Violence: Religious Riot in Sixteenth-Century France." *Past and Present* 59 (1973): 51–91.

De Armas, Frederick A. *The Return of Astraea: An Astral-Imperial Myth in Calderón.* Studies in Romance Languages, vol. 32. Lexington: University Press of Kentucky, 1986.

De Lauretis, Teresa. "The Violence of Rhetoric: Considerations on Representation and Gender." In her *Technologies of Gender: Essays on Theory, Film, and Fiction,* 31–50. Bloomington: Indiana University Press, 1987.

De Rentiis, Dina. "Cervantes's *La fuerza de la sangre* and the Force of Negation." In *Cervantes's "Exemplary Novels" and the Advantage of Writing,* edited by Michael Nerlich and Nicholas Spadaccini, 157–74. Hispanic Issues, vol. 6. Minneapolis, Minn.: Prisma Institute, 1990.

Deyermond, Alan. *El "Cantar de Mio Cid" y la épica medieval española.* Barcelona: Sirmio, 1987.

Deyermond, Alan, and David Hook. "The *Afrenta de Corpes* and Other Stories." *La Corónica* 10, no. 1 (1981): 12–37.

Diez Borque, José María. *Sociología de la comedia española del siglo XVII.* Madrid: Cátedra, 1976.

Dio Cassius. *Roman History.* Translated by Herbert Baldwin Foster. Vol. 1 of 6 vols. Troy, N.Y.: Pafraets, 1905–1906.

Dionysius of Halicarnassus. *The Roman Antiquitites.* Translated by Edward Spelman. 4 vols. London, 1758.

Dixon, Victor. "El santo rey David y *Los cabellos de Absalón.*" In *Hacia Calderón: Tercer Coloquio Anglogermano, 1973,* edited by Hans Flasche, 84–98. Hamburger Romanistische Studien, vol. 39. Berlin: Walter de Gruyter, 1976.

———. "'Su Majestad habla, en fin, como quien tanto ha acertado': La conclusión ejemplar de *Fuente Ovejuna.*" *Criticón* 42 (1988): 155–68.

Donaldson, Ian. *The Rapes of Lucretia: A Myth and Its Transformations.* Oxford: Clarendon Press, 1982.

Douglas, Mary. *Purity and Danger: An Analysis of the Concepts of Pollution and Taboo.* London: Ark, 1984 [1966].

DuBois, Page. *Centaurs and Amazons: Women and the Pre-History of the Great Chain of Being.* Ann Arbor: University of Michigan Press, 1982.

Dunn, Peter. "Honour and the Christian Background in Calderón." *Critical Essays on the Theatre of Calderón,* edited by Bruce W. Wardropper, 24–60. New York: New York University Press, 1965.

Eagleton, Terry. *The Rape of Clarissa.* Minneapolis: University of Minnesota Press, 1982.

Edgerton, Samuel Y., Jr. "*Maniera* and the *Mannaia:* Decorum and Decapitation in the Sixteenth Century." In *The Meaning of Mannerism,* edited by Franklin W. Robinson and Stephen G. Nichols Jr., 67–103. Hanover, N.H.: University Press of New England, 1972.

Edwards, Gwynne. "Calderón's *Los cabellos de Absalón:* A Reappraisal." *Bulletin of Hispanic Studies* 48 (1971): 218–38.

―――. "The Closed World of *El alcalde de Zalamea.*" In *Critical Perspectives on Calderón de la Barca,* edited by Frederick A. de Armas, David M. Gitlitz, and José A. Madrigal, 53–67. Lincoln, Nebr.: Society of Spanish and Spanish-American Studies, 1981.

―――. *The Prison and the Labyrinth: Studies in Calderonian Tragedy.* Cardiff: University of Wales Press, 1978.

El Saffar, Ruth S. *Beyond Fiction: The Recovery of the Feminine in the Novels of Cervantes.* Berkeley: University of California Press, 1984.

―――. *Novel to Romance: A Study of Cervantes's "Novelas ejemplares."* Baltimore, Md.: Johns Hopkins University Press, 1974.

―――. *Rapture Encaged: The Suppression of the Feminine in Western Culture.* London: Routledge, 1994.

Escribano, Jean Schneider. "The Function of Classical Myth in the Theater of Guillén de Castro." Ph.D. diss., Emory University, 1971.

Euripides. *The Bacchae.* Translated by William Arrowsmith. In *Euripides V: The Complete Greek Tragedies,* edited by David Grene and Richard Lattimore. Chicago: University of Chicago Press, 1959, 142–228.

Evans, Peter W. "Pedro Crespo y el Capitán." In *Hacia Calderón: Quinto Coloquio Anglogermano, Oxford 1978,* edited by Hans Flasche and R. D. F. Pring-Mill, 48–54. Wiesbaden, Germany: Franz Steiner Verlag, 1982.

Ferguson, Frances. "Rape and the Rise of the Novel." In *Misogyny, Misandry, and Misanthropy,* edited by R. Howard Bloch and Frances Ferguson, 88–112. Berkeley: University of California Press, 1989.

Fineman, Joel. "Shakespeare's *Will:* The Temporality of Rape." In *Misogyny, Misandry, and Misanthropy,* edited by R. Howard Bloch and Frances Ferguson, 25–76. Berkeley: University of California Press, 1989.

Fischer, Susan L. "Art-within-Art: The Significance of the Hercules Painting in *El pintor de su deshonra.*" In *Critical Perspectives on Calderón de la Barca,* edited by Frederick A. de Armas, David M. Gitlitz, and José A. Madrigal, 69–77. Lincoln, Nebr.: Society of Spanish and Spanish-American Studies, 1981.

———. "*Fuente Ovejuna* on the Rack: Interrogation of a Carnivalesque Theatre of Terror." *Hispanic Review* 65 (1997): 61–92.

Flor nueva de romances viejos, edited by R. Menéndez Pidal. Madrid: Revista de Archivos, Bibliotecas y Museos, 1928.

Fokkelman, J. P. *Narrative Art and Poetry in the Books of Samuel: A Full Interpretation Based on Stylistic and Structural Analyses.* Studia Semitica Neerladica, no. 20. 4 vols. Assen, Netherlands: Van Gorcum, 1981.

Foley, Helene. "Medea's Divided Self." *Classical Antiquity* 8 (April 1989): 61–85.

Fontenrose, Joseph. "The Sorrows of Ino and of Procne." *Transactions and Proceedings of the American Philological Association (TAPA)* 78 (1948): 125–67.

Forcione, Alban K. *Cervantes and the Humanist Vision: A Study of Four Exemplary Novels.* Princeton, N.J.: Princeton University Press, 1982.

Fothergill-Payne, Louise. "Unas reflexiones sobre el duelo de honor y la deshonra de la mujer en *El alcalde de Zalamea.*" In *Hacia Calderón: Octavo Coloquio Anglogermano, 1987,* edited by Hans Flasche. Archivum Calderonianum, vol. 5. Stuttgart: Franz Steiner Verlag, 1988, 221–26.

Fox, Dian. *Refiguring the Hero: From Peasant to Noble in Lope de Vega and Calderón.* University Park: Pennsylvania State University Press, 1991.

Freud, Sigmund. "Fetishism" [1927]. In *Sexuality and the Psychology of Love*, edited by Philip Rieff. New York: Macmillan, 1963, 214–19.

———. *Group Psychology and the Analysis of the Ego* [1921]. In *A General Selection from the Works of Sigmund Freud*, 169–209, edited by John Rickman, M.D. New York: Doubleday, 1957.

———. "Medusa's Head." In *Sexuality and the Psychology of Love*, edited by Philip Rieff. New York: Macmillan, 1963, 212–13.

———. *Psychopathology of Everyday Life*. In *The Basic Writings of Sigmund Freud*. Translated and edited A. A. Brill. New York: Random House, 1938, 35–178.

———. "Some Psychological Consequences of the Anatomical Distinction between the Sexes" [1925]. In *Sexuality and the Psychology of Love*, edited by Philip Rieff. New York: Macmillan, 1963, 183–93.

———. "The Taboo of Virginity" [1918]. In *Sexuality and the Psychology of Love*, edited by Philip Rieff. New York: Macmillan, 1963, 70–86.

———. *Totem and Taboo* [1912–1913]. In *The Basic Writings of Sigmund Freud*. Translated and edited A. A. Brill. New York: Random House, 1938, 807–930.

Friedman, Edward H. "Cervantes' 'La fuerza de la sangre' and the Rhetoric of Power." In *Cervantes's "Exemplary Novels" and the Advantage of Writing*, edited by Michael Nerlich and Nicholas Spadaccini. Hispanic Issues, vol. 6. Minneapolis, Minn.: Prisma Institute, 1990, 125–56.

———. "Guillén de Castro's *Progne y Filomena*: Between the Classic and the Comedia." *Neophilologus* 72 (1988): 213–17.

Galinsky, G. Karl. *The Herakles Theme: The Adaptation of the Hero in Literature from Homer to the Twentieth Century*. Totowa, N.J.: Rowman and Littlefield, 1972.

García Lorca, Federico. *Five Plays: Comedies and Tragicomedies*. Translated by James Graham-Lujan and Richard L. O'Connell. New York: New Directions, 1963.

———. *Selected Poems*, edited by Christopher Maurer. London: Penguin, 1997.

Giacoman, Helmy F. "En torno a *Los cabellos de Absalón* de Pedro Calderón de la Barca." *Revista de Filología* 80 (1968): 343–53.

Gillet, Joseph E. "Lucrecia-Necia." *Hispanic Review* 15 (1947): 120–36.

Girard, René. *The Scapegoat*. Translated by Yvonne Freccero. Baltimore, Md.: Johns Hopkins University Press, 1986.

———. *Violence and the Sacred.* Translated by Patrick Gregory. Baltimore, Md.: Johns Hopkins University Press, 1977.

Gitlitz, David M. "Symmetry and Lust in Cervantes' 'La fuerza de la sangre.'" In *Studies in Honor of Everett W. Hesse,* edited by William C. McCrary and José Madrigal. Lincoln, Nebr.: Society of Spanish and Spanish-American Studies, 1981, 113–22.

Gould, Cecil. *The Paintings of Correggio.* Ithaca, N.Y.: Cornell University Press, 1976.

Gould, John. "Law, Custom and Myth: Aspects of the Social Position of Women in Classical Athens." *Journal of Hellenic Studies* 100 (1980): 38–59.

Goytisolo, Juan. "El mundo erótico de María de Zayas." *Cuadernos de Ruedo Ibérico* no. 39–40 (1972). Rpt. *Disidencias.* Barcelona: Seix-Barral, 1977, 63–115.

Gracián, Baltasar. *The Critick.* Translated by Paul Rycaut. London, 1681.

———. *El Criticón.* In *Obras completas,* edited by Arturo del Hoyo. Madrid: Aguilar, 1967, 519–1013.

Graham, Jorie. "Self-Portrait as Demeter and Persephone." In *The End of Beauty,* 59–63. New York: Ecco Press, 1987.

Gravdal, Kathryn. *Ravishing Maidens: Writing Rape in Medieval French Literature and Law.* Philadelphia: University of Pennsylvania Press, 1991.

Greenblatt, Stephen. "Filthy Rites." *Daedalus* 3, no. 3 (1982): 1–16.

Greer, Margaret Rich. *The Play of Power: Mythological Court Dramas of Calderón de la Barca.* Princeton, N.J.: Princeton University Press, 1991.

Grieve, Patricia. *Desire and Death in the Spanish Sentimental Romance, 1440–1550.* Newark, Del.: Juan de la Cuesta, 1987.

Güntert, Georges. "Relección de *Peribáñez.*" *Revista de Filología Española* 54 (1971): 37–52.

Haddon, Alfred C. *Magic and Fetishism.* London: Constable, 1921.

Hagan, Harry. "Deception as Motif and Theme in 2 Sm 9–20; 1 Kgs 1–2." *Biblica* 60 (1979): 301–26.

Hainsworth, Georges. *Les "Novelas ejemplares" de Cervantes en France au XVIIe siècle.* New York: Burt Franklin, 1971 [1933].

Hart, Thomas R., Jr. "The Infantes de Carrión." *Bulletin of Hispanic Studies* 33 (1956): 17–24.

Herman, Dianne. "The Rape Culture." In *Women: A Feminist Perspective,* edited by Jo Freeman. 3d ed. Palo Alto, Calif.: Mayfield Publishing Co., 1984, 20–38.

Hernández-Araico, Susana. *Ironía y tragedia en Calderón.* Potomac, Md.: Scripta Humanistica, 1986.

Herodotus. *The Nine Books of the History of Herodotus.* Translated by Peter Edmund Laurent (from the text of Thomas Gaisford). 2 vols. Oxford: Henry Slatter, 1846.

Hertz, Neil. "Medusa's Head: Male Hysteria under Political Pressure." *Representations* 4 (1983): 27–54.

Hesse, Everett W. "Imágenes de la sexualidad en *La venganza de Tamar* de Tirso." *Bulletin of the Comediantes* 41, no. 2 (1989): 163–72.

————. "The Incest Motif in Tirso's 'La venganza de Tamar.'" *Hispania* 47, no. 2 (1964): 268–76.

————. "The 'Terrible Mother' Image in Calderón's *Eco y Narciso.*" *Romance Notes* 1, no. 2 (1960): 133–36.

————. *Tirso's Art in "La venganza de Tamar": Tragedy of Sex and Violence.* York, S.C.: Spanish Literature Publishing Co., 1991.

Huarte de San Juan, Juan. *Examen de los ingenios para las ciencias,* edited by Estéban Torre. Madrid: Nacional, 1976.

Irigaray, Luce. *This Sex Which Is Not One.* Translated by Catherine Porter with Carolyn Burke. Ithaca, N.Y.: Cornell University Press, 1985.

Jacobus, Mary. "Judith, Holofernes, and the Phallic Woman." In *Reading Woman: Essays in Feminist Criticism,* 110–36. New York: Columbia University Press, 1986.

Jones, Anny Brooksbank. "The Incubus and I: Unbalancing Acts in Moix's *Julia.*" *Bulletin of Hispanic Studies* 72 (1995): 73–85.

Joplin, Patricia Klindienst. "Ritual Work on Human Flesh: Livy's Lucretia and the Rape of the Body Politic." *Helios* 17, no. 1 (1990): 51–70.

————. "The Voice of the Shuttle Is Ours." *Stanford Literature Review* 1 (Spring 1984): 25–53.

Kahn, Coppélia. "*Lucrece:* The Sexual Politics of Subjectivity." In *Rape and Representation,* edited by Lynn A. Higgins and Brenda R. Silver. New York: Columbia University Press, 1991, 141–59.

Kaplan, Louise J. *Female Perversions: The Temptations of Emma Bovary.* New York: Doubleday, 1991.

Kaufman, Gershen. *The Psychology of Shame: Theory and Treatment of Shame-Based Syndromes.* 2d ed. New York: Springer, 1996 [1989].

Kolodny, Annette. "A Map for Rereading: Or, Gender and the Interpretation of Literary Texts." *New Literary History* 11 (1980): 451–67.

Kristeva, Julia. *Powers of Horror: An Essay on Abjection.* Translated by Leon S. Roudiez. New York: Columbia University Press, 1982.

Lacan, Jacques. *The Four Fundamental Concepts of Psycho-Analysis,* edited by Jacques-Alain Miller. Translated by Alan Sheridan. New York: W. W. Norton, 1977 [1973].

Lacarra, María Eugenia. *El "Poema de mio Cid": Realidad histórica e ideología.* Madrid: Porrúa, 1980.

Laplanche, Jean, and Jean-Bertrand Pontalis. "Fantasy and the Origins of Sexuality." In *Formations of Fantasy,* edited by Victor Burgin, James Donald, and Cora Kaplan. London and New York: Methuen, 1986, 5–34.

Larson, Catherine. *Language and the "Comedia."* Lewisburg, Pa.: Bucknell University Press, 1991.

Larson, Donald R. *The Honor Plays of Lope de Vega.* Cambridge: Harvard University Press, 1977.

Laymon, Charles M., ed. *The Interpreter's One-Volume Commentary on the Bible.* Nashville and New York: Abingdon Press, 1971.

Leach, Edmund. "The Legitimacy of Solomon: Some Structural Aspects of Old Testament History." In *Genesis as Myth and Other Essays,* 25–83. London: Cape Editions, 1969. First appeared in *European Journal of Sociology* 7 (1966): 58–101.

Leavitt, Sturgis E. "Some Aspects of the Grotesque in the Drama of the Siglo de Oro." *Hispania* 18, no. 1 (1935): 72–86.

Leo, Ulrich. "La 'Afrenta de Corpes,' novela psicológica." *Nueva Revista de Filología Española* 13 (1959): 291–304.

León, Luis de. *The Perfect Wife.* Translated by Alice Philena Hubbard. Denton, Tex.: College Press, Texas State College for Women, 1943.

Levisi, Margarita. "La función de lo visual en 'La fuerza de la sangre.'" *Hispanófila* 49 (1973): 59–67.

Lévi-Strauss, Claude. *The Elementary Structures of Kinship.* Edited by Rodney Needham. Translated by James Harle Bell, John Richard von Sturmer, and Rodney Needham. Rev. ed. Boston: Beacon, 1969.

———. *Structural Anthropology.* 1958. Translated by Claire Jacobson and Brooke Grundfest Schoepf, vol. 1. New York: Basic Books, 1963.

Livy, Titus. *The Early History of Rome.* Translated by Aubrey de Sélincourt. London: Penguin, 1960.

López-Vázquez, Alfredo Rodríguez. "*La venganza de Tamar:* Colaboración entre Tirso y Calderón." *Revista CAUCE* [Seville], no. 5 (November 1982): 73–85.

Lorch, Lavinia. "Human Time and the Magic of the *Carmen:* Metamorphosis as an Element of Rhetoric in Ovid's *Metamorphoses.*" *Philosophy and Rhetoric* 15, no. 4 (1982): 262–73.

MacCurdy, Raymond R. *Francisco de Rojas Zorrilla and the Tragedy.* University of New Mexico Publications in Language and Literature, 13. Albuquerque: University of New Mexico Press, 1958.

Machiavelli. *The Discourses,* edited by Bernard Crick. Translated by Leslie J. Walker, S.J. Harmondsworth, U.K.: Penguin, 1970.

MacKay, Angus, and Geraldine McKendrick. "The Crowd in Theater and the Crowd in History: *Fuenteovejuna.*" *Renaissance Drama,* n.s., 17 (1986): 125–47.

Maravall, José Antonio. *Culture of the Baroque: Analysis of a Historical Structure.* Translated by Terry Cochran. Theory and History of Literature, vol. 25. Minneapolis: University of Minnesota Press, 1986.

———. "Maquiavelo y Maquiavelismo en España." *Boletín de la Real Academia de la Historia* 165 (1969): 183–218.

Martínez Nadal, Rafael. *"El público": Amor, teatro y caballos en la obra de Federico García Lorca.* Oxford: Dolphin, 1970.

Martínez Vidal, Enrique. "Katharsis and Comic Relief in Rojas Zorrrilla's *Progne y Filomena.*" In *Josep María Solà-Solé: Homage, Homenaje, Homenatge,* edited by Antonio Torres-Alcalá and others. Barcelona: Puvill, 1984, 85–90.

Marx, Karl. *Capital: A Critique of Political Economy.* Translated by Ben Fowkes. Vol. 1. New York: Vintage, 1976.

Mayberry, Nancy K. "Tirso's *La venganza de Tamar:* Second Part of a Trilogy?" *Bulletin of Hispanic Studies* 55 (1978): 119–27.

McKendrick, Melveena. *Woman and Society in the Spanish Drama of the Golden Age: A Study of the "Mujer Varonil."* Cambridge, U.K.: Cambridge University Press, 1974.

Meinecke, Friedrich. *Machiavellism: The Doctrine of Raison d'Etat and Its Place in Modern History.* Translated by Douglas Scott. New York: Praeger, 1965 [1957].

Merrick, C. A. "Neoplatonic Allegory in Calderón's *Las fortunas de Andrómeda y Perseo.*" *Modern Language Review* 67 (1972): 319–27.

Metford, J. C. J. "Tirso de Molina's Old Testament Plays." *Bulletin of Hispanic Studies* 27 (1950): 149–63.

Metzger, Deena. "It Is Always the Woman Who Is Raped." *American Journal of Psychiatry* 133, no. 4 (1976): 405–8.

Mills, S. P. "The Sorrows of Medea." *Classical Philology* 75 (1980): 289–96.

Mitchell, Phyllis Patteson. "When Sacred and Secular Intersect: Calderón's *El pintor de su deshonra, comedia* and *auto.*" *Bulletin of the Comediantes* 48, no. 2 (1996): 353–66.

Moix, Ana María. *Julia.* Barcelona: Seix Barral, 1969.

———. *Walter, ¿por qué te fuiste?* Barcelona: Barral, 1972.

Morby, Edwin S. "The *Hércules* of Francisco López de Zárate." *Hispanic Review* 30 (1962): 116–32.

Morley, S. Griswold, and Courtney Bruerton. *Cronología de las comedias de Lope de Vega.* Translated by María Rosa Cartes. Madrid: Gredos, 1968.

Mujica, Barbara. "The Rapist and His Victim: Calderón's *No hay cosa como callar.*" *Hispania* 62 (1979): 30–46.

Mulvey, Laura. "Visual Pleasure and Narrative Cinema." *Screen* 16, no. 3 (1975): 6–18.

Nelson, Leslie. "Velázquez's *Bodegones a lo divino.*" M.A. thesis, Bryn Mawr College, 1987.

Nepaulsingh, Colbert I. "The Afrenta de Corpes and the Martyrological Tradition." *Hispanic Review* 51 (1983): 205–21.

Nichols, Geraldine Cleary. "*Julia:* 'This Is the Way the World Ends' (T. S. Eliot, 'The Hollow Men')." In *Novelistas femeninas de la postguerra española,* edited by Janet W. Pérez. Madrid: Studia Humanitatis, 1983, 113–24.

O'Conner, Thomas A. "Hércules y el mito masculino: La posición 'feminista' de *Fieras afemina Amor.*" In *Estudios sobre el Siglo de Oro en homenaje a Raymond R. MacCurdy,* edited by Angel González, Tamara Holzapfel, and Alfred Rodríguez. Madrid: Cátedra, 1983, 171–80.

———. *Myth and Mythology in the Theater of Pedro Calderón de la Barca.* San Antonio, Tex.: Trinity University Press, 1988.

———. "On Love and the Human Condition: A Prolegomenon to Calderón's Mythological Plays." In *Calderón de la Barca at the Tercentenary: Comparative Views,* edited by Wendell M. Aycock and Sydney P. Cravens. Lubbock: Texas Tech University Press, 1982, 119–34.

————. "The Politics of Rape and *Fineza* in Calderonian Myth Plays." In *The Perception of Women in Spanish Theater of the Golden Age,* edited by Anita K. Stoll and Dawn L. Smith Lewisburg, Pa.: Bucknell University Press, 1991, 170–83..

————. "Violación, amor y entereza en *Fortunas de Andrómeda y Perseo* de Calderón de la Barca." In *Homenaje a Gonzalo Torrente Ballester,* 573–82. Salamanca: Biblioteca de la Caja de Ahorros de M. de P. de Salamanca, 1981.

Orcastegui Gros, Carmen. "La mujer aragonesa en la legislación foral de la Edad Media." In *Las mujeres medievales y su ámbito jurídico,* 115–23. Actas de las Segundas Jornadas de Investigación Interdisciplinaria, Seminario de Estudios de la Mujer. Madrid: Universidad Autónoma de Madrid, 1983.

Ordóñez, Elizabeth J. "The Woman and Her Text in the Works of María de Zayas and Ana Caro." *Revista de Estudios Hispánicos* 19, no. 1 (1985): 3–15.

Ovid. *Metamorphoses.* Translated by Frank Justus Miller. Loeb Classical Library. 2 vols. 3d ed. 1916; rpt. Cambridge, Mass.: Harvard University Press; London: William Heinemann, 1977.

Parker, A. A. "Henry VIII in Shakespeare and Calderón." *Modern Language Review* 43 (1948): 327–52.

Parker, Patricia A. *Literary Fat Ladies: Rhetoric, Gender, Property.* London, New York: Methuen, 1987.

Parry, Hugh. "Ovid's *Metamorphoses:* Violence in a Pastoral Landscape." *Transactions and Proceedings of the American Philological Association* 95 (1964): 268–82.

Paterson, Alan K. G. "The Comic and Tragic Melancholy of Juan Roca: A Study of Calderón's *El pintor de su deshonra.*" *Forum for Modern Language Studies* 5, no. 3 (1969): 244–61.

————. "Juan Roca's Northern Ancestry: A Study of Art Theory in Calderón's *El pintor de su deshonra.*" *Forum for Modern Language Studies* 7, no. 3 (1971): 195–210.

————. "The Textual History of Tirso's *La venganza de Tamar.*" *Modern Language Review* 63 (1968): 381–91.

Patton, Elizabeth. "From *Tulliola* to *Polyphemia:* Women and the Rhetoric of Renaissance Pedagogy." Ph.D. diss., Columbia University, 1994.

Pedraza Jiménez, Felipe B. "Sexo, poder y relaciones afectivas en *Los cabellos de Absalón.*" In *Calderón: Actas del "Congreso Internacional sobre Calderón y el teatro español del Siglo de Oro,"* edited by Luciano García Lorenzo. Madrid: C.S.I.C., 1983, 1:549–60.

Pérez de Moya, Juan. *Philosophia secreta*, edited by Eduardo Gómez de Baquero. 2 vols. Los clásicos olvidados, vols. 6 and 7. Madrid: Blass, 1928.

Phillips, Anthony. "*Nebalah*—a Term for Serious Disorderly and Unruly Conduct." *Vetus Testamentum* 25, no. 2 (1975): 237–42.

Piercy, Marge. "Rape Poem." In *Living in the Open. Circles on the Water. Selected Poems of Marge Piercy,* 164–65. New York: Knopf, 1994.

Pietz, William. "The Problem of the Fetish, I." *Res* 9 (Spring 1985): 5–17.

———. "The Problem of the Fetish, II: The Origin of the Fetish." *Res* 13 (Spring 1987): 23–45.

———. "The Problem of the Fetish, IIIa: Bosman's Guinea and the Enlightenment Theory of Fetishism." *Res* 16 (Autumn 1988): 105–23.

Piluso, Robert V. "'La fuerza de la sangre': Un análisis estructural." *Hispania* 47 (1964): 485–90.

Pinta Llorente, Miguel de la, and José María de Palacio y de Palacio. *Procesos inquisitoriales contra la familia judía de Juan Luis Vives. Vol. 1, Proceso contra la memoria y fama de Blanquina March, madre del humanista Juan Luis Vives (1528–1529).* Instituto B. Arias Montano. Madrid: C.S.I.C., 1964.

The Poem of the Cid. Translated by Rita Hamilton and Janet Perry. London: Penguin, 1984.

Pope, Alexander. "An Essay on Criticism." In *The Poems of Alexander Pope,* edited by E. Audra and Aubrey Williams. London: Methuen, 1961, 1:239–326.

Prudentius. *Crowns of Martyrdom.* In *Prudentius.* Translated by H. J. Thomson. Loeb Classical Library. Cambridge, Mass.: Harvard University Press, 1949, 2: 98–345.

Quevedo, Francisco de. *The Swindler.* In *Two Spanish Picaresque Novels. "Lazarillo de Tormes" and "The Swindler."* Translated by Michael Alpert. Harmondsworth, U.K.: Penguin, 1969.

Quina, Kathryn, and Nancy L. Carlson. *Rape, Incest, and Sexual Harassment: A Guide for Helping Survivors.* New York: Praeger, 1989.

Randel, Mary Gaylord. "The Portrait and the Creation of Peribáñez." *Romanische Forshungen* 85 (1973): 145–58.

Rank, Otto. *The Incest Theme in Literature and Legend: Fundamentals of a Psychology of Literary Creation.* Translated by Gregory C. Richter. Baltimore, Md.: Johns Hopkins University Press, 1992.

Rape: A Crime of War. Directed by Shelley Saywell. Produced by Silva Basmajian. National Film Board of Canada, 1996.

Ridout, George. "The Rape of Tamar: A Rhetorical Analysis of 2 Sam 13: 1–22." In *Rhetorical Criticism: Essays in Honor of James Muilenburg,* edited by Jared J. Jackson and Martin Kessler. Pittsburgh Theological Monograph Series, vol. 1. Pittsburgh: Pickwick Press, 1974, 75–84.

Rivière, Joan. "Womanliness as a Masquerade." In *Formations of Fantasy,* edited by Victor Burgin, James Donald, and Cora Kaplan. London and New York: Methuen, 1986, 35–44.

Rojas Zorrilla, Francisco de. *Cada qual lo que le toca y La viña de Nabot,* edited by Américo Castro. Teatro Antiguo Español, vol. 2. Madrid: Sucesores de Hernando, 1917.

———. *Lucrecia y Tarquino,* edited by Raymond R. MacCurdy. Albuquerque: University of New Mexico Press, 1963.

———. *Progne y Filomena,* edited by Alfred Rodríguez and Saúl E. Roll-Vélez. Ibérica, vol. 8. New York: Peter Lang, 1994. Also available in *Comedias escogidas,* edited by Ramón de Mesonero Romanos. *Biblioteca de Autores Españoles,* vol. 54. Madrid: Rivadeneira, 1952, 39–60.

Romancero general ó Colección de romances castellanos anteriores al siglo XVIII, edited by Agustín Durán, vol. 2. *Biblioteca de Autores Españoles.* Madrid: Rivadeneyra, 1882, 16.

Rubin, Gayle. "The Traffic in Women: Notes on the 'Political Economy' of Sex." In *Toward an Anthropology of Women,* edited by Rayna Reiter. New York: Monthly Review Press, 1975, 157–210.

Ruggiero, Guido. *The Boundaries of Eros: Sex, Crime and Sexuality in Renaissance Venice.* New York: Oxford University Press, 1985.

Ruiz de Alarcón, Juan. *La crueldad por el honor.* In *Obras completas,* edited by Agustín Millares Carlo. Mexico City: Fondo de Cultura Económica, 1959, 2: 826–915.

Ruiz Ramón, Francisco. "En torno al sentido trágico de *Los cabellos de Absalón,* de Calderón." *Segismundo,* nos. 21–22 (1975): 155–70.

Salomon, Noël. *Recherches sur le thème paysan dans la "comedia" au temps de Lope de Vega.* Bordeaux: Féret et Fils, 1965.

Sánchez de Viana, Pedro, trans. *Las transformaciones* with *Anotaciones.* By Ovid. Valladolid: Diego Fernández de Cordoba, 1589.

Scafuro, Adele. "Discourses of Sexual Violation in Mythic Accounts and Dramatic Versions of 'The Girl's Tragedy.'" *Differences* 2, no. 1 (1990): 126–59.

Scarry, Elaine. *The Body in Pain: The Making and Unmaking of the World.* New York and Oxford: Oxford University Press, 1985.

Schevill, Rodolfo, and Adolfo Bonilla [y San Martín]. "Introducción." In *Novelas ejemplares,* by Miguel de Cervantes. Madrid: n.p., 1925, 3: 371–406.

Schumm, Sandra J. "Progressive Schizophrenia in Ana María Moix's *Julia.*" *Revista Canadiense de Estudios Hispánicos* 19, no. 1 (1994): 149–71.

Scott, Nina M. "Honor and Family in 'La fuerza de la sangre.'" In *Studies in Honor of Ruth Lee Kennedy,* edited by Vern G. Williamsen and A. F. Michael Atlee. Estudios de Hispanófila, vol. 46. Chapel Hill, N.C.: Hispanófila, 1977, 125–32.

Sedgwick, Eve. *Between Men: Homosexual Desire and the English Novel.* New York: Columbia University Press, 1985.

Segal, Charles Paul. *Landscape in Ovid's "Metamorphoses": A Study in the Transformations of a Literary Symbol.* Wiesbaden, Germany: Franz Steiner, 1969.

Segura Graiño, Cristina. "Aproximación a la legislación medieval sobre la mujer andaluza: El fuero de Ubeda." In *Las mujeres medievales y su ámbito jurídico,* 87–94. Actas de las Segundas Jornadas de Investigación Interdisciplinaria, Seminario de Estudios de la Mujer. Madrid: Universidad Autónoma de Madrid, 1983.

Selig, Karl-Ludwig. "Some Observations on 'La fuerza de la sangre.'" *Modern Language Notes* 87 (1972): 121–25.

Shainess, Natalie. "Psychological Significance of Rape." *New York State Journal of Medicine* 76, no. 12 (1976): 2044–48.

Shakespeare, William. *Hamlet.* Folger Library General Reader's Shakespeare, edited by Louis B. Wright and Virginia A. LaMar. New York: Washington Square Press, 1958.

———. *The Rape of Lucrece.* In *The Sonnets and Poems of Shakespeare,* edited by Oscar James Campbell. New York: Schocken, 1964, 279–332.

Shergold, N. D., and J. E. Varey. "Some Early Calderón Dates." *Bulletin of Hispanic Studies* 38 (1961): 274–86.

Sicroff, Albert. *Los estatutos de limpieza de sangre. Controversias entre los siglos XV y XVII.* Translated by Mauro Armiño. Madrid: Taurus, 1985 [1979].

Slaniceanu, Adriana. "The Calculating Woman in Cervantes' 'La fuerza de la sangre.'" *Bulletin of Hispanic Studies* 64 (1987): 101–10.

Sloman, A. E. *The Dramatic Craftmanship of Calderón: His Use of Earlier Plays.* Oxford: Dolphin, 1958.

Smith, Colin. "On the Distinctiveness of the *Poema de Mio Cid.*" In *"Mio Cid" Studies,* edited by A. D. Deyermond. London: Tamesis, 1977, 161–94.

———, and Roger M. Walker. "Did the Infantes de Carrión Intend to Kill the Cid's Daughters?" *Bulletin of Hispanic Studies* 56 (1979): 1–10.

Sobré, J. M. "Calderón's Rebellion? Notes on *El alcalde de Zalamea.*" *Bulletin of Hispanic Studies* 54 (1977): 215–22.

Sophocles. *Antigone.* Translated by Elizabeth Wyckoff. In *Sophocles,* edited by David Grene and Richmond Lattimore. Chicago: University of Chicago Press, 1954, 1: 157–206.

Soufas, Christopher, Jr. "Ana María Moix and the 'Generation of 1968'; *Julia* as (Anti-)Generational (Anti-)Manifesto." In *Nuevos y novísimos: Algunas perspectivas críticas sobre la narrativa española desde la década de los 60,* edited by Ricardo Landeira and Luis T. González-del-Valle. Boulder, Colo.: Society of Spanish and Spanish-American Studies, 1987, 217–28.

Soufas, Teresa Scott. "Calderón's Melancholy Wife Murderers." *Hispanic Review* 52 (1984): 181–203.

———. *Dramas of Distinction: A Study of Plays by Golden Age Women.* Lexington: University Press of Kentucky, 1997.

Spiegel, D. "Multiple Personality as a Post-Traumatic Stress Disorder." In *Psychiatric Clinics of North America: Multiple Personality,* edited by B. C. Braun. Philadelphia: Saunders, 1984, 7: 101–10.

Stallybrass, Peter. "Patriarchal Territories: The Body Enclosed." In *Rewriting the Renaissance: The Discourses of Sexual Difference in Early Modern Europe,* edited by Margaret W. Ferguson, Maureen Quilligan, and Nancy J. Vickers. Chicago: University of Chicago Press, 1986, 123–42.

———, and Allon White. *The Politics and Poetics of Transgression.* Ithaca, N.Y.: Cornell University Press, 1986.

Stein, Louise K. *Songs of Mortals, Dialogue of the Gods: Music and Theatre in Seventeenth Century Spain.* Oxford: Clarendon Press; New York: Oxford University Press, 1993.

Sternberg, Meir. *The Poetics of Biblical Narrative: Ideological Literature and the Drama of Reading.* Bloomington: Indiana University Press, 1985.

Stimpson, Catharine R. "Shakespeare and the Soil of Rape." In *The Woman's Part: Feminist Criticism of Shakespeare,* edited by Carolyn Ruth Swift Lenz, Gayle Greene, and Carol Thomas Neely. Urbana and Chicago: University of Illinois Press, 1980, 56–64.

Stoll, Anita K. "'Venid a ver tan raro portento': The Staging of *Los cabellos de Absalón.*" In *The Calderonian Stage: Body and Soul,* edited by Manuel Delgado Morales. Lewisburg, Pa.: Bucknell University Press, 1997, 69–80.

Stoller, Robert J. *Observing the Erotic Imagination.* New Haven, Conn.: Yale University Press, 1985.

———. *Sexual Excitement: Dynamics of Erotic Life.* New York: Pantheon, 1979.

Stone, Lawrence. "Sex in the West." *New Republic,* 8 July 1985, 25–37.

Stratton, Jon. *The Virgin Text: Fiction, Sexuality, and Ideology.* Oklahoma Project for Discourse and Theory, vol. 1. Norman and London: University of Oklahoma Press, 1987.

Stroud, Matthew D. "The Resocialization of the *Mujer Varonil* in Three Plays by Vélez." In *Antigüedad y actualidad de Luis Vélez de Guevara,* edited by C. George Peale. Purdue University Monographs in Romance Languages, vol. 10. Amsterdam: John Benjamins, 1983, 111–26.

Sullivan, Henry W. "The Incest Motif in Tirsian Drama: A Lacanian View." In *Parallel Lives: Spanish and English National Drama, 1580–1680,* edited by Louise and Peter Fothergill-Payne. Lewisburg, Pa.: Bucknell University Press, 1991, 180–92.

———. "El motivo del incesto en el drama de Tirso: Una orientación Lacaniana." In *Tirso de Molina: Immagine e Rappresentazione,* edited by Laura Dolfi. Segundo Coloquio Internacional, 1989. Naples: Edizioni Scientifiche Italiane, 1991, 207–17.

———. "Sibling Symmetry and the Incest Taboo in Tirso's *Habladme en entrando.*" *Revista Canadiense de Estudios Hispánicos* 10, no. 2 (1986): 261–78.

Taylor, Simon. "The Phobic Object: Abjection in Contemporary Art." In *Abject Art: Repulsion and Desire in American Art,* 59–83. Exhibition catalogue, Whitney Museum of American Art (23 June–29 August 1993). Independent Study Papers, vol. 3. New York: Whitney Museum of American Art, 1993.

Temkin, Jennifer. "Women, Rape and Law Reform." In *Rape,* edited by Sylvana Tomaselli and Roy Porter. Oxford: Basil Blackwell, 1986, 16–40.

Ter Horst, Robert. "The Second Self: Painting and Sculpture in the Plays of Calderón." In *Calderón de la Barca at the Tercentenary: Comparative Views,* edited by Wendell M. Aycock and Sydney P. Cravens. Lubbock: Texas Tech University Press, 1982, 175–92.

Thomas, Michael. "El desdoblamiento psíquico como factor dinámico en *Julia,* de Ana María Moix." *Novelistas femeninas de la postguerra española,* edited by Janet W. Pérez. Madrid: Studia Humanitatis, 1983, 103–11.

Timoneda, Juan de. "Tragicomedia llamada *Filomena* (*La Turiana*)." In *Obras completas,* edited by D. M. Menéndez y Pelayo. La Sociedad de Bibliófilos Valencianos. Valencia: Domenech, 1911, 1: 207–62,.

Tirso de Molina (Fray Gabriel Téllez). *La dama del olivar.* In *Obras completas dramáticas*, edited by Blanca de los Ríos. Madrid: Aguilar, c. 1947; 4th ed. 1989, 2: 227–72.

―――. *La Santa Juana (Segunda Parte).* In *Obras completas dramáticas,* edited by Blanca de los Ríos. Madrid: Aguilar, c. 1947; 4th ed. 1989, 1: 825–65,.

―――. *Tamar's Revenge.* Translated by John Lyon. Warminster, United Kingdom: Aris & Phillips, 1988.

―――. *La venganza de Tamar,* edited by A. K. G. Paterson. Cambridge, U.K.: Cambridge University Press, 1969.

Trachman, Sadie Edith. *Cervantes' Women of Literary Tradition.* New York: Instituto de las Españas en los Estados Unidos, 1932.

Trambaioli, Marcela. "Una obra mitológica de corral: *Progne y Filomena* de Rojas Zorrilla." *Bulletin of the Comediantes* 48, no. 2 (1996): 275–94.

Trible, Phyllis. *Texts of Terror: Literary-Feminist Readings of Biblical Narratives.* Philadelphia: Fortress Press, 1984.

Ulrich, Leo. "La 'afrenta de Corpes,' novela psicológica." *Nueva Revista de Filología Hispánica* 13 (1959): 291–304.

Urrea, Pedro Manuel de, and Fernández de Hijar. *Penitencia de amor* [Burgos, 1514], edited by R. Foulché-Delbosc. Barcelona: "L'Avenç"; Madrid: M. Murillo, 1902.

Van Duyn, Mona. "Leda" and "Leda Reconsidered." In *No More Masks: An Anthology of Poems by Women,* edited by Florence Howe and Ellen Bass. Garden City, N.Y.: Anchor, 1973, 129–32.

Vasari, Giorgio. *Lives of the Artists.* Translated by George Bull. 2 vols. London: Penguin, 1987.

Vega Carpio, Lope Félix de. *El Alcalde de Zalamea.* In *Obras escogidas,* edited by Federico Carlos Sainz de Robles. Madrid: Aguilar, 1955, 3: 1399–1426.

————. *Fuente Ovejuna.* Translated by Victor Dixon. Hispanic Classics. Warminster, United Kingdom: Aris & Phillips, 1989.

————. *The King the Greatest Alcalde.* In *Four Plays by Lope de Vega.* Translated by John Garrett Underhill. New York: Charles Scribner's Sons, 1936, 103–87.

————. *La limpieza no manchada.* Salamanca: Gráficas Cervantes, 1972.

————. *The New Art of Writing Plays.* Translated by William T. Brewster. New York. Dramatic Museum of Columbia University, 1914.

————. *El niño inocente de la Guardia,* edited by Anthony J. Farrell. London: Tamesis, 1985.

————. *Peribáñez and the Comendador of Ocaña.* Translated by James Lloyd. Warminster, United Kingdom: Aris & Phillips, 1990.

————. *El príncipe despeñado. Obras de Lope de Vega.* Introduction by M. Menéndez y Pelayo. La Real Academia Española. Madrid: Sucesores de Rivadeneyra, 1893. Vol. 8, second section: 121–59.

————. *El príncipe despeñado,* edited by María Soledad de Ciria Matilla. Pamplona, Spain: Gobierno de Navarra, 1992.

————. *El robo de Dina. Obras de Lope de Vega. Biblioteca de Autores Españoles,* edited by Marcelino Menéndez y Pelayo. Madrid: Atlas, 1963, 8: 7–50.

Vélez de Guevara, Luis. *La serrana de la Vera,* edited by R. Menéndez Pidal and María Goyri de Menéndez Pidal. Teatro Antiguo Español, vol. l. Madrid: Sucesores de Hernando, 1916.

Vickers, Nancy J. "'This Heraldry in Lucrece' Face.'" In *The Female Body in Western Culture,* edited by Susan Rubin Suleiman. Cambridge, Mass.: Harvard University Press, 1986, 209–22.

Vives, Juan Luis. *De Institutione Feminae Christianae (On the Education of the Christian Woman). Liber Primus* [In English and Latin], edited by C. Fantazzi and C. Matheeussen. Translated by C. Fantazzi. 2 vols: vol. 6 (book 1) and 7 (books 2 and 3) of *Selected Works of J. L. Vives.* Leiden, Netherlands: E. J. Brill, 1996, 1998.

————. *De Institutione Feminae Christianae (Formación de la mujer cristiana).* Translated by Joaquín Beltrán Serra. Valencia, Spain: Ajuntament de Valencia, 1994.

————. *Formación de la mujer cristiana (Institutio Foeminae Christianae, 1523)*. In *Obras completas*, edited by Lorenzo Riber. Madrid: Aguilar, 1947, 1: 985–1175.

————. *In pseudodialecticos*. Edited and translated by Charles Fantazzi. Studies in Medieval and Reformation Thought, vol. 27. Leiden, Netherlands: E. J. Brill, 1979.

Voragine, Jacobus de. *The Golden Legend*. Translated by Granger Ryan and Helmut Ripperger. New York: Arno, 1969.

Walcot, Peter. "Herodotus on Rape." *Arethusa* 11 (Spring–Fall 1978): 137–47.

Walker, Roger M. "A Possible Source for the 'Afrenta de Corpes' Episode in the 'Poema de mio Cid.'" *Modern Language Review* 72 (1977): 335–47.

Walsh, John K. "Religious Motifs in the Early Spanish Epic." *Revista Hispánica Moderna* 36 (1970–1971): 165–72.

Wardropper, Bruce W. "The Unconscious Mind in Calderón's *El pintor de su deshonra*." *Hispanic Review* 18 (1950): 285–301.

Welles, Marcia L. "María de Zayas y Sotomayor and Her *novela cortesana:* A Re-Evaluation." *Bulletin of Hispanic Studies* 55 (1978): 301–10.

Wenham, G. J. "Why Does Sexual Intercourse Defile (*Lev.*15.18)?" *Zeitschrift für die Alttestamentliche Wissenschaft* 95 (1983): 432–34.

Wertenbaker, Timberlake. *The Love of the Nightingale* and *The Grace of Mary Traverse*. London: Faber and Faber, 1989.

Wethey, Harold E. *The Paintings of Titian*. Vol. 3, *The Mythological and Historical Paintings*. London: Phaídon, 1975.

Williamsen, Amy R. "Woman as Subject: Violation and Volition in Cervantes and Zayas." Paper presented at the meeting of the Modern Language Association, Chicago, 1990.

Wilson, Diana. *Allegories of Love: A Study of Cervantes's "Persiles and Sigismunda."* Princeton, N.J.: Princeton University Press, 1991.

————. "Cervantes's Last Romance: Deflating the Myth of Female Sacrifice." *Cervantes* 3 (1983): 103–20.

Wilson, Edward M. "Hacia una interpretación de *El pintor de su deshonra*." *Abaco* 3 (1970): 49–85.

Wilson, William E. *Guillén de Castro*. New York: Twayne, 1973.

Wolfthal, Diane. "The 'Heroic' Rape." Unpublished essay, 1987.

———. "A 'Hue and a Cry': Medieval Rape Imagery and Its Transformation." *Art Bulletin* 75. no. 1 (1993): 39–64.

Yeats, William Butler. *The Variorum Edition of the Poems of W. B. Yeats*, edited by Peter Allt and Russell K. Alspach. 5th ed. New York: Macmillan, 1971.

Zayas y Sotomayor, María de. *The Disenchantments of Love.* Translated by H. Patsy Boyer. Albany: State University of New York Press, 1997.

———. *The Enchantments of Love: Amorous and Exemplary Novels.* Translated by H. Patsy Boyer. Berkeley: University of California Press, 1990.

Zeitlin, Froma. "Configurations of Rape in Greek Myth." In *Rape,* edited by Sylvana Tomaselli and Roy Porter. Oxford: Basil Blackwell, 1986, 122–51.

———. "Playing the Other: Theater, Theatricality, and the Feminine in Greek Drama." *Representations* 11 (1985): 63–94.

INDEX

MARCIA L. WELLES is professor of Spanish at Barnard College. Her previous works include *Style and Structure in Gracián's "El Criticón"* (1976) and *Arachne's Tapestry: The Transformation of Myth in Seventeenth-Century Spain* (1986).